MW00397660

The Complete Air Fryer Cookbook for Beginners

1001 Easy and Affordable Air Fryer Recipes for Busy People on a Budget

By Gerald M. Stanley

Tabel of Content

Chapter 8 Appetizers and Snacks 68

Chapter 9 Poultry   82

Chapter 10 Red Meats 104

Chapter 11 Fish and Seafood 125

Chapter 12 Desserts   145

Chapter 13 Holiday Specials 157

Chapter 14 Fast and Easy Everyday Favorites   165

Introduction

The air fryer is a countertop convection oven that produces superheated air to cook foods that are similar to deep-frying only you don't smother your food with oil. While it is similar to a convection oven, the air is evenly distributed throughout the perforated basket that creates an intense environment that cooks the food more efficiently resulting in a crispy brown exterior and moist interior. In order to be able to achieve delicious air-fried foods, it is crucial to understand how this nifty kitchen appliance works.

In this cookbook, I will tell you all about the Air Fryer, including features, benefits, tips on how to use successfully, maintenance and cleaning of Air Fryer etc.

The most important thing is the large quantity of recipes, there are listed by follow category:

- Sauces, Dip and Dressing
- Breakfast
- Wraps and Sandwiches
- Casseroles, Frittatas and Quiches
- Vegetables
- Appetizers and Snacks
- Poultry
- Red Meats
- Fish and Seafood
- Desserts

I also selected some favorites recipes for special holiday and fast & easy recipes for busy people. You can cook whatever you want, I believe you will love it.

Chapter 1 The Basics of Air Fryer

Air fryers work similarly to convection ovens. It has a high-powered fan that allows hot air to circulate in the cooking chamber. The fan helps distribute heat around the food so that it cooks food evenly within a short span of time. The circulating hot air also carries natural oils from food so and distributes it all around the food to give that deep-fried effect without having to use a lot of oil. Moreover, the hot circulating air also encourages the maillard reaction no food as it produces high heat and dry environment that allows the proteins, fats, and carbohydrates to brown and improve the flavor of your food.

Features and Functions of Air Fryers

Depending on the brand of air fryers that you have, most air fryers come with general features and functions. Below is the general feature of air fryers that allow you to cook foods healthy and delicious meals.

- **Temperature Control Dial:** The temperature control dial allows you to select frying temperatures from 1750F to 4000F. The control dial can be adjusted during the entire cooking period.

- **Power Indicators:** Power indicators are located on the Control Panel of the air fryer. The control power indicates power indicators. The red power light indicates that the machine is turned on.

- **Automatic Timer Button:** Air fryers also come with an automatic timer button that will immediately turn off the machine once the cooking time is over. The machine usually gives off a beep sound to set off the timer.

- **Pre-Cooked Buttons:** Pre-cooked buttons are shortcut functions that are specifically designed to cook certain kinds of foods including fish and poultry. Other air fryers come with baking functions that allow you to cook baked goods.

How to Use It

Air fryers are not created equally thus the features can vary from model or brand to the other. For

instance, parts of some air fryers may be dishwasher safe while others are not. It is for this reason that it is crucial to read your appliance manual before using it. That way, you will get to know more about what your air fryer can and cannot do. Reading the safety information ensures that you do not misuse your air fryer in any way.

Reading the user manual also provides you instructions on how to use your air fryer properly. This also includes the type of accessories that you need to use in order to successfully make different dishes using this unconventional kitchen appliance. Now when it comes to general tips on using your air fryer, there are certain tips that you need to know. Below are some tips on how to use your air fryer. These tips are applicable for most models of air fryer that are available in the market:

- **Cook your food between 145°F to 160°F:** Cook food using this temperature range to ensure that your food is cooked through and that you avoid the risk for contracting food-borne diseases.

- **Check your device's wattage:** The higher the wattage often means the shorter the cooking time. For most recipes, the total cooking time can vary by a minute or two so it is crucial to follow the recipe book to avoid overcooking your food.

- **Start with the shortest cooking time:** Opt for the shortest cooking time as indicated in your recipe book. Constantly check for doneness and increase the cooking time as needed. This may be challenging but you will eventually learn how to adjust the cooking time on your air fryer to get your food done.

- **Constantly check your food if you are new to air frying:** This is especially true if you are new to cooking with an air fryer.

Benefits of Air Fryer

Cooking with an air fryer is touted to be good for your health. The reason for this is that you can use less oil but still get the same effects similar when cooking with a deep fryer. But more than being able to cook delicious fried foods with less oil, below are the benefits of cooking with an air fryer.

- **May aid to weight loss:** Because you can use less oil with the air fryer, it is a great kitchen appliance for people who want to lose weight or maintain a healthy weight without the need for you to sacrifice your favorite "fried" comfort foods.

- **Fewer mess:** Unlike cooking in a deep fryer, there is too little mess involved when cooking with the air fryer. Gone are the days when you have to suffer from oil splattering all over your kitchen. But more than anything else, you don't need to use too many pots, pans, baking sheets, and others as you only need the air fryer basket to cook your food. And because you save yourself from being splattered with hot oil, air fryers are very safe.

- **Portable and practical:** The air fryer is a great kitchen device for people who have a small kitchen or living in an RV as it does not take too much space, unlike conventional convection ovens.

- **Easy to operate:** Air fryers are very easy to use. It does not come with complicated buttons so anyone can operate the device even kitchen neophytes. It also comes with automatic cooking functions so there is no guesswork when it comes to choosing the right cooking setting for a particular food that you are making.

- **Faster cooking time:** People who are always on the go can also benefit from air fryers. The convection cooking mechanism of air fryers allows you to cook food faster than conventional ovens. Moreover, cooking with air fryers does not only require you to preheat the air fryer prior to cooking your food so you can save more time spending in the kitchen and more time doing other equally important things.

Choose a Right Air Fryer for You

With so many people wanting to go into the healthier route, buying air fryers is definitely becoming a trend these days. So, if you are one of the many people who are contemplating buying an air fryer, below is a buying guide for you to choose the perfect air fryer that fits your needs.

- **Size:** If you have limited kitchen space, then selecting small air fryers that will fit on the countertop is very important. When buying an air fryer, check for the dimension of the model that you are planning to buy and make sure that they fit your kitchen or anywhere you want to store your air fryer.

- **Capacity:** Know how much food you will be making in your household. If you run a large household, opting for air fryers that have large capacities is your best option. Regular sizes of air fryers often have capacities of 3.7 quarts while larger air fryers can hold as much as 5.8 to 6 capacities. If you are planning to use the air fryer for four or more people, then opting for large size air fryers is your best option.

- **Features:** Different models come with a wide variety of features. Before buying your air fryer, make sure that you decide on which features you want to have in your air fryer. Whether you opt for air fryers with digital or manual controls is a matter of personal preference. While manual air fryers come with simple control knobs, air fryers with digital controls may come with pre-set cooking functions as well as timers. If you are going to use your air fryer to cook different kinds of foods, then you may opt for the air fryer with a pre-set digital cooking function. If you are mainly going to use it to air fry food, then the manual air fryer is your best bet.

- **Accessories:** Different models of air fryers also come with different accessories. These accessories allow you to cook different kinds of food using one kitchen appliance. But you have to remember that buying more accessories for your air fryer can cost more money. But if you don't have enough money to splurge on accessories, you can still optimize your air fryer by using heat-proof dishes to cook casseroles and baked goodies as long as they will fit inside the air fryer basket.

- **Warranty options:** Before you buy an air fryer, it is crucial to do due diligence on the warranty options that different brands and models offer. Regardless of whether you choose a familiar brand name or not, find something that offers good warranty options. Warranty options for air fryers can vary from 30 days to 2 years. You can find the warranty period of air fryers from the user annual but you can also search for such information from the company website.

- **Price:** The price of air fryers is also another thing that you have to consider before you buy one. However, haven't you noticed that different shops (online and brick and mortar) sell the same model of air fryers at different prices? Thus, if you are looking for good air fryers that are not too expensive, you can scout for air fryers from different shops to compare prices.

Step-by-Step Air Frying Prep

While air fryers are very innovative kitchen appliance, you still need to do certain preparations to optimize your air fryer. Below is a list of air frying preps that you can follow to successfully create delicious dishes using your air fryer.

- **Put your air fryer on a stable surface:** For safety purposes, place your air fryer on a stable and heat-resistant surface. Moreover, make sure that there are at least five inches of space behind the air fryer for ventilation.

- **Spray oil on food:** Most recipes designed for air fryers require a small amount of oil. Brushing oil on food can often lead to using more oil than necessary. Instead, use an oil spray bottle to conveniently coat your food with oil. There are many types of cooking oil that you can spray on your food but vegetable oil or olive oil always works for air fryers due to their high burning point.

- **Preheat the air fryer:** Preheat the air fryer if recommended by your model. In general, preheating the air fryer requires only about 5 minutes but make sure to read your air fryer manual just to make sure that this step is indeed necessary or not.

- **Slice food into portions that will fit the air fryer:** When cooking with the air fryer, make sure that you slice food into portions that will fit inside the fryer basket. Moreover, make sure that you do not overcrowd the air fryer basket. Creating spaces in between your food allows the air to properly circulate your food for even browning.

- **Use proper breading:** When air frying food, make sure that you use the right breading. When breading your food, make sure that you coat it first with flour, eggs, and bread crumbs before misting or spraying it with cooking oil.

- **Always remember to monitor your food:** In most cases, people tend to forget about this part. Monitoring your food by opening the fryer basket and checking halfway through the cooking time is important so that you don't burn your food. This is also crucial when you are cooking frozen foods.

- **Different food requires different cooking techniques:** It is crucial to take note that different kinds of foods require different cooking techniques in your air fryer. For instance, vegetables needed to be shaken vigorously or halfway through the cooking time.

- **Always start with a clean air fryer:** When cooking foods that are naturally greasy, make sure that you start with a clean air fryer. Remove any oil that has been stuck at the bottom of the air fryer. During the cooking process, make sure that you also empty the frying basket oi oil halfway through the cooking time as excess oil can cause too much smoke that can even burn your food.

- **Create an aluminum sling:** Getting your air fryer accessories in and out of the air fryer basket can be difficult especially when the air fryer is hot. To facilitate the transfer, you can use a long aluminum foil folded into a sling and placing it at the bottom of the baking dish so that you can easily lift it once the cooking time ends.

Tips On Using Your Air Fryer

The success of using your air fryer comes with practice and understanding how this kitchen appliance works. Using your air fryer is no rocket science but it still pays to know how to use it properly to optimize its use. This section will discuss tips on how you can use your air fryer properly.

- **Get to know your kitchen device:** Before using your new air fryer, it is crucial that you read the manual that includes safety and cooking information. As much as possible, do not use the machine that violates the manufacturer's instruction. Information such as using the right cooking temperature and the factors that affect the cooking time including size and wattage of your machine.

- **Cook in batches:** Cook food in batches for best results. Moreover, cut foods into uniform pieces so that they will cook evenly. Stacking your food on top of the other is counter-productive as it will prevent the heat from circulating the food. If you have to cook a lot of food, cooking in batches may mean that the first batch may be too cool before the second batch is done cooking. What you can do is that once all of the batches are done, you can reheat the first batch quickly before serving.

Air Fryer Cleaning

The air fryer needs regular cleaning after every use. This is to ensure that no grease will accumulate inside the air fryer that may eventually cause excessive smoking in the air fryer. To clean your air fryer, below are tips that you can follow:

- **Do not use an abrasive cleaning cloth when wiping the interior part of your air fryer basket:** The interior of the appliance has a non-stick coating. Do not use an abrasive material to clean them otherwise it will remove the non-stick coating. Use a damp kitchen towel instead. Use warm water and liquid detergent to remove the grease: To remove the grease, use liquid detergent to remove the grease as grease cuts through fat and grime.

- **Pay attention to the heating element:** The heating element including the fan inside the air fryer is exposed to grime and dirt. Make sure that you pay extra attention by cleaning it with a brush.

- **Push the cord into the cord and store inside the compartment:** Keeping the cord in place prevents it from getting loose and being damaged.

- **Put inside the dishwasher the washable parts:** Read the instruction manual to know which parts are washable.

Chapter 2 Air Fryer Cooking Guide

Air frying should make meal prep easy. But it is still crucial to know what ingredients you can use to cook your food. Below are ingredients that you can use for your air fryer.

- **Flour:** Flour such as all-purpose flour can be used for breading and cooking pastries and baked goodies.

- **Sugar:** Sugar is used to flavor desserts, sauces, and marinades. They are very versatile and considered a kitchen staple. Other sweeteners that you can use include honey, maple syrup, and many others.

- **Oils and fat:** Oils and fats can be used in making air fried foods. There are many fats and oils that you can use including butter, rapeseed oil, and coconut oil. Choose those that will match the recipe that you need.

- **Eggs:** Eggs are versatile ingredients that you can use to make a lot of air fried foods. You can use them for making casseroles, baked goods, and as an egg wash for many foods.

- **Spices:** Foods are flavorful when they are made with spices. You have the option to use different spices when making your food. A wide array of spices can be used to cook food including garlic, black pepper, paprika, salt, mustard, and many others.

- **Meats:** All types of meats can be cooked in an air fryer. Chicken, turkey, lamb, beef, pork, fish, and game meat can be used. However, when using your air fryer to cook meats, make sure that you slice the meat in portions that fit inside the air fryer and trim unnecessary fats to avoid burning your food.

- **Vegetables:** Many vegetables can be cooked in an air fryer. Cook roasted vegetables such as potatoes, roasted potatoes, carrots, beans, asparagus, peas, and even kale in the air fryer.

The thing is that there are so many things that you can cook using your air fryer except for soups, sauces, chowder, pasta, and any foods coated with wet batter.

All about Oil And Fat

While oils are not necessarily needed in cooking with air fryers, it is still important to know about oils and fats. After all, some recipes call for misting oil all over the ingredients to give it a browned roasted effect. When choosing the right oil for air fryers, it is critical to use those that come with a high smoke point. This section will discuss the good fats and bad fats that you can use when making air fried foods:

Good Fats

- **Saturated fats:** Recent studies indicate that there is no correlation between heart disease and saturated fats. Saturated fats contain medium-chain triglycerides that increase high-density lipoproteins (good fat). Examples of saturated fats include coconut oil, palm oil, and butter. Red meat also naturally contains saturated fats

- **Monounsaturated fatty acids:** Monounsaturated fats increases the amount of good cholesterol in the body. Health benefits of this fat include lowering blood pressure and decreasing the risk of developing heart diseases. Monounsaturated fats are sourced from avocado, extra virgin olive oil, lard, and macadamia nut.

- **Polyunsaturated fatty acids:** Omega-3 and Omega-6 oils are examples of polyunsaturated fats. They are sourced from chia seeds, flaxseed, salmon, extra virgin olive oil, sesame seeds, and walnuts. They can help improve cardiovascular health and mental health.

- **Naturally-occurring trans fats:** While trans-fat have quite a bad reputation, naturally-occurring trans-fat have health benefits such as protection against inflammation that can lead to cancer, obesity, and diabetes. Sources of natural healthy fats include grass-fed butter and yogurt.

Bad Fats

- **Processed Trans and Polyunsaturated Fats:** Processed trans-fat are present in sweet snacks and many processed foods. Foods that contain processed trans and polyunsaturated fats may increase the risk for cancer, heart disease, and many other inflammatory health issues.

Hints For Air Fryer Success

Cooking your meals in an air fryer is easy but there are many tips that you can follow to ensure your air fryer success. Below are some tips that can ensure your success.

- **Never go beyond the 2/3 mark when filling the fryer basket:** As a rule of thumb, make sure that you do not go over the 2/3 mark of the basket. This is to prevent the fryer basket from being too overcrowded so that air can still circulate your food for even cooking.

- **Be wary of excessive smoking:** While it is natural for foods with high-fat content to produce smoke, excessive smoking can be an indication of electrical malfunction. Although the air fryer is an intuitive machine that can work without supervision, it is still best to constantly check for such things to ensure safety and success when cooking

- with an air fryer.

How To Eat Healthy Air-Fried Foods?

Cooking healthy foods with an air fryer is not difficult at all. But just because you have omitted using oil does not mean that food is already healthy. For instance, to add more flavor, people might use more salt or sugar to get that feeling of satiety that oil provides. Thus, below are tips for eating healthier using your air fryer.

- **Avoid air frying processed items:** Air frying processed items such as chicken nuggets, processed fish fingers, and others defeat the purpose of healthy cooking and eating using an air fryer as they contain high salt.

- **Cook natural and unprocessed foods:** If you truly want to eat healthy using your air fryer, it is best to cook foods that are natural and unprocessed.

- **Avoid adding too much salt or sugar to food:** Avoid using too much salt and sugar on your air fried foods. Excessive consumption of salt and sugar can lead to diseases like hypertension and diabetes.

- **Do not overcook your vegetables:** When cooking vegetables, make sure that you do not overcook your food. Overcooking often leads to the loss of nutrients in your food.

Converting Recipes for Air Fryer Use

As there are not too many recipes that are designed for air fryers, it is crucial that you know how to convert conventional recipes so that you can cook them in your air fryer. Below are tips on how you convert recipes to air fryers.

- **Adjust the heat:** The heat produced by the air fryer is more intense compared to a conventional oven. If you are cooking using an air fryer, reduce the suggested temperature by 250F to 500F. For instance, if the food package calls for cooking in the oven for 4500F, you can cook for 4000F instead.

- **Adjust the time:** You can also cut the cooking time to 20% s instead of cooking for 10 minutes as indicated in conventional recipes, you can cook it in your air fryer for 8 minutes.

About The Recipes

Designing recipes for air fryer is a great way for you to extend the use of your air fryer. This is especially true if you cannot find air fryer recipes of your favorite foods. Below are tips on how to design recipes using the air fryer.

- **Maximize your accessories:** Maximize your air fryer accessories by incorporating them into your recipes. For instead, use your grill pan for making steaks and hamburgers. You can also use your layer rack to make kabobs or your barrel pan to make fried rice.

- **Include nutritional information:** Always include the nutritional information in your recipes such as calories, total fat, saturated fat, cholesterol, sodium, carbohydrates, fiber, and protein. It is also crucial to include cooking time and serving size. By including the nutritional information, this will let you know the nutritional value of your food.

- **Include the recipe category:** Include the recipe category in your recipes. These include fast recipes, a vegetarian, gluten-free, family favorite, or a personal favorite. This is important to easily organize the recipes.

- **Clean up after every use:** Cleaning up after every use is crucial as the presence of grease in the bottom of the air fryer. As mentioned earlier, accumulation of grease can cause smoking that will not only affect the flavor of your food but may cause your food to also burn.

- **Use the right accessories:** Using the air fryer is not complicated at all and using the right accessories, can help you extend the functionality of your air fryer. These accessories include baking pans and muffin cups that will fit inside the air fryer so that you can cook baked goodies, casseroles, and many others. Another accessory that you can use is air fryer grill pans that will give you the effect of grilled marks on your food.

Air Fryer Safety Tips

The air fryer is designed to be safe similar to other types of modern kitchen appliances available to date. Unlike conventional deep fryers, cooking with air fryers does not involve hot oil splattering all over the place. So, what makes air fryers safe? They come with safety features including a thermostat and lid to keep the hot air inside. But aside from having safety features, below are some tips on air fryer safety.

- **Avoid touching the air fryer when cooking:** Although air fryers come with an insulated body, they can still get hot during the entire cooking time. Thus, avoid touching the air fryer when cooking. You can also use mitts or pot holders to touch in should you need to open the air fryer basket.

- **Avoid immersing the air fryer in water:** Water and electricity do not really mix well. Make sure that the wiring of the air fryer does not come into contact with water otherwise electric shocks can occur. If the air fryer has damaged its electrical wiring, make sure that you replace the damaged parts before using it.

- **Use the air fryer with supervision:** Always keep children and people with reduced physical and mental capabilities to use the air fryer alone.

- **Keep wires in place:** Do not let the wires dangle all over the place especially if you have kids and pets running around the kitchen.

- **Do not place the air fryer on top of the burner:** Do not put the air fryer on top of a burner especially a burner with an open flame.

- **Make sure that the frying basket is locked in position:** Make sure that the air frying basket is locked in to place to avoid falling off when the air fryer is on.

Air fryers are generally safe and different models come with varying safety instructions. Make sure that you read the instruction manual for basic safety tips.

Chapter 3 Sauces, Dips, and Dressings

Balsamic-Dijon Dressing

Prep time: 5 minutes | Cook time: 0 minutes | Makes 1 cup

2 tablespoons Dijon mustard
¼ cup balsamic
vinegar
¾ cup olive oil

1. Put all ingredients in a jar with a tight-fitting lid. Put on the lid and shake vigorously until thoroughly combined. Refrigerate until ready to use and shake well before serving.

Creamy Cashew Vodka Sauce

Prep time: 15 minutes | Cook time: 5 minutes | Makes 3 cups

¾ cup raw cashews
¼ cup boiling water
1 tablespoon olive oil
4 garlic cloves, minced
1½ cups unsweetened almond milk
1 tablespoon arrowroot powder
1 teaspoon salt
1 tablespoon nutritional yeast
1¼ cups marinara sauce

1. Put the cashews in a heatproof bowl and add boiling water to cover. Let soak for 10 minutes. Drain the cashews and place them in a blender. Add ¼ cup boiling water and blend for 1 to 2 minutes or until creamy. Set aside.
2. In a small saucepan, heat the olive oil over medium heat. Add the garlic and sauté for 2 minutes until golden. Whisk in the almond milk, arrowroot powder, and salt. Bring to a simmer. Continue to simmer, whisking frequently, for about 5 minutes or until the sauce thickens.
3. Carefully transfer the hot almond milk mixture to the blender with the cashews. Blend for 30 seconds to combine, then add the nutritional yeast and marinara sauce. Blend for 1 minute or until creamy.

Chimichurri Sauce

Prep time: 15 minutes | Cook time: 0 minutes | Makes 2 cups

1 cup minced fresh parsley
½ cup minced fresh cilantro
¼ cup minced fresh mint leaves
¼ cup minced garlic (about 6 cloves)
2 tablespoons minced
fresh oregano leaves
1 teaspoon fine Himalayan salt
1 cup olive oil or avocado oil
½ cup red wine vinegar
Juice of 1 lemon

1. Thoroughly mix the parsley, cilantro, mint leaves, garlic, oregano leaves, and salt in a medium bowl. Add the olive oil, vinegar, and lemon juice and whisk to combine.
2. Store in an airtight container in the refrigerator and shake before using.
3. You can serve the chimichurri over vegetables, poultry, meats, and fish. It also can be used as a marinade, dipping sauce, or condiment.

Creamy Coconut-Lemon Dressing

Prep time: 5 minutes | Cook time: 0 minutes | Makes about 1 cup

8 ounces (227 g) plain coconut yogurt
2 tablespoons chopped fresh parsley
2 tablespoons freshly
squeezed lemon juice
1 tablespoon snipped fresh chives
½ teaspoon salt
Pinch freshly ground black pepper

1. Stir together the coconut yogurt, parsley, lemon juice, chives, salt, and pepper in a medium bowl until completely mixed.
2. Transfer to an airtight container and refrigerate until ready to use.
3. This dressing perfectly pairs with spring mix greens, grilled chicken or even your favorite salad.

Lemony Cashew Pesto

Prep time: 10 minutes | Cook time: 0 minutes | Makes 1 cup

¼ cup raw cashews
Juice of 1 lemon
2 garlic cloves
⅓ red onion (about 2 ounces / 56 g in total)

1 tablespoon olive oil
4 cups basil leaves, packed
1 cup wheatgrass
¼ cup water
¼ teaspoon salt

1. Put the cashews in a heatproof bowl and add boiling water to cover. Soak for 5 minutes and then drain.
2. Put all ingredients in a blender and blend for 2 to 3 minutes or until fully combined.

Homemade Creamy Ranch Dressing

Prep time: 5 minutes | Cook time: 0 minutes | Serves 8

1 cup plain Greek yogurt
¼ cup chopped fresh dill
2 tablespoons chopped fresh chives

Zest of 1 lemon
1 garlic clove, minced
½ teaspoon sea salt
⅛ teaspoon freshly cracked black pepper

1. Mix together the yogurt, dill, chives, lemon zest, garlic, sea salt, and pepper in a small bowl and whisk to combine.
2. Serve chilled.

Vegan Cashew Ranch Dressing

Prep time: 15 minutes | Cook time: 0 minutes | Serves 12

1 cup cashews, soaked in warm water for at least 1 hour
½ cup water
2 tablespoons freshly squeezed lemon juice

1 tablespoon vinegar
1 teaspoon garlic powder
1 teaspoon onion powder
2 teaspoons dried dill

1. In a food processor, combine the cashews, water, lemon juice, vinegar, garlic powder, and onion powder. Blend until creamy and smooth. Add the dill and pulse a few times until combined.

Homemade Peanut-Lime Dressing

Prep time: 5 minutes | Cook time: 0 minutes | Serves 8

1 cup lite coconut milk
¼ cup freshly squeezed lime juice
¼ cup creamy peanut butter
2 tablespoons low-

sodium soy sauce or tamari
3 garlic cloves, minced
1 tablespoon grated fresh ginger

1. Place all the ingredients in a food processor or blender and process until completely mixed and smooth.
2. It's delicious served over grilled chicken or tossed with noodles and green onions.

Easy Homemade Hummus

Prep time: 5 minutes | Cook time: 0 minutes | Serves 2

1 (19-ounce / 539-g) can chickpeas, drained and rinsed
¼ cup tahini
3 tablespoons cold water
2 tablespoons freshly squeezed lemon juice

1 garlic clove
½ teaspoon turmeric powder
⅛ teaspoon black pepper
Pinch pink Himalayan salt, to taste

1. Combine all the ingredients in a food processor and blend until smooth.

Lemony Dijon Vinaigrette

Prep time: 5 minutes | Cook time: 0 minutes | Makes about 6 tablespoons

¼ cup extra-virgin olive oil
1 garlic clove, minced
2 tablespoons freshly squeezed lemon juice
1 teaspoon Dijon

mustard
½ teaspoon raw honey
¼ teaspoon salt
¼ teaspoon dried basil

1. Place all the ingredients in a mason jar. Cover and shake vigorously until thoroughly mixed and well emulsified.
2. Serve chilled.

Garlicky Lime Tahini Dressing

Prep time: 5 minutes | Cook time: 0 minutes | Makes about ¾ cup

1/3 cup tahini
3 tablespoons filtered water
2 tablespoons freshly squeezed lime juice
1 tablespoon apple cider vinegar

1 teaspoon lime zest
1½ teaspoons raw honey
¼ teaspoon garlic powder
¼ teaspoon salt

1. Whisk together the tahini, water, vinegar, lime juice, lime zest, honey, salt, and garlic powder in a small bowl until well emulsified.
2. Serve immediately, or refrigerate in an airtight container for to 1 week.

Maple Ginger Sauce

Prep time: 5 minutes | Cook time: 5 minutes | Makes 2/3 cup

3 tablespoons ketchup
2 tablespoons water
2 tablespoons maple syrup
1 tablespoon rice vinegar
2 teaspoons peeled

minced fresh ginger root
2 teaspoons soy sauce (or tamari, which is a gluten-free option)
1 teaspoon cornstarch

1. In a small saucepan over medium heat, combine all the ingredients and stir continuously for 5 minutes, or until slightly thickened. Enjoy warm or cold.

Simple Kale and Almond Pesto

Prep time: 15 minutes | Cook time: 0 minutes | Makes about 1 cup

2 cups chopped kale leaves, rinsed well and stemmed
½ cup toasted almonds
2 garlic cloves
3 tablespoons extra-virgin olive oil
3 tablespoons freshly

squeezed lemon juice
2 teaspoons lemon zest
1 teaspoon salt
½ teaspoon freshly ground black pepper
¼ teaspoon red pepper flakes

1. Place all the ingredients in a food processor and pulse until smoothly puréed.
2. It tastes great with the eggs, salads, soup, pasta, cracker, and sandwiches.

Mexican Pico de Gallo

Prep time: 5 minutes | Cook time: 0 minutes | Serves 2

3 large tomatoes, chopped
½ small red onion, diced
1/8 cup chopped fresh cilantro
3 garlic cloves, chopped

2 tablespoons chopped pickled jalapeño pepper
1 tablespoon lime juice
¼ teaspoon pink Himalayan salt (optional)

1. In a medium bowl, combine all the ingredients and mix with a wooden spoon.

Tangy Balsamic Berry Vinaigrette

Prep time: 15 minutes | Cook time: 0 minutes | Makes about 1½ cups

1 cup mixed berries, thawed if frozen
½ cup balsamic vinegar
1/3 cup extra-virgin olive oil
2 tablespoons freshly squeezed lemon or lime juice

1 tablespoon lemon or lime zest
1 tablespoon Dijon mustard
1 tablespoon raw honey or maple syrup
1 teaspoon salt
½ teaspoon freshly ground black pepper

1. Place all the ingredients in a blender and purée until thoroughly mixed and smooth.
2. You can serve it over a bed of greens, grilled meat, or fresh fruit salad.

Chapter 4 Breakfasts

Bacon and Broccoli Florets Bread Pudding

Prep time: 15 minutes | Cook time: 48 minutes | Serves 2 to 4

½ pound (227 g) thick cut bacon, cut into ¼-inch pieces
3 cups brioche bread, cut into ½-inch cubes
2 tablespoons butter, melted
3 eggs
1 cup milk
½ teaspoon salt
Freshly ground black pepper, to taste
1 cup frozen broccoli florets, thawed and chopped
1½ cups grated Swiss cheese

1. Air fry the bacon for 8 minutes until crispy, shaking the basket a few times to help it air fry evenly. Remove the bacon and set it aside on a paper towel.
2. Air fry the brioche bread cubes at 400ºF (204ºC) for 2 minutes to dry and toast lightly.
3. Butter a cake pan. Combine all the remaining ingredients in a large bowl and toss well. Transfer the mixture to the buttered cake pan, cover with aluminum foil and refrigerate the bread pudding overnight, or for at least 8 hours.
4. Remove the cake pan from the refrigerator an hour before you plan to bake and let it sit on the countertop to come to room temperature.
5. Transfer the covered cake pan to the basket of the air fryer, lowering the pan into the basket. Fold the ends of the aluminum foil over the top of the pan before returning the basket to the air fryer.
6. Bake at 330ºF (166ºC) for 20 minutes. Remove the foil and air fry for an additional 20 minutes. If the top browns a little too much before the custard has set, simply return the foil to the pan. The bread pudding has cooked through when a skewer inserted into the center comes out clean.
7. Serve warm.

Fast Banana Churros with Oatmeal

Prep time: 15 minutes | Cook time: 15 minutes | Serves 2

For the Churros:
1 large yellow banana, peeled, cut in half lengthwise, then cut in half widthwise
2 tablespoons whole-wheat pastry flour
⅛ teaspoon sea salt
2 teaspoons oil
(sunflower or melted coconut)
1 teaspoon water
Cooking spray
1 tablespoon coconut sugar
½ teaspoon cinnamon

For the Oatmeal:
¾ cup rolled oats
1½ cups water

To make the churros
1. Put the 4 banana pieces in a medium-size bowl and add the flour and salt. Stir gently. Add the oil and water. Stir gently until evenly mixed. You may need to press some coating onto the banana pieces.
2. Spray the air fryer basket with the oil spray. Put the banana pieces in the air fryer basket and air fry at 340ºF (171ºC) for 5 minutes. Remove, gently turn over, and air fry for another 5 minutes or until browned.
3. In a medium bowl, add the coconut sugar and cinnamon and stir to combine. When the banana pieces are nicely browned, spray with the oil and place in the cinnamon-sugar bowl. Toss gently with a spatula to coat the banana pieces with the mixture.

To make the oatmeal
1. While the bananas are cooking, make the oatmeal. In a medium pot, bring the oats and water to a boil, then reduce to low heat. Simmer, stirring often, until all the water is absorbed, about 5 minutes. Put the oatmeal into two bowls.
2. Top the oatmeal with the coated banana pieces and serve immediately.

Fast Apple and Walnut Muffins

Prep time: 15 minutes | Cook time: 10 minutes | Makes 8 muffins

1 cup flour	pancake syrup, plus
1/3 cup sugar	2 teaspoons
1 teaspoon baking	2 tablespoons
powder	melted butter, plus 2
1/4 teaspoon baking	teaspoons
soda	3/4 cup unsweetened
1/4 teaspoon salt	applesauce
1 teaspoon cinnamon	1/2 teaspoon vanilla
1/4 teaspoon ginger	extract
1/4 teaspoon nutmeg	1/4 cup chopped
1 egg	walnuts
2 tablespoons	1/4 cup diced apple

1. In a large bowl, stir together the flour, sugar, baking powder, baking soda, salt, cinnamon, ginger, and nutmeg.
2. In a small bowl, beat egg until frothy. Add syrup, butter, applesauce, and vanilla and mix well.
3. Pour egg mixture into dry ingredients and stir just until moistened.
4. Gently stir in nuts and diced apple.
5. Divide batter among 8 parchment paper-lined muffin cups.
6. Put 4 muffin cups in air fryer basket and bake at 330ºF (166ºC) for 10 minutes.
7. Repeat with remaining 4 muffins or until toothpick inserted in center comes out clean.
8. Serve warm.

Crispy Avocado Quesadillas

Prep time: 10 minutes | Cook time: 11 minutes | Serves 4

4 eggs	4 tablespoons salsa
2 tablespoons skim	2 ounces (57 g)
milk	Cheddar cheese,
Salt and ground black	grated
pepper, to taste	1/2 small avocado,
Cooking spray	peeled and thinly
4 flour tortillas	sliced

1. Beat together the eggs, milk, salt, and pepper.
2. Spray a baking pan lightly with cooking spray and add egg mixture.

3. Bake at 270ºF (132ºC) for 8 minutes, stirring every 1 to 2 minutes, until eggs are scrambled to the liking. Remove and set aside.
4. Spray one side of each tortilla with cooking spray. Flip over.
5. Divide eggs, salsa, cheese, and avocado among the tortillas, covering only half of each tortilla.
6. Fold each tortilla in half and press down lightly. Increase the temperature of the air fryer to 390ºF (199ºC).
7. Put 2 tortillas in air fryer basket and air fry for 3 minutes or until cheese melts and outside feels slightly crispy. Repeat with remaining two tortillas.
8. Cut each cooked tortilla into halves. Serve warm.

Asparagus Spears and Cheese Strata

Prep time: 10 minutes | Cook time: 14 to 19 minutes | Serves 4

6 asparagus spears,	2 tablespoons
cut into 2-inch pieces	chopped flat-leaf
1 tablespoon water	parsley
2 slices whole-	1/2 cup grated Havarti
wheat bread, cut into	or Swiss cheese
1/2-inch cubes	Pinch salt
4 eggs	Freshly ground black
3 tablespoons whole	pepper, to taste
milk	Cooking spray

1. Add the asparagus spears and 1 tablespoon of water in a baking pan and transfer to the air fryer basket. Bake for 3 to 5 minutes until crisp-tender. Remove the asparagus from the pan and drain on paper towels. Spritz the pan with cooking spray.
2. Place the bread and asparagus in the pan.
3. Whisk together the eggs and milk in a medium mixing bowl until creamy. Fold in the parsley, cheese, salt, and pepper and stir to combine. Pour this mixture into the baking pan.
4. Bake at 330ºF (166ºC) for 11 to 14 minutes or until the eggs are set and the top is lightly browned.
5. Let cool for 5 minutes before slicing and serving.

Cheesy Bacon and Egg Bread Cups

Prep time: 10 minutes | Cook time: 8 to 12 minutes | Serves 4

4 (3-by-4-inch) crusty rolls
4 thin slices Gouda or Swiss cheese mini wedges
5 eggs
2 tablespoons heavy cream
3 strips precooked bacon, chopped
½ teaspoon dried thyme
Pinch salt
Freshly ground black pepper, to taste

1. On a clean work surface, cut the tops off the rolls. Using your fingers, remove the insides of the rolls to make bread cups, leaving a ½-inch shell. Place a slice of cheese onto each roll bottom.
2. Whisk together the eggs and heavy cream in a medium bowl until well combined. Fold in the bacon, thyme, salt, and pepper and stir well.
3. Scrape the egg mixture into the prepared bread cups.
4. Transfer the bread cups to the basket and bake at 330°F (166°C) for 8 to 12 minutes, or until the eggs are cooked to your preference.
5. Serve warm.

Oatmeal Banana Bread Pudding

Prep time: 10 minutes | Cook time: 16 to 20 minutes | Serves 4

2 medium ripe bananas, mashed
½ cup low-fat milk
2 tablespoons maple syrup
2 tablespoons peanut butter
1 teaspoon vanilla
extract
1 teaspoon ground cinnamon
2 slices whole-grain bread, cut into bite-sized cubes
¼ cup quick oats
Cooking spray

1. Spritz a baking dish lightly with cooking spray.
2. Mix the bananas, milk, maple syrup, peanut butter, vanilla, and cinnamon in a large mixing bowl and stir until well incorporated.
3. Add the bread cubes to the banana mixture and stir until thoroughly coated. Fold in the oats and stir to combine.

4. Transfer the mixture to the baking dish. Wrap the baking dish in aluminum foil.
5. Air fry in the air fryer at 350°F (177°C) for 10 to 12 minutes until heated through.
6. Remove the foil and cook for an additional 6 to 8 minutes, or until the pudding has set.
7. Let the pudding cool for 5 minutes before serving.

Panko-Crusted Grit and Ham Fritters

Prep time: 15 minutes | Cook time: 20 minutes | Serves 6 to 8

4 cups water
1 cup quick-cooking grits
¼ teaspoon salt
2 tablespoons butter
2 cups grated Cheddar cheese, divided
1 cup finely diced ham
1 tablespoon chopped chives
Salt and freshly ground black pepper, to taste
1 egg, beaten
2 cups panko bread crumbs
Cooking spray

1. Bring the water to a boil in a saucepan. Whisk in the grits and ¼ teaspoon of salt, and cook for 7 minutes until the grits are soft. Remove the pan from the heat and stir in the butter and 1 cup of the grated Cheddar cheese. Transfer the grits to a bowl and let them cool for 10 to 15 minutes.
2. Stir the ham, chives and the rest of the cheese into the grits and season with salt and pepper to taste. Add the beaten egg and refrigerate the mixture for 30 minutes.
3. Put the panko bread crumbs in a shallow dish. Measure out ¼-cup portions of the grits mixture and shape them into patties. Coat all sides of the patties with the panko bread crumbs, patting them with the hands so the crumbs adhere to the patties. You should have about 16 patties. Spritz both sides of the patties with cooking spray.
4. In batches of 5 or 6, air fry the fritters at 400°F (204°C) for 8 minutes. Using a flat spatula, flip the fritters over and air fry for another 4 minutes.
5. Serve hot.

Sausage and Tater Tot Casserole

Prep time: 5 minutes | Cook time: 17 to 19 minutes | Serves 4

4 eggs
1 cup milk
Salt and pepper, to taste
12 ounces (340 g) ground chicken sausage
1 pound (454 g) frozen tater tots, thawed
¾ cup grated Cheddar cheese
Cooking spray

1. Whisk together the eggs and milk in a medium bowl. Season with salt and pepper to taste and stir until mixed. Set aside.
2. Place a skillet over medium-high heat and spritz with cooking spray. Place the ground sausage in the skillet and break it into smaller pieces with a spatula or spoon. Cook for 3 to 4 minutes until the sausage starts to brown, stirring occasionally. Remove from heat and set aside.
3. Coat a baking pan with cooking spray.
4. Arrange the tater tots in the baking pan. Bake in the air fryer at 400ºF (204ºC) for 6 minutes. Shake the basket and stir in the egg mixture and cooked sausage. Bake for another 6 minutes.
5. Scatter the cheese on top of the tater tots. Continue to bake for 2 to 3 minutes more until the cheese is bubbly and melted.
6. Let the mixture cool for 5 minutes and serve warm.

Sweet Banana Bread

Prep time: 10 minutes | Cook time: 22 minutes | Makes 3 loaves

3 ripe bananas, mashed
1 cup sugar
1 large egg
4 tablespoons (½ stick) unsalted butter,
melted
1½ cups all-purpose flour
1 teaspoon baking soda
1 teaspoon salt

1. Coat the insides of 3 mini loaf pans with cooking spray.
2. In a large mixing bowl, mix the bananas and sugar.
3. In a separate large mixing bowl, combine the egg, butter, flour, baking soda, and salt and mix well.
4. Add the banana mixture to the egg and flour mixture. Mix well.
5. Divide the batter evenly among the prepared pans.
6. Set the mini loaf pans into the air fryer basket.
7. Bake in the air fryer at 310ºF (154ºC) for 22 minutes. Insert a toothpick into the center of each loaf; if it comes out clean, they are done.
8. When the loaves are cooked through, remove the pans from the air fryer basket. Turn out the loaves onto a wire rack to cool.
9. Serve warm.

Peanut Butter and Jelly Sandwich

Prep time: 5 minutes | Cook time: 6 minutes | Serves 4

½ cup cornflakes, crushed
¼ cup shredded coconut
8 slices oat nut bread or any whole-grain, oversize bread
6 tablespoons peanut
butter
2 medium bananas, cut into ½-inch-thick slices
6 tablespoons pineapple preserves
1 egg, beaten
Cooking spray

1. In a shallow dish, mix the cornflake crumbs and coconut.
2. For each sandwich, spread one bread slice with 1½ tablespoons of peanut butter. Top with banana slices. Spread another bread slice with 1½ tablespoons of preserves. Combine to make a sandwich.
3. Using a pastry brush, brush top of sandwich lightly with beaten egg. Sprinkle with about 1½ tablespoons of crumb coating, pressing it in to make it stick. Spray with cooking spray.
4. Turn sandwich over and repeat to coat and spray the other side.
5. Air frying 2 at a time, place sandwiches in air fryer basket and air fry at 360ºF (182ºC) for 6 minutes or until coating is golden brown and crispy.
6. Cut the cooked sandwiches in half and serve warm.

Cheesy Bacon and Veggies Casserole

Prep time: 10 minutes | Cook time: 14 minutes | Serves 4

6 slices bacon	½ cup chopped green
6 eggs	bell pepper
Salt and pepper, to	½ cup chopped onion
taste	¾ cup shredded
Cooking spray	Cheddar cheese

1. Place the bacon in a skillet over medium-high heat and cook each side for about 4 minutes until evenly crisp. Remove from the heat to a paper towel-lined plate to drain. Crumble it into small pieces and set aside.
2. Whisk the eggs with the salt and pepper in a medium bowl.
3. Spritz a baking pan with cooking spray.
4. Place the whisked eggs, crumbled bacon, green bell pepper, and onion in the prepared pan. Bake in the air fryer at 400ºF (204ºC) for 6 minutes.
5. Scatter the Cheddar cheese all over and bake for 2 minutes more.
6. Allow to sit for 5 minutes and serve on plates.

Cream Cheese Glazed Cinnamon Rolls

Prep time: 10 minutes | Cook time: 9 minutes | Serves 8

1 pound (454 g)	¾ cup brown sugar
frozen bread dough,	1½ tablespoons
thawed	ground cinnamon
¼ cup butter, melted	
Cream Cheese Glaze:	
4 ounces (113 g)	1¼ cups powdered
cream cheese,	sugar
softened	½ teaspoon vanilla
2 tablespoons butter,	extract
softened	

1. Let the bread dough come to room temperature on the counter. On a lightly floured surface, roll the dough into a 13-inch by 11-inch rectangle. Position the rectangle so the 13-inch side is facing you. Brush the melted butter all over the dough, leaving a 1-inch border uncovered along the edge farthest away from you.
2. Combine the brown sugar and cinnamon in a small bowl. Sprinkle the mixture evenly over the buttered dough, keeping the 1-inch border uncovered. Roll the dough into a log, starting with the edge closest to you. Roll the dough tightly, rolling evenly, and push out any air pockets. When you get to the uncovered edge of the dough, press the dough onto the roll to seal it together.
3. Cut the log into 8 pieces, slicing slowly with a sawing motion so you don't flatten the dough. Turn the slices on their sides and cover with a clean kitchen towel. Let the rolls sit in the warmest part of the kitchen for 1½ to 2 hours to rise.
4. To make the glaze, place the cream cheese and butter in a microwave-safe bowl. Soften the mixture in the microwave for 30 seconds at a time until it is easy to stir. Gradually add the powdered sugar and stir to combine. Add the vanilla extract and whisk until smooth. Set aside.
5. When the rolls have risen. Transfer 4 of the rolls to the air fryer basket. Air fry at 350ºF (177ºC) for 5 minutes. Turn the rolls over and air fry for another 4 minutes. Repeat with the remaining 4 rolls.
6. Let the rolls cool for two minutes before glazing. Spread large dollops of cream cheese glaze on top of the warm cinnamon rolls, allowing some glaze to drip down the side of the rolls. Serve warm.

Fast Sourdough Croutons

Prep time: 5 minutes | Cook time: 6 minutes | Makes 4 cups

4 cups cubed	thyme leaves
sourdough bread,	¼ teaspoon salt
1-inch cubes	Freshly ground black
1 tablespoon olive oil	pepper, to taste
1 teaspoon fresh	

1. Combine all ingredients in a bowl.
2. Toss the bread cubes into the air fryer and air fry at 400ºF (204ºC) for 6 minutes, shaking the basket once or twice while they cook.
3. Serve warm.

Maple Blueberry Cobbler

Prep time: 5 minutes | Cook time: 15 minutes | Serves 4

¾ teaspoon baking powder
⅓ cup whole-wheat pastry flour
Dash sea salt
⅓ cup unsweetened nondairy milk
2 tablespoons maple

syrup
½ teaspoon vanilla
Cooking spray
½ cup blueberries
¼ cup granola
Nondairy yogurt, for topping (optional)

1. Spritz a baking pan with cooking spray.
2. Mix together the baking powder, flour, and salt in a medium bowl. Add the milk, maple syrup, and vanilla and whisk to combine.
3. Scrape the mixture into the prepared pan. Scatter the blueberries and granola on top.
4. Transfer the pan to the air fryer and bake at 347ºF (175ºC) for 15 minutes, or until the top begins to brown and a knife inserted in the center comes out clean.
5. Let the cobbler cool for 5 minutes and serve with a drizzle of nondairy yogurt.

Simple Buttermilk Biscuits

Prep time: 5 minutes | Cook time: 5 minutes | Makes 12 biscuits

2 cups all-purpose flour, plus more for dusting the work surface
1 tablespoon baking powder
¼ teaspoon baking soda

2 teaspoons sugar
1 teaspoon salt
6 tablespoons cold unsalted butter, cut into 1-tablespoon slices
¾ cup buttermilk

1. Spray the air fryer basket with olive oil.
2. In a large mixing bowl, combine the flour, baking powder, baking soda, sugar, and salt and mix well.
3. Using a fork, cut in the butter until the mixture resembles coarse meal.
4. Add the buttermilk and mix until smooth.
5. Dust more flour on a clean work surface. Turn the dough out onto the work surface and roll it out until it is about ½ inch thick.

6. Using a 2-inch biscuit cutter, cut out the biscuits. Put the uncooked biscuits in the greased air fryer basket in a single layer.
7. Bake at 360ºF (182ºC) for 5 minutes. Transfer the cooked biscuits from the air fryer to a platter.
8. Cut the remaining biscuits. Bake the remaining biscuits.
9. Serve warm.

Chocolate, Banana, and Walnut Bread

Prep time: 10 minutes | Cook time: 30 minutes | Serves 4

¼ cup cocoa powder
6 tablespoons plus 2 teaspoons all-purpose flour, divided
½ teaspoon kosher salt
¼ teaspoon baking soda
1½ ripe bananas
1 large egg, whisked
¼ cup vegetable oil

½ cup sugar
3 tablespoons buttermilk or plain yogurt (not Greek)
½ teaspoon vanilla extract
6 tablespoons chopped white chocolate
6 tablespoons chopped walnuts

1. Mix together the cocoa powder, 6 tablespoons of the flour, salt, and baking soda in a medium bowl.
2. Mash the bananas with a fork in another medium bowl until smooth. Fold in the egg, oil, sugar, buttermilk, and vanilla, and whisk until thoroughly combined. Add the wet mixture to the dry mixture and stir until well incorporated.
3. Combine the white chocolate, walnuts, and the remaining 2 tablespoons of flour in a third bowl and toss to coat. Add this mixture to the batter and stir until well incorporated. Pour the batter into a baking pan and smooth the top with a spatula.
4. Bake in the air fryer at 310ºF (154ºC) for about 30 minutes. Check the bread for doneness: If a toothpick inserted into the center of the bread comes out clean, it's done.
5. Remove from the air fryer and allow to cool on a wire rack for 10 minutes before serving.

Fast Coffee Doughnuts

Prep time: 5 minutes | Cook time: 6 minutes | Serves 6

¼ cup sugar
½ teaspoon salt
1 cup flour
1 teaspoon baking powder
¼ cup coffee
1 tablespoon aquafaba
1 tablespoon sunflower oil

1. In a large bowl, combine the sugar, salt, flour, and baking powder.
2. Add the coffee, aquafaba, and sunflower oil and mix until a dough is formed. Leave the dough to rest in and the refrigerator.
3. Remove the dough from the fridge and divide up, kneading each section into a doughnut.
4. Put the doughnuts inside the air fryer. Air fry at 400ºF (204ºC) for 6 minutes.
5. Serve immediately.

Potatoes with Bell Peppers and Onions

Prep time: 10 minutes | Cook time: 35 minutes | Serves 4

1 pound (454 g) red potatoes, cut into ½-inch dices
1 large red bell pepper, cut into ½-inch dices
1 large green bell pepper, cut into ½-inch dices
1 medium onion, cut into ½-inch dices
1½ tablespoons extra-virgin olive oil
1¼ teaspoons kosher salt
¾ teaspoon sweet paprika
¾ teaspoon garlic powder
Freshly ground black pepper, to taste

1. Mix together the potatoes, bell peppers, onion, oil, salt, paprika, garlic powder, and black pepper in a large mixing and toss to coat.
2. Transfer the potato mixture to the air fryer basket and air fry at 350ºF (177ºC) for about 35 minutes, or until the potatoes are nicely browned. Shake the basket three times during cooking.
3. Remove from the basket to a plate and serve warm.

Fast Ham and Corn Muffins

Prep time: 10 minutes | Cook time: 6 minutes | Makes 8 muffins

¾ cup yellow cornmeal
¼ cup flour
1½ teaspoons baking powder
¼ teaspoon salt
1 egg, beaten
2 tablespoons canola oil
½ cup milk
½ cup shredded sharp Cheddar cheese
½ cup diced ham

1. In a medium bowl, stir together the cornmeal, flour, baking powder, and salt.
2. Add the egg, oil, and milk to dry ingredients and mix well.
3. Stir in shredded cheese and diced ham.
4. Divide batter among 8 parchment paper-lined muffin cups.
5. Put 4 filled muffin cups in air fryer basket and bake at 390ºF (199ºC) for 5 minutes.
6. Reduce temperature to 330ºF (166ºC) and bake for 1 minute or until a toothpick inserted in center of the muffin comes out clean.
7. Repeat steps 6 and 7 to bake remaining muffins.
8. Serve warm.

Super Veggies Omelet

Prep time: 10 minutes | Cook time: 13 minutes | Serves 2

2 teaspoons canola oil
4 eggs, whisked
3 tablespoons plain milk
1 teaspoon melted butter
1 red bell pepper, seeded and chopped
1 green bell pepper, seeded and chopped
1 white onion, finely chopped
½ cup baby spinach leaves, roughly chopped
½ cup Halloumi cheese, shaved
Kosher salt and freshly ground black pepper, to taste

1. Grease a baking pan with canola oil.
2. Put the remaining ingredients in the baking pan and stir well.
3. Transfer to the air fryer and bake at 350ºF (177ºC) for 13 minutes.
4. Serve warm.

Air-Fried Cheesy Hash Brown Casserole

Prep time: 15 minutes | Cook time: 30 minutes | Serves 4

3½ cups frozen hash browns, thawed
1 teaspoon salt
1 teaspoon freshly ground black pepper
3 tablespoons butter, melted
1 (10.5-ounce / 298-

g) can cream of chicken soup
½ cup sour cream
1 cup minced onion
½ cup shredded sharp Cheddar cheese
Cooking spray

1. Put the hash browns in a large bowl and season with salt and black pepper. Add the melted butter, cream of chicken soup, and sour cream and stir until well incorporated. Mix in the minced onion and cheese and stir well.
2. Spray a baking pan with cooking spray.
3. Spread the hash brown mixture evenly into the baking pan.
4. Place the pan in the air fryer basket and bake at 325°F (163°C) for 30 minutes until browned.
5. Cool for 5 minutes before serving.

Chicken and Apple Patties

Prep time: 15 minutes | Cook time: 8 to 12 minutes | Makes 8 patties

1 Granny Smith apple, peeled and finely chopped
2 tablespoons apple juice
2 garlic cloves, minced
1 egg white

⅓ cup minced onion
3 tablespoons ground almonds
⅛ teaspoon freshly ground black pepper
1 pound (454 g) ground chicken breast

1. Combine all the ingredients except the chicken in a medium mixing bowl and stir well.
2. Add the chicken breast to the apple mixture and mix with your hands until well incorporated.
3. Divide the mixture into 8 equal portions and shape into patties. Arrange the patties in the air fryer basket. You may

need to work in batches depending on the size of your air fryer basket.
4. Air fry at 330°F (166°C) for 8 to 12 minutes, or until a meat thermometer inserted in the center of the chicken reaches at least 165°F (74°C).
5. Remove from the air fryer to a plate and repeat with the remaining patties.
6. Let the chicken cool for 5 minutes and serve warm.

Creamy Coconut Brown Rice Porridge

Prep time: 5 minutes | Cook time: 23 minutes | Serves 1 or 2

½ cup cooked brown rice
1 cup canned coconut milk
¼ cup unsweetened shredded coconut
¼ cup packed dark brown sugar
4 large Medjool

dates, pitted and roughly chopped
½ teaspoon kosher salt
¼ teaspoon ground cardamom
Heavy cream, for serving (optional)

1. Place all the ingredients except the heavy cream in a baking pan and stir until blended.
2. Transfer the pan to the air fryer and bake at 375°F (191°C) for about 23 minutes until the porridge is thick and creamy. Stir the porridge halfway through the cooking time.
3. Remove from the air fryer and ladle the porridge into bowls.
4. Serve hot with a drizzle of the cream, if desired.

Golden French Toast Sticks

Prep time: 10 minutes | Cook time: 6 minutes | Serves 4

2 eggs
½ cup milk
⅛ teaspoon salt
½ teaspoon pure vanilla extract
¾ cup crushed cornflakes

6 slices sandwich bread, each slice cut into 4 strips
Maple syrup, for dipping
Cooking spray

1. In a small bowl, beat together the eggs,

milk, salt, and vanilla.
2. Put crushed cornflakes on a plate or in a shallow dish.
3. Dip bread strips in egg mixture, shake off excess, and roll in cornflake crumbs.
4. Spray both sides of bread strips with oil.
5. Put bread strips in air fryer basket in a single layer.
6. Air fry at 390ºF (199ºC) for 6 minutes or until golden brown.
7. Repeat steps 5 and 6 to air fry remaining French toast sticks.
8. Serve with maple syrup.

Cheesy Broccoli Quiche

Prep time: 5 minutes | Cook time: 10 minutes | Serves 4

1 cup broccoli florets
¾ cup chopped roasted red peppers
1¼ cups grated Fontina cheese
6 eggs
¾ cup heavy cream
½ teaspoon salt
Freshly ground black pepper, to taste
Cooking spray

1. Spritz a baking pan with cooking spray.
2. Add the broccoli florets and roasted red peppers to the pan and scatter the grated Fontina cheese on top.
3. In a bowl, beat together the eggs and heavy cream. Sprinkle with salt and pepper. Pour the egg mixture over the top of the cheese. Wrap the pan in foil.
4. Transfer the pan to the air fryer and air fry at 325ºF (163ºC) for 8 minutes. Remove the foil and continue to cook another 2 minutes until the quiche is golden brown.
5. Rest for 5 minutes before cutting into wedges and serve warm.

Crispy Egg and Avocado Burrito

Prep time: 10 minutes | Cook time: 3 to 5 minutes | Serves 4

4 low-sodium whole-wheat flour tortillas
Filling:
1 hard-boiled egg, chopped
2 hard-boiled egg
whites, chopped
1 ripe avocado, peeled, pitted, and chopped
1 red bell pepper, chopped
1 (1.2-ounce / 34-g) slice low-sodium, low-fat American cheese, torn into pieces
3 tablespoons low-sodium salsa, plus additional for serving (optional)

Special Equipment:
4 toothpicks (optional), soaked in water for at least 30 minutes

1. Make the filling: Combine the egg, egg whites, avocado, red bell pepper, cheese, and salsa in a medium bowl and stir until blended.
2. Assemble the burritos: Arrange the tortillas on a clean work surface and place ¼ of the prepared filling in the middle of each tortilla, leaving about 1½-inch on each end unfilled. Fold in the opposite sides of each tortilla and roll up. Secure with toothpicks through the center, if needed.
3. Transfer the burritos to the air fryer basket and air fry at 390ºF (199ºC) for 3 to 5 minutes, or until the burritos are crisp and golden brown.
4. Allow to cool for 5 minutes and serve with salsa, if desired.

Pumpkin English Muffin

Prep time: 10 minutes | Cook time: 10 minutes | Serves 2

2 eggs
½ cup milk
2 cups flour
2 tablespoons cider vinegar
2 teaspoons baking powder
1 tablespoon sugar
1 cup pumpkin purée
1 teaspoon cinnamon powder
1 teaspoon baking soda
1 tablespoon olive oil

1. Crack the eggs into a bowl and beat with a whisk. Combine with the milk, flour, cider vinegar, baking powder, sugar, pumpkin purée, cinnamon powder, and baking soda, mixing well.
2. Grease a baking tray with oil. Add the mixture and transfer into the air fryer. Bake at 300ºF (149ºC) for 10 minutes.
3. Serve warm.

Golden Maple Walnut Pancake

Prep time: 10 minutes | Cook time: 20 minutes | Serves 4

3 tablespoons melted butter, divided
1 cup flour
2 tablespoons sugar
1½ teaspoons baking powder
¼ teaspoon salt
1 egg, beaten
¾ cup milk
1 teaspoon pure vanilla extract
½ cup roughly chopped walnuts
Maple syrup or fresh sliced fruit, for serving

1. Grease a baking pan with 1 tablespoon of melted butter.
2. Mix together the flour, sugar, baking powder, and salt in a medium bowl. Add the beaten egg, milk, the remaining 2 tablespoons of melted butter, and vanilla and stir until the batter is sticky but slightly lumpy.
3. Slowly pour the batter into the greased baking pan and scatter with the walnuts.
4. Place the pan in the air fryer basket and bake at 330ºF (166ºC) for 20 minutes until golden brown and cooked through.
5. Let the pancake rest for 5 minutes and serve topped with the maple syrup or fresh fruit, if desired.

Vanilla Soufflé

Prep time: 10 minutes | Cook time: 22 minutes | Serves 4

⅓ cup butter, melted
¼ cup flour
1 cup milk
1 ounce (28 g) sugar
4 egg yolks
1 teaspoon vanilla extract
6 egg whites
1 teaspoon cream of tartar
Cooking spray

1. In a bowl, mix the butter and flour until a smooth consistency is achieved.
2. Pour the milk into a saucepan over medium-low heat. Add the sugar and allow to dissolve before raising the heat to boil the milk.
3. Pour in the flour and butter mixture and stir rigorously for 7 minutes to eliminate any lumps. Make sure the mixture thickens. Take off the heat and allow to cool for 15 minutes.
4. Spritz 6 soufflé dishes with cooking spray.
5. Put the egg yolks and vanilla extract in a separate bowl and beat them together with a fork. Pour in the milk and combine well to incorporate everything.
6. In a smaller bowl mix the egg whites and cream of tartar with a fork. Fold into the egg yolks-milk mixture before adding in the flour mixture. Transfer equal amounts to the 6 soufflé dishes.
7. Put the dishes in the air fryer and bake at 320ºF (160ºC) for 15 minutes.
8. Serve warm.

Cheesy Frittata with Avocado Dressing

Prep time: 10 minutes | Cook time: 20 minutes | Serves 2 or 3

½ cup cherry tomatoes, halved
Kosher salt and freshly ground black pepper, to taste
6 large eggs, lightly beaten
½ cup corn kernels, thawed if frzoen
¼ cup milk
1 tablespoon finely chopped fresh dill
½ cup shredded Monterey Jack cheese
Avocado Dressing:
1 ripe avocado, pitted and peeled
2 tablespoons fresh lime juice
¼ cup olive oil
1 scallion, finely chopped
8 fresh basil leaves, finely chopped

1. Put the tomato halves in a colander and lightly season with salt. Set aside for 10 minutes to drain well. Pour the tomatoes into a large bowl and fold in the eggs, corn, milk, and dill. Sprinkle with salt and pepper and stir until mixed.
2. Pour the egg mixture into a baking pan. Transfer the pan to the air fryer and bake at 300ºF (149ºC) for 15 minutes.
3. Scatter the cheese on top. Increase the air fryer temperature to 315ºF (157ºC) and continue to cook for another 5 minutes, or until the frittata is puffy and set.
4. Meanwhile, make the avocado dressing: Mash the avocado with the lime juice in a medium bowl until smooth. Mix in the olive oil, scallion, and basil and stir until well incorporated.
5. Let the frittata cool for 5 minutes and serve alongside the avocado dressing.

Mushroom, Squash, and Pepper Toast

Prep time: 10 minutes | Cook time: 10 minutes | Serves 4

1 tablespoon olive oil
1 red bell pepper, cut into strips
2 green onions, sliced
1 cup sliced button or cremini mushrooms
1 small yellow
squash, sliced
2 tablespoons softened butter
4 slices bread
½ cup soft goat cheese

1. Brush the air fryer basket with the olive oil.
2. Put the red pepper, green onions, mushrooms, and squash inside the air fryer, give them a stir and air fry at 350ºF (177ºC) for 7 minutes or the vegetables are tender, shaking the basket once throughout the cooking time.
3. Remove the vegetables and set them aside.
4. Spread the butter on the slices of bread and transfer to the air fryer, butter-side up. Brown for 3 minutes.
5. Remove the toast from the air fryer and top with goat cheese and vegetables. Serve warm.

Brown Sugar Nut and Seed Muffins

Prep time: 15 minutes | Cook time: 10 minutes | Makes 8 muffins

½ cup whole-wheat flour, plus 2 tablespoons
¼ cup oat bran
2 tablespoons flaxseed meal
¼ cup brown sugar
½ teaspoon baking soda
½ teaspoon baking powder
¼ teaspoon salt
½ teaspoon cinnamon
½ cup buttermilk
2 tablespoons melted butter
1 egg
½ teaspoon pure vanilla extract
½ cup grated carrots
¼ cup chopped pecans
¼ cup chopped walnuts
1 tablespoon pumpkin seeds
1 tablespoon sunflower seeds
Cooking spray

Special Equipment:
16 foil muffin cups, paper liners removed

1. In a large bowl, stir together the flour, bran, flaxseed meal, sugar, baking soda, baking powder, salt, and cinnamon.
2. In a medium bowl, beat together the buttermilk, butter, egg, and vanilla. Pour into flour mixture and stir just until dry ingredients moisten. Do not beat.
3. Gently stir in carrots, nuts, and seeds.
4. Double up the foil cups so you have 8 total and spritz with cooking spray.
5. Put 4 foil cups in air fryer basket and divide half the batter among them.
6. Bake at 330ºF (166ºC) for 10 minutes or until a toothpick inserted in center comes out clean.
7. Repeat step 7 to bake remaining 4 muffins.
8. Serve warm.

Spinach, Mushroom and Leek Frittata

Prep time: 10 minutes | Cook time: 20 to 23 minutes | Serves 2

4 large eggs
4 ounces (113 g) baby bella mushrooms, chopped
1 cup (1 ounce / 28-g) baby spinach, chopped
½ cup (2 ounces / 57-g) shredded Cheddar cheese
⅓ cup (from 1 large) chopped leek, white part only
¼ cup halved grape tomatoes
1 tablespoon 2% milk
¼ teaspoon dried oregano
¼ teaspoon garlic powder
½ teaspoon kosher salt
Freshly ground black pepper, to taste
Cooking spray

1. Lightly spritz a baking dish with cooking spray.
2. Whisk the eggs in a large bowl until frothy. Add the mushrooms, baby spinach, cheese, leek, tomatoes, milk, oregano, garlic powder, salt, and pepper and stir until well blended. Pour the mixture into the prepared baking dish.
3. Put the baking dish in the air fryer basket and bake at 300ºF (149ºC) until the center is puffed up and the top is golden brown, about 20 to 23 minutes.
4. Let the frittata cool for 5 minutes before slicing to serve.

Cheesy Western Omelet

Prep time: 5 minutes | Cook time: 18 to 21 minutes | Serves 2

¼ cup chopped bell pepper, green or red
¼ cup chopped onion
¼ cup diced ham
1 teaspoon butter
4 large eggs
2 tablespoons milk
⅛ teaspoon salt
¾ cup shredded sharp Cheddar cheese

1. Put the bell pepper, onion, ham, and butter in a baking pan and mix well.
2. Air fry in the air fryer at 390ºF (199ºC) for 1 minute. Stir and continue to cook for an additional 4 to 5 minutes until the veggies are softened.
3. Meanwhile, whisk together the eggs, milk, and salt in a bowl.
4. Pour the egg mixture over the veggie mixture. Reduce the air fryer temperature to 360ºF (182ºC) and bake for 13 to 15 minutes more, or until the top is lightly golden browned and the eggs are set.
5. Scatter the omelet with the shredded cheese. Bake for another 1 minute until the cheese has melted.
6. Let the omelet cool for 5 minutes before serving.

Easy Potato Rolls

Prep time: 15 minutes | Cook time: 20 minutes | Serves 5

5 large potatoes, boiled and mashed
Salt and ground black pepper, to taste
½ teaspoon mustard seeds
1 tablespoon olive oil
2 small onions, chopped
2 sprigs curry leaves
½ teaspoon turmeric powder
2 green chilis, seeded and chopped
1 bunch coriander, chopped
8 slices bread, brown sides discarded

1. Put the mashed potatoes in a bowl and sprinkle on salt and pepper. Set to one side.
2. Fry the mustard seeds in olive oil over a medium-low heat in a skillet, stirring continuously, until they sputter.

3. Add the onions and cook until they turn translucent. Add the curry leaves and turmeric powder and stir. Cook for a further 2 minutes until fragrant.
4. Remove the pan from the heat and combine with the potatoes. Mix in the green chilies and coriander.
5. Wet the bread slightly and drain of any excess liquid.
6. Spoon a small amount of the potato mixture into the center of the bread and enclose the bread around the filling, sealing it entirely. Continue until the rest of the bread and filling is used up. Brush each bread roll with some oil and transfer to the basket of the air fryer.
7. Air fry at 400ºF (204ºC) for 15 minutes, gently shaking the air fryer basket at the halfway point to ensure each roll is cooked evenly.
8. Serve immediately.

Vegetable Parmesan Frittata

Prep time: 10 minutes | Cook time: 8 to 12 minutes | Serves 4

½ cup chopped red bell pepper
⅓ cup grated carrot
⅓ cup minced onion
1 teaspoon olive oil
1 egg
6 egg whites
⅓ cup 2% milk
1 tablespoon shredded Parmesan cheese

1. Mix together the red bell pepper, carrot, onion, and olive oil in a baking pan and stir to combine.
2. Transfer the pan to the air fryer and bake at 350ºF (177ºC) for 4 to 6 minutes until the veggies are soft. Shake the basket once during cooking.
3. Meantime, whisk together the egg, egg whites, and milk in a medium bowl until creamy.
4. When the veggies are done, pour the egg mixture over the top. Scatter with the Parmesan cheese.
5. Bake for an additional 4 to 6 minutes, or until the eggs are set and the top is golden around the edges.
6. Allow the frittata to cool for 5 minutes before slicing and serving.

Classic Berry Dutch Baby Pancake

Prep time: 10 minutes | Cook time: 12 to 16 minutes | Serves 4

1 tablespoon unsalted butter, at room temperature
1 egg
2 egg whites
½ cup 2% milk
½ cup whole-wheat pastry flour

1 teaspoon pure vanilla extract
1 cup sliced fresh strawberries
½ cup fresh raspberries
½ cup fresh blueberries

1. Grease a baking pan with the butter.
2. Using a hand mixer, beat together the egg, egg whites, milk, pastry flour, and vanilla in a medium mixing bowl until well incorporated.
3. Pour the batter into the pan and bake in the air fryer at 330ºF (166ºC) for 12 to 16 minutes, or until the pancake puffs up in the center and the edges are golden brown.
4. Allow the pancake to cool for 5 minutes and serve topped with the berries.

Ritzy Orange Glazed Rolls

Prep time: 15 minutes | Cook time: 8 minutes | Makes 8 rolls

3 ounces (85 g) low-fat cream cheese
1 tablespoon low-fat sour cream or plain yogurt
2 teaspoons sugar
¼ teaspoon pure vanilla extract
¼ teaspoon orange extract
1 can (8 count) organic crescent roll dough
¼ cup chopped walnuts

¼ cup dried cranberries
¼ cup shredded, sweetened coconut
Butter-flavored cooking spray
Orange Glaze:
½ cup powdered sugar
1 tablespoon orange juice
¼ teaspoon orange extract
Dash of salt

1. Cut a circular piece of parchment paper slightly smaller than the bottom of the air fryer basket. Set aside.
2. In a small bowl, combine the cream cheese, sour cream or yogurt, sugar, and vanilla and orange extracts. Stir until smooth.

3. Separate crescent roll dough into 8 triangles and divide cream cheese mixture among them. Starting at wide end, spread cheese mixture to within 1 inch of point.
4. Sprinkle nuts and cranberries evenly over cheese mixture.
5. Starting at wide end, roll up triangles, then sprinkle with coconut, pressing in lightly to make it stick. Spray tops of rolls with butter-flavored cooking spray.
6. Put parchment paper in air fryer basket, and place 4 rolls on top, spaced evenly.
7. Air fry at 300ºF (149ºC) for 8 minutes, until rolls are golden brown and cooked through.
8. Repeat steps 7 and 8 to air fry remaining 4 rolls. You should be able to use the same piece of parchment paper twice.
9. In a small bowl, stir together ingredients for glaze and drizzle over warm rolls. Serve warm.

Sugar-Free Sausage and Cheese Quiche

Prep time: 5 minutes | Cook time: 25 minutes | Serves 4

12 large eggs
1 cup heavy cream
Salt and black pepper, to taste
12 ounces (340 g)

sugar-free breakfast sausage
2 cups shredded Cheddar cheese
Cooking spray

1. Coat a casserole dish with cooking spray.
2. Beat together the eggs, heavy cream, salt and pepper in a large bowl until creamy. Stir in the breakfast sausage and Cheddar cheese.
3. Pour the sausage mixture into the prepared casserole dish and bake at 375ºF (191ºC) for 25 minutes, or until the top of the quiche is golden brown and the eggs are set.
4. Remove from the air fryer and let sit for 5 to 10 minutes before serving.

Cheesy Olives and Kale Baked Eggs

Prep time: 5 minutes | Cook time: 10 to 12 minutes | Serves 2

1 cup roughly chopped kale leaves, stems and center ribs removed
¼ cup grated pecorino cheese
¼ cup olive oil
1 garlic clove, peeled
3 tablespoons whole almonds
Kosher salt and freshly ground black pepper, to taste
4 large eggs
2 tablespoons heavy cream
3 tablespoons chopped pitted mixed olives

1. Place the kale, pecorino, olive oil, garlic, almonds, salt, and pepper in a small blender and blitz until well incorporated.
2. One at a time, crack the eggs in a baking pan. Drizzle the kale pesto on top of the egg whites. Top the yolks with the cream and swirl together the yolks and the pesto.
3. Transfer the pan to the air fryer basket and bake at 300ºF (149ºC) for 10 to 12 minutes, or until the top begins to brown and the eggs are set.
4. Allow the eggs to cool for 5 minutes. Scatter the olives on top and serve warm.

Cheesy Spinach Omelet

Prep time: 10 minutes | Cook time: 10 minutes | Serves 1

1 teaspoon olive oil
3 eggs
Salt and ground black pepper, to taste
1 tablespoon ricotta cheese
¼ cup chopped spinach
1 tablespoon chopped parsley

1. Grease the air fryer basket with olive oil..
2. In a bowl, beat the eggs with a fork and sprinkle salt and pepper.
3. Add the ricotta, spinach, and parsley and then transfer to the air fryer. Bake at 330ºF (166ºC) for 10 minutes or until the egg is set.
4. Serve warm.

Homemade Soft Pretzels

Prep time: 10 minutes | Cook time: 6 minutes | Makes 24 pretzels

2 teaspoons yeast
1 cup water, warm
1 teaspoon sugar
1 teaspoon salt
2½ cups all-purpose flour
2 tablespoons butter,
melted, plus more as needed
1 cup boiling water
1 tablespoon baking soda
Coarse sea salt, to taste

1. Combine the yeast and water in a small bowl. Combine the sugar, salt and flour in the bowl of a stand mixer. With the mixer running and using the dough hook, drizzle in the yeast mixture and melted butter and knead dough until smooth and elastic, about 10 minutes. Shape into a ball and let the dough rise for 1 hour.
2. Punch the dough down to release any air and divide the dough into 24 portions.
3. Roll each portion into a skinny rope using both hands on the counter and rolling from the center to the ends of the rope. Spin the rope into a pretzel shape (or tie the rope into a knot) and place the tied pretzels on a parchment lined baking sheet.
4. Combine the boiling water and baking soda in a shallow bowl and whisk to dissolve. Let the water cool so you can put the hands in it. Working in batches, dip the pretzels (top side down) into the baking soda mixture and let them soak for 30 seconds to a minute. Then remove the pretzels carefully and return them (top side up) to the baking sheet. Sprinkle the coarse salt on the top.
5. Air fry in batches at 350ºF (177ºC) for 3 minutes per side. When the pretzels are finished, brush them generously with the melted butter and enjoy them warm.

Chapter 5 Wraps and Sandwiches

Cheesy Potato and Black Bean Burritos

Prep time: 15 minutes | Cook time: 1 hour | Makes 6 burritos

2 sweet potatoes, peeled and cut into a small dice
1 tablespoon vegetable oil
Kosher salt and ground black pepper, to taste
6 large flour tortillas
1 (16-ounce / 454-g) can refried black beans, divided
1½ cups baby spinach, divided
6 eggs, scrambled
¾ cup grated Cheddar cheese, divided
¼ cup salsa
¼ cup sour cream
Cooking spray

1. Put the sweet potatoes in a large bowl, then drizzle with vegetable oil and sprinkle with salt and black pepper. Toss to coat well.
2. Place the potatoes in the air fryer and air fry at 400°F (204°C) for 10 minutes or until lightly browned. Shake the basket halfway through.
3. Unfold the tortillas on a clean work surface. Divide the black beans, spinach, air fried sweet potatoes, scrambled eggs, and cheese on top of the tortillas.
4. Fold the long side of the tortillas over the filling, then fold in the shorter side to wrap the filling to make the burritos.
5. Work in batches, wrap the burritos in the aluminum foil and put in the air fryer to air fry at 350°F (177°C) for 20 minutes. Flip the burritos halfway through.
6. Remove the burritos from the air fryer and put back to the air fryer. Spritz with cooking spray and air fry for 5 more minutes or until lightly browned. Repeat with remaining burritos.
7. Remove the burritos from the air fryer and spread with sour cream and salsa. Serve immediately.

Mexican Paprika Chicken Burgers

Prep time: 15 minutes | Cook time: 20 minutes | Serves 6 to 8

4 skinless and boneless chicken breasts
1 small head of cauliflower, sliced into florets
1 jalapeño pepper
3 tablespoons smoked paprika
1 tablespoon thyme
1 tablespoon oregano
1 tablespoon mustard powder
1 teaspoon cayenne pepper
1 egg
Salt and ground black pepper, to taste
2 tomatoes, sliced
2 lettuce leaves, chopped
6 to 8 brioche buns, sliced lengthwise
¾ cup taco sauce
Cooking spray

1. In a blender, add the cauliflower florets, jalapeño pepper, paprika, thyme, oregano, mustard powder and cayenne pepper and blend until the mixture has a texture similar to breadcrumbs.
2. Transfer ¾ of the cauliflower mixture to a medium bowl and set aside. Beat the egg in a different bowl and set aside.
3. Add the chicken breasts to the blender with remaining cauliflower mixture. Sprinkle with salt and pepper. Blend until finely chopped and well mixed.
4. Remove the mixture from the blender and form into 6 to 8 patties. One by one, dredge each patty in the reserved cauliflower mixture, then into the egg. Dip them in the cauliflower mixture again for additional coating.
5. Place the coated patties into the air fryer basket and spritz with cooking spray. Air fry at 350°F (177°C) for 20 minutes or until golden and crispy. Flip halfway through to ensure even cooking.
6. Transfer the patties to a clean work surface and assemble with the buns, tomato slices, chopped lettuce leaves and taco sauce to make burgers. Serve and enjoy.

Crispy Cheesy Wontons

Prep time: 5 minutes | Cook time: 6 minutes | Serves 4

2 ounces (57 g) cream cheese, softened	16 square wonton wrappers
1 tablespoon sugar	Cooking spray

1. Spritz the air fryer basket with cooking spray.
2. In a mixing bowl, stir together the cream cheese and sugar until well mixed. Prepare a small bowl of water alongside.
3. On a clean work surface, lay the wonton wrappers. Scoop ¼ teaspoon of cream cheese in the center of each wonton wrapper. Dab the water over the wrapper edges. Fold each wonton wrapper diagonally in half over the filling to form a triangle.
4. Arrange the wontons in the air fryer basket. Spritz the wontons with cooking spray. Air fry at 350ºF (177ºC) for 6 minutes, or until golden brown and crispy. Flip once halfway through to ensure even cooking.
5. Divide the wontons among four plates. Let rest for 5 minutes before serving.

BBQ Bacon and Bell Pepper Sandwich

Prep time: 10 minutes | Cook time: 6 minutes | Serves 4

⅓ cup spicy barbecue sauce	1 yellow bell pepper, sliced
2 tablespoons honey	3 pita pockets, cut in half
8 slices cooked bacon, cut into thirds	1¼ cups torn butter lettuce leaves
1 red bell pepper, sliced	2 tomatoes, sliced

1. In a small bowl, combine the barbecue sauce and the honey. Brush this mixture lightly onto the bacon slices and the red and yellow pepper slices.
2. Put the peppers into the air fryer basket and roast at 350ºF (177ºC) for 4 minutes. Then shake the basket, add the bacon, and roast for 2 minutes or until the bacon is browned and the peppers are tender.
3. Fill the pita halves with the bacon, peppers, any remaining barbecue sauce, lettuce, and tomatoes, and serve immediately.

Bulgogi Burgers with Korean Mayo

Prep time: 15 minutes | Cook time: 10 minutes | Serves 4

For the Burgers:

1 pound (454 g) 85% lean ground beef	1 tablespoon soy sauce
2 tablespoons gochujang	1 tablespoon toasted sesame oil
¼ cup chopped scallions	2 teaspoons sugar
2 teaspoons minced garlic	½ teaspoon kosher salt
2 teaspoons minced fresh ginger	4 hamburger buns
	Cooking spray

For the Korean Mayo:

1 tablespoon gochujang	¼ cup chopped scallions
¼ cup mayonnaise	1 tablespoon toasted sesame oil
2 teaspoons sesame seeds	

1. Combine the ingredients for the burgers, except for the buns, in a large bowl. Stir to mix well, then wrap the bowl in plastic and refrigerate to marinate for at least an hour.
2. Divide the meat mixture into four portions and form into four balls. Bash the balls into patties.
3. Arrange the patties in the air fryer and spritz with cooking spray. Air fry at 350ºF (177ºC) for 10 minutes or until golden brown. Flip the patties halfway through.
4. Meanwhile, combine the ingredients for the Korean mayo in a small bowl. Stir to mix well.
5. Remove the patties from the air fryer and assemble with the buns, then spread the Korean mayo over the patties to make the burgers. Serve immediately.

Golden Samosas with Chutney

Prep time: 30 minutes | Cook time: 1 hour 10 minutes | Makes 16 samosas

Dough:

4 cups all-purpose flour, plus more for flouring the work surface
¼ cup plain yogurt

½ cup cold unsalted butter, cut into cubes
2 teaspoons kosher salt
1 cup ice water

Filling:

2 tablespoons vegetable oil
1 onion, diced
1½ teaspoons coriander
1½ teaspoons cumin
1 clove garlic, minced
1 teaspoon turmeric

1 teaspoon kosher salt
½ cup peas, thawed if frozen
2 cups mashed potatoes
2 tablespoons yogurt
Cooking spray

Chutney:

1 cup mint leaves, lightly packed
2 cups cilantro leaves, lightly packed
1 green chile pepper, deseeded and minced
½ cup minced onion

Juice of 1 lime
1 teaspoon granulated sugar
1 teaspoon kosher salt
2 tablespoons vegetable oil

1. Put the flour, yogurt, butter, and salt in a food processor. Pulse to combine until grainy. Pour in the water and pulse until a smooth and firm dough forms.
2. Transfer the dough on a clean and lightly floured working surface. Knead the dough and shape it into a ball. Cut in half and flatten the halves into 2 discs. Wrap them in plastic and let sit in refrigerator until ready to use.
3. Meanwhile, make the filling: Heat the vegetable oil in a saucepan over medium heat.
4. Add the onion and sauté for 5 minutes or until lightly browned.
5. Add the coriander, cumin, garlic, turmeric, and salt and sauté for 2 minutes or until fragrant.
6. Add the peas, potatoes, and yogurt and stir to combine well. Turn off the heat and allow to cool.
7. Meanwhile, combine the ingredients for the chutney in a food processor. Pulse to mix well until glossy. Pour the chutney in a bowl and refrigerate until ready to use.
8. Make the samosas: Remove the dough discs from the refrigerator and cut each disc into 8 parts. Shape each part into a ball, then roll the ball into a 6-inch circle. Cut the circle in half and roll each half into a cone.
9. Scoop up 2 tablespoons of the filling into the cone, press the edges of the cone to seal and form into a triangle. Repeat with remaining dough and filling.
10. Arrange four samosas each batch in the air fryer and spritz with cooking spray. Air fry at 360ºF (182ºC) for 15 minutes or until golden brown and crispy. Flip the samosas halfway through.
11. Serve the samosas with the chutney.

Golden Cabbage and Pork Gyoza

Prep time: 10 minutes | Cook time: 10 minutes per batch | Makes 48 gyozas

1 pound (454 g) ground pork
1 small head Napa cabbage (about 1 pound / 454 g), sliced thinly and minced
½ cup minced scallions
1 teaspoon minced fresh chives
1 teaspoon soy sauce

1 teaspoon minced fresh ginger
1 tablespoon minced garlic
1 teaspoon granulated sugar
2 teaspoons kosher salt
48 to 50 wonton or dumpling wrappers
Cooking spray

1. Make the filling: Combine all the ingredients, except for the wrappers in a large bowl. Stir to mix well.
2. Unfold a wrapper on a clean work surface, then dab the edges with a little water. Scoop up 2 teaspoons of the filling mixture in the center.
3. Make the gyoza: Fold the wrapper over to filling and press the edges to seal. Pleat the edges if desired. Repeat with remaining wrappers and fillings.
4. Arrange the gyozas in the air fryer and spritz with cooking spray. Air fry at 360ºF (182ºC) for 10 minutes or until golden brown. Flip the gyozas halfway through. Work in batches to avoid overcrowding.
5. Serve immediately.

Fast Steak and Seeds Burgers

Prep time: 15 minutes | Cook time: 10 minutes | Serves 4

1 teaspoon cumin seeds	salt
1 teaspoon mustard seeds	2 teaspoons ground black pepper
1 teaspoon coriander seeds	1 pound (454 g) 85% lean ground beef
1 teaspoon dried minced garlic	2 tablespoons Worcestershire sauce
1 teaspoon dried red pepper flakes	4 hamburger buns
1 teaspoon kosher	Mayonnaise, for serving
	Cooking spray

1. Put the seeds, garlic, red pepper flakes, salt, and ground black pepper in a food processor. Pulse to coarsely ground the mixture.
2. Put the ground beef in a large bowl. Pour in the seed mixture and drizzle with Worcestershire sauce. Stir to mix well.
3. Divide the mixture into four parts and shape each part into a ball, then bash each ball into a patty.
4. Arrange the patties in the air fryer and air fry at 350ºF (177ºC) for 10 minutes or until the patties are well browned. Flip the patties with tongs halfway through.
5. Assemble the buns with the patties, then drizzle the mayo over the patties to make the burgers. Serve immediately.

Cheesy Salsa Chicken Taquitos

Prep time: 15 minutes | Cook time: 12 minutes | Serves 4

1 cup cooked chicken, shredded	Mozzarella cheese
¼ cup Greek yogurt	Salt and ground black pepper, to taste
¼ cup salsa	4 flour tortillas
1 cup shredded	Cooking spray

1. Combine all the ingredients, except for the tortillas, in a large bowl. Stir to mix well.
2. Make the taquitos: Unfold the tortillas on a clean work surface, then scoop up 2 tablespoons of the chicken mixture in the middle of each tortilla. Roll the tortillas up to wrap the filling.

3. Arrange the taquitos in the air fryer and spritz with cooking spray.
4. Air fry at 380ºF (193ºC) for 12 minutes or until golden brown and the cheese melts. Flip the taquitos halfway through.
5. Serve immediately.

Crispy Crabmeat Wontons

Prep time: 10 minutes | Cook time: 10 minutes per batch | Serves 6 to 8

24 wonton wrappers, thawed if frozen
Cooking spray
For the Filling:

5 ounces (142 g) lump crabmeat, drained and patted dry	1½ teaspoons toasted sesame oil
4 ounces (113 g) cream cheese, at room temperature	1 teaspoon Worcestershire sauce
2 scallions, sliced	Kosher salt and ground black pepper, to taste

1. Spritz the air fryer basket with cooking spray.
2. In a medium-size bowl, place all the ingredients for the filling and stir until well mixed. Prepare a small bowl of water alongside.
3. On a clean work surface, lay the wonton wrappers. Scoop 1 teaspoon of the filling in the center of each wrapper. Wet the edges with a touch of water. Fold each wonton wrapper diagonally in half over the filling to form a triangle.
4. Arrange the wontons in the air fryer basket. Spritz the wontons with cooking spray. Work in batches, 6 to 8 at a time. Air fry at 350ºF (177ºC) for 10 minutes, or until crispy and golden brown. Flip once halfway through.
5. Serve immediately.

Homemade Sloppy Joes

Prep time: 10 minutes | Cook time: 17 to 19 minutes | Makes 4 large sandwiches or 8 sliders

1 pound (454 g) very lean ground beef
1 teaspoon onion powder
1/3 cup ketchup
1/4 cup water
1/2 teaspoon celery seed
1 tablespoon lemon juice
1½ teaspoons brown sugar
1¼ teaspoons low-sodium Worcestershire sauce
½ teaspoon salt (optional)
½ teaspoon vinegar
⅛ teaspoon dry mustard
Hamburger or slider buns, for serving
Cooking spray

1. Spray the air fryer basket with cooking spray.
2. Break raw ground beef into small chunks and pile into the basket. Roast for 5 minutes. Stir to break apart and roast at 390°F (199°C) for 3 minutes. Stir and roast for 2 to 4 minutes longer, or until meat is well done.
3. Remove the meat from the air fryer, drain, and use a knife and fork to crumble into small pieces.
4. Give your air fryer basket a quick rinse to remove any bits of meat.
5. Place all the remaining ingredients, except for the buns, in a baking pan and mix together. Add the meat and stir well.
6. Bake at 330°F (166°C) for 5 minutes. Stir and bake for 2 minutes.
7. Scoop onto buns. Serve hot.

Chicken and Veggies Pita Sandwich

Prep time: 10 minutes | Cook time: 9 to 11 minutes | Serves 4

2 boneless, skinless chicken breasts, cut into 1-inch cubes
1 small red onion, sliced
1 red bell pepper, sliced
1/3 cup Italian salad
dressing, divided
½ teaspoon dried thyme
4 pita pockets, split
2 cups torn butter lettuce
1 cup chopped cherry tomatoes

1. Place the chicken, onion, and bell pepper in the air fryer basket. Drizzle with 1 tablespoon of the Italian salad dressing, add the thyme, and toss.
2. Bake at 380°F (193°C) for 9 to 11 minutes, or until the chicken is 165°F (74°C) on a food thermometer, stirring once during cooking time.
3. Transfer the chicken and vegetables to a bowl and toss with the remaining salad dressing.
4. Assemble sandwiches with the pita pockets, butter lettuce, and cherry tomatoes. Serve immediately.

Golden Cheesy Potato Taquitos

Prep time: 5 minutes | Cook time: 6 minutes per batch | Makes 12 taquitos

2 cups mashed potatoes
½ cup shredded
Mexican cheese
12 corn tortillas
Cooking spray

1. Line the baking pan with parchment paper.
2. In a bowl, combine the potatoes and cheese until well mixed. Microwave the tortillas on high heat for 30 seconds, or until softened. Add some water to another bowl and set alongside.
3. On a clean work surface, lay the tortillas. Scoop 3 tablespoons of the potato mixture in the center of each tortilla. Roll up tightly and secure with toothpicks if necessary.
4. Arrange the filled tortillas, seam side down, in the prepared baking pan. Spritz the tortillas with cooking spray. Air fry at 400°F (204°C) for 6 minutes, or until crispy and golden brown, flipping once halfway through the cooking time. You may need to work in batches to avoid overcrowding.
5. Serve hot.

Cheesy Mixed Greens Sandwich

Prep time: 15 minutes | Cook time: 10 to 13 minutes | Serves 4

1½ cups chopped mixed greens
2 garlic cloves, thinly sliced
2 teaspoons olive oil

2 slices low-sodium low-fat Swiss cheese
4 slices low-sodium whole-wheat bread
Cooking spray

1. In a baking pan, mix the greens, garlic, and olive oil. Air fry at 400ºF (204ºC) for 4 to 5 minutes, stirring once, until the vegetables are tender. Drain, if necessary.
2. Make 2 sandwiches, dividing half of the greens and 1 slice of Swiss cheese between 2 slices of bread. Lightly spray the outsides of the sandwiches with cooking spray.
3. Bake the sandwiches in the air fryer for 6 to 8 minutes, turning with tongs halfway through, until the bread is toasted and the cheese melts.
4. Cut each sandwich in half and serve.

Crispy Cheesy Shrimp Sandwich

Prep time: 10 minutes | Cook time: 5 to 7 minutes | Serves 4

1¼ cups shredded Colby, Cheddar, or Havarti cheese
1 (6-ounce / 170-g) can tiny shrimp, drained
3 tablespoons

mayonnaise
2 tablespoons minced green onion
4 slices whole grain or whole-wheat bread
2 tablespoons softened butter

1. In a medium bowl, combine the cheese, shrimp, mayonnaise, and green onion, and mix well.
2. Spread this mixture on two of the slices of bread. Top with the other slices of bread to make two sandwiches. Spread the sandwiches lightly with butter.
3. Air fry at 400ºF (204ºC) for 5 to 7 minutes, or until the bread is browned and crisp and the cheese is melted.
4. Cut in half and serve warm.

Eggplant Parmesan Hoagies

Prep time: 15 minutes | Cook time: 12 minutes | Makes 3 hoagies

6 peeled eggplant slices (about ½ inch thick and 3 inches in diameter)
¼ cup jarred pizza sauce

6 tablespoons grated Parmesan cheese
3 Italian sub rolls, split open lengthwise, warmed
Cooking spray

1. Arrange the eggplant slices in the air fryer and spritz with cooking spray.
2. Air fry at 350ºF (177ºC) for 10 minutes or until lightly wilted and tender. Flip the slices halfway through.
3. Divide and spread the pizza sauce and cheese on top of the eggplant slice and air fry over 375ºF (191ºC) for 2 more minutes or until the cheese melts.
4. Assemble each sub roll with two slices of eggplant and serve immediately.

Cheesy Lamb Hamburgers

Prep time: 15 minutes | Cook time: 16 minutes | Makes 4 burgers

1½ pounds (680 g) ground lamb
¼ cup crumbled feta
1½ teaspoons tomato paste
1½ teaspoons minced garlic
1 teaspoon ground dried ginger
1 teaspoon ground

coriander
¼ teaspoon salt
¼ teaspoon cayenne pepper
4 kaiser rolls or hamburger buns, split open lengthwise, warmed
Cooking spray

1. Combine all the ingredients, except for the buns, in a large bowl. Coarsely stir to mix well.
2. Shape the mixture into four balls, then pound the balls into four 5-inch diameter patties.
3. Arrange the patties in the air fryer and spritz with cooking spray. Air fry at 375ºF (191ºC) for 16 minutes or until well browned. Flip the patties halfway through.
4. Assemble the buns with patties to make the burgers and serve immediately.

Pork, Carrot, and Onion Momos

Prep time: 20 minutes | Cook time: 10 minutes per batch | Serves 4

2 tablespoons olive oil
1 pound (454 g) ground pork
1 shredded carrot

1 onion, chopped
1 teaspoon soy sauce
16 wonton wrappers
Salt and ground black pepper, to taste

1. Heat the olive oil in a nonstick skillet over medium heat until shimmering.
2. Add the ground pork, carrot, onion, soy sauce, salt, and ground black pepper and sauté for 10 minutes or until the pork is well browned and carrots are tender.
3. Unfold the wrappers on a clean work surface, then divide the cooked pork and vegetables on the wrappers. Fold the edges around the filling to form momos. Nip the top to seal the momos.
4. Arrange the momos in the air fryer and spritz with cooking spray. Air fry at 320ºF (160ºC) for 10 minutes or until the wrappers are lightly browned. Work in batches to avoid overcrowding.
5. Serve immediately.

Crispy Salsa Verde Chicken Empanadas

Prep time: 25 minutes | Cook time: 24 minutes | Makes 12 empanadas

1 cup boneless, skinless rotisserie chicken breast meat, chopped finely
¼ cup salsa verde
²⁄₃ cup shredded Cheddar cheese
1 teaspoon ground cumin
1 teaspoon ground

black pepper
2 purchased refrigerated pie crusts, from a minimum 14.1-ounce box
1 large egg
2 tablespoons water
Cooking spray

1. Combine the chicken meat, salsa verde, Cheddar, cumin, and black pepper in a large bowl. Stir to mix well. Set aside.
2. Unfold the pie crusts on a clean work surface, then use a large cookie cutter to cut out 3½-inch circles as much as possible.
3. Roll the remaining crusts to a ball and flatten into a circle which has the same thickness of the original crust. Cut out more 3½-inch circles until you have 12 circles in total.
4. Make the empanadas: Divide the chicken mixture in the middle of each circle, about 1½ tablespoons each. Dab the edges of the circle with water. Fold the circle in half over the filling to shape like a half-moon and press to seal, or you can press with a fork.
5. Whisk the egg with water in a small bowl.
6. Arrange six of the empanadas in the air fryer and spritz with cooking spray. Brush with whisked egg. Air fry at 350ºF (177ºC) for 12 minutes or until golden and crispy. Flip the empanadas halfway through..
7. Serve immediately.

Thai Curry Pork Sliders

Prep time: 10 minutes | Cook time: 14 minutes | Makes 6 sliders

1 pound (454 g) ground pork
1 tablespoon Thai curry paste
1½ tablespoons fish sauce
¼ cup thinly sliced scallions, white and green parts
2 tablespoons minced

peeled fresh ginger
1 tablespoon light brown sugar
1 teaspoon ground black pepper
6 slider buns, split open lengthwise, warmed
Cooking spray

1. Combine all the ingredients, except for the buns in a large bowl. Stir to mix well.
2. Divide and shape the mixture into six balls, then bash the balls into six 3-inch-diameter patties.
3. Arrange the patties in the air fryer and spritz with cooking spray. Air fry at 375ºF (191ºC) for 14 minutes or until well browned. Flip the patties halfway through.
4. Assemble the buns with patties to make the sliders and serve immediately.

Cheesy Mayo Tuna Muffin

Prep time: 8 minutes | Cook time: 4 to 8 minutes | Serves 4

1 (6-ounce / 170-g) can chunk light tuna, drained
¼ cup mayonnaise
2 tablespoons mustard
1 tablespoon lemon juice

2 green onions, minced
3 English muffins, split with a fork
3 tablespoons softened butter
6 thin slices Provolone or Muenster cheese

1. In a small bowl, combine the tuna, mayonnaise, mustard, lemon juice, and green onions. Set aside.
2. Butter the cut side of the English muffins. Bake, butter-side up, in the air fryer at 390ºF (199ºC) for 2 to 4 minutes, or until light golden brown. Remove the muffins from the air fryer basket.
3. Top each muffin with one slice of cheese and return to the air fryer. Bake for 2 to 4 minutes or until the cheese melts and starts to brown.
4. Remove the muffins from the air fryer, top with the tuna mixture, and serve.

Air-Fried Turkey Sliders with Chive Mayo

Prep time: 10 minutes | Cook time: 15 minutes | Serves 6

12 burger buns
For the Turkey Sliders:
¾ pound (340 g) turkey, minced
1 tablespoon oyster sauce
¼ cup pickled jalapeno, chopped
2 tablespoons chopped scallions
For the Chive Mayo:
1 tablespoon chives
1 cup mayonnaise

Cooking spray

1 tablespoon chopped fresh cilantro
1 to 2 cloves garlic, minced
Sea salt and ground black pepper, to taste

Zest of 1 lime
1 teaspoon salt

1. Combine the ingredients for the turkey sliders in a large bowl. Stir to mix well. Shape the mixture into 6 balls, then bash the balls into patties.
2. Arrange the patties in the air fryer and spritz with cooking spray. Air fry at 365ºF (185ºC) for 15 minutes or until well browned. Flip the patties halfway through.
3. Meanwhile, combine the ingredients for the chive mayo in a small bowl. Stir to mix well.
4. Smear the patties with chive mayo, then assemble the patties between two buns to make the sliders. Serve immediately.

Turkey and Veggies Hamburger

Prep time: 10 minutes | Cook time: 20 minutes | Serves 4

1 cup leftover turkey, cut into bite-sized chunks
1 leek, sliced
1 Serrano pepper, deveined and chopped
2 bell peppers, deveined and chopped
2 tablespoons Tabasco sauce
½ cup sour cream

1 heaping tablespoon fresh cilantro, chopped
1 teaspoon hot paprika
¾ teaspoon kosher salt
½ teaspoon ground black pepper
4 hamburger buns
Cooking spray

1. Mix all the ingredients, except for the buns, in a large bowl. Toss to combine well.
2. Pour the mixture in the baking pan and place in the air fryer. Bake at 385ºF (196ºC) for 20 minutes or until the turkey is well browned and the leek is tender.
3. Assemble the hamburger buns with the turkey mixture and serve immediately.

Vegetable Pita Sandwich

Prep time: 10 minutes | Cook time: 9 to 12 minutes | Serves 4

1 baby eggplant, peeled and chopped
1 red bell pepper, sliced
½ cup diced red onion
½ cup shredded carrot
1 teaspoon olive oil

1/3 cup low-fat Greek yogurt
½ teaspoon dried tarragon
2 low-sodium whole-wheat pita breads, halved crosswise

1. In a baking pan, stir together the eggplant, red bell pepper, red onion, carrot, and olive oil. Put the vegetable mixture into the air fryer basket and roast for 7 to 9 minutes, stirring once, until the vegetables are tender. Drain if necessary.
2. In a small bowl, thoroughly mix the yogurt and tarragon until well combined.
3. Stir the yogurt mixture into the vegetables. Stuff one-fourth of this mixture into each pita pocket.
4. Place the sandwiches in the air fryer and bake at 390ºF (199ºC) for 2 to 3 minutes, or until the bread is toasted.
5. Serve immediately.

Chapter 6 Casseroles, Frittatas, and Quiches

Cheesy Broccoli, Carrot, and Tomato Quiche

Prep time: 6 minutes | Cook time: 14 minutes | Serves 4

4 eggs
1 teaspoon dried thyme
1 cup whole milk
1 steamed carrot, diced
2 cups steamed broccoli florets
2 medium tomatoes, diced

¼ cup crumbled feta cheese
1 cup grated Cheddar cheese
1 teaspoon chopped parsley
Salt and ground black pepper, to taste
Cooking spray

1. Spritz a baking pan with cooking spray.
2. Whisk together the eggs, thyme, salt, and ground black pepper in a bowl and fold in the milk while mixing.
3. Put the carrots, broccoli, and tomatoes in the prepared baking pan, then spread with feta cheese and ½ cup Cheddar cheese. Pour the egg mixture over, then scatter with remaining Cheddar on top.
4. Put the pan in the air fryer. Bake at 350ºF (177ºC) for 14 minutes or until the eggs are set and the quiche is puffed.
5. Remove the quiche from the air fryer and top with chopped parsley, then slice to serve.

Baked Chicken Divan

Prep time: 5 minutes | Cook time: 24 minutes | Serves 4

4 chicken breasts
Salt and ground black pepper, to taste
1 head broccoli, cut into florets
½ cup cream of

mushroom soup
1 cup shredded Cheddar cheese
½ cup croutons
Cooking spray

1. Spritz the air fryer basket with cooking spray.
2. Put the chicken breasts in the air fryer and sprinkle with salt and ground black pepper.

3. Air fry at 390ºF (199ºC) for 14 minutes or until well browned and tender. Flip the breasts halfway through the cooking time.
4. Remove the breasts from the air fryer and allow to cool for a few minutes on a plate, then cut the breasts into bite-size pieces.
5. Combine the chicken, broccoli, mushroom soup, and Cheddar cheese in a large bowl. Stir to mix well.
6. Spritz a baking pan with cooking spray. Pour the chicken mixture into the pan. Spread the croutons over the mixture.
7. Place the baking pan in the air fryer. Bake for 10 minutes or until the croutons are lightly browned and the mixture is set.
8. Remove the baking pan from the air fryer and serve immediately.

Fast Chorizo, Corn, and Potato Frittata

Prep time: 8 minutes | Cook time: 12 minutes | Serves 4

2 tablespoons olive oil
1 chorizo, sliced
4 eggs
½ cup corn
1 large potato, boiled and cubed

1 tablespoon chopped parsley
½ cup feta cheese, crumbled
Salt and ground black pepper, to taste

1. Heat the olive oil in a nonstick skillet over medium heat until shimmering.
2. Add the chorizo and cook for 4 minutes or until golden brown.
3. Whisk the eggs in a bowl, then sprinkle with salt and ground black pepper.
4. Mix the remaining ingredients in the egg mixture, then pour the chorizo and its fat into a baking pan. Pour in the egg mixture.
5. Place the pan in the air fryer. Bake at 330ºF (166ºC) for 8 minutes or until the eggs are set.
6. Serve immediately.

Baked Mediterranean Quiche

Prep time: 10 minutes | Cook time: 30 minutes | Serves 4

4 eggs
¼ cup chopped Kalamata olives
½ cup chopped tomatoes
¼ cup chopped onion
½ cup milk
1 cup crumbled feta
cheese
½ tablespoon chopped oregano
½ tablespoon chopped basil
Salt and ground black pepper, to taste
Cooking spray

1. Spritz a baking pan with cooking spray.
2. Whisk the eggs with remaining ingredients in a large bowl. Stir to mix well.
3. Pour the mixture into the prepared baking pan, then place the pan in the air fryer.
4. Bake at 340ºF (171ºC) for 30 minutes or until the eggs are set and a toothpick inserted in the center comes out clean. Check the doneness of the quiche during the last 10 minutes of baking.
5. Serve immediately.

Herbed Cheddar Scallion and Parsley Frittata

Prep time: 10 minutes | Cook time: 20 minutes | Serves 4

½ cup shredded Cheddar cheese
½ cup half-and-half
4 large eggs
2 tablespoons chopped scallion greens
2 tablespoons
chopped fresh parsley
½ teaspoon kosher salt
½ teaspoon ground black pepper
Cooking spray

1. Spritz a baking pan with cooking spray.
2. Whisk together all the ingredients in a large bowl, then pour the mixture into the prepared baking pan.
3. Set the pan in the air fryer and bake at 300ºF (149ºC) for 20 minutes or until set.
4. Serve immediately.

Fata Kale Frittata

Prep time: 5 minutes | Cook time: 11 minutes | Serves 2

1 cup kale, chopped
1 teaspoon olive oil
4 large eggs, beaten
Kosher salt, to taste
2 tablespoons water
3 tablespoons crumbled feta
Cooking spray

1. Spritz an air fryer baking pan with cooking spray.
2. Add the kale to the baking pan and drizzle with olive oil. Arrange the pan in the air fryer. Broil at 360ºF (182ºC) for 3 minutes.
3. Meanwhile, combine the eggs with salt and water in a large bowl. Stir to mix well.
4. Make the frittata: When the broiling time is complete, pour the eggs into the baking pan and spread with feta cheese. Reduce the temperature to 300ºF (149ºC).
5. Bake for 8 minutes or until the eggs are set and the cheese melts.
6. Remove the baking pan from the air fryer and serve the frittata immediately.

Shrimp and Veggies Casserole

Prep time: 15 minutes | Cook time: 22 minutes | Serves 4

1 pound (454 g) shrimp, cleaned and deveined
2 cups cauliflower, cut into florets
2 green bell pepper,
sliced
1 shallot, sliced
2 tablespoons sesame oil
1 cup tomato paste
Cooking spray

1. Spritz a baking pan with cooking spray.
2. Arrange the shrimp and vegetables in the baking pan. Then, drizzle the sesame oil over the vegetables. Pour the tomato paste over the vegetables.
3. Bake at 360ºF (182ºC) for 10 minutes in the air fryer. Stir with a large spoon and bake for a further 12 minutes.
4. Serve warm.

Homemade Keto Cheese Quiche

Prep time: 20 minutes | Cook time: 1 hour | Serves 8

Crust:

1¼ cups blanched almond flour	Parmesan cheese
1 large egg, beaten	¼ teaspoon fine sea salt
1¼ cups grated	

Filling:

4 ounces (113 g) cream cheese	pepper
1 cup shredded Swiss cheese	¾ teaspoon fine sea salt
⅓ cup minced leeks	1 tablespoon unsalted butter, melted
4 large eggs, beaten	Chopped green onions, for garnish
½ cup chicken broth	Cooking spray
⅛ teaspoon cayenne	

1. Spritz a pie pan basket with cooking spray.
2. Combine the flour, egg, Parmesan, and salt in a large bowl. Stir to mix until a satiny and firm dough forms.
3. Arrange the dough between two grease parchment papers, then roll the dough into a $\frac{1}{16}$-inch thick circle.
4. Make the crust: Transfer the dough into the prepared pie pan and press to coat the bottom, then arrange the pie pan in the air fryer.
5. Bake at 325ºF (163ºC) for 12 minutes or until the edges of the crust are lightly browned.
6. Meanwhile, combine the ingredient for the filling, except for the green onions in a large bowl.
7. Pour the filling over the cooked crust and cover the edges of the crust with aluminum foil. Bake for 15 more minutes, then reduce the heat to 300ºF (149ºC) and bake for another 30 minutes or until a toothpick inserted in the center comes out clean.
8. Remove the pie pan from the air fryer and allow to cool for 10 minutes before serving.

Pork Sausage Quiche Cups

Prep time: 15 minutes | Cook time: 16 minutes | Makes 10 quiche cups

4 ounces (113 g) ground pork sausage	Cooking spray
3 eggs	4 ounces (113 g) sharp Cheddar cheese, grated
¾ cup milk	

Special Equipment:
20 foil muffin cups

1. Spritz the air fryer basket with cooking spray.
2. Divide sausage into 3 portions and shape each into a thin patty.
3. Put patties in air fryer basket and air fry at 390ºF (199ºC) for 6 minutes.
4. While sausage is cooking, prepare the egg mixture. Combine the eggs and milk in a large bowl and whisk until well blended. Set aside.
5. When sausage has cooked fully, remove patties from the basket, drain well, and use a fork to crumble the meat into small pieces.
6. Double the foil cups into 10 sets. Remove paper liners from the top muffin cups and spray the foil cups lightly with cooking spray.
7. Divide crumbled sausage among the 10 muffin cup sets.
8. Top each with grated cheese, divided evenly among the cups.
9. Put 5 cups in air fryer basket.
10. Pour egg mixture into each cup, filling until each cup is at least ⅔ full.
11. Bake for 8 minutes and test for doneness. A knife inserted into the center shouldn't have any raw egg on it when removed.
12. Repeat steps 8 through 11 for the remaining quiches.
13. Serve warm.

Lush Vegetable Frittata

Prep time: 15 minutes | Cook time: 21 minutes | Serves 2

4 eggs
¼ cup milk
Sea salt and ground black pepper, to taste
1 zucchini, sliced
½ bunch asparagus, sliced
½ cup mushrooms, sliced
½ cup spinach, shredded
½ cup red onion, sliced
½ tablespoon olive oil
5 tablespoons feta cheese, crumbled
4 tablespoons Cheddar cheese, grated
¼ bunch chives, minced

1. In a bowl, mix the eggs, milk, salt and pepper.
2. Over a medium heat, sauté the vegetables for 6 minutes with the olive oil in a nonstick pan.
3. Put some parchment paper in the base of a baking tin. Pour in the vegetables, followed by the egg mixture. Top with the feta and grated Cheddar.
4. Transfer the baking tin to the air fryer and bake at 320ºF (160ºC) for 15 minutes. Remove the frittata from the air fryer and leave to cool for 5 minutes.
5. Top with the minced chives and serve.

Hearty Beef and Bean Casserole

Prep time: 15 minutes | Cook time: 31 minutes | Serves 4

1 tablespoon olive oil
½ cup finely chopped bell pepper
½ cup chopped celery
1 onion, chopped
2 garlic cloves, minced
1 pound (454 g) ground beef
1 can diced tomatoes
½ teaspoon parsley
½ tablespoon chili powder
1 teaspoon chopped cilantro
1½ cups vegetable broth
1 (8-ounce / 227-g) can cannellini beans
Salt and ground black pepper, to taste

1. Heat the olive oil in a nonstick skillet over medium heat until shimmering.
2. Add the bell pepper, celery, onion, and garlic to the skillet and sauté for 5 minutes or until the onion is translucent.

3. Add the ground beef and sauté for an additional 6 minutes or until lightly browned.
4. Mix in the tomatoes, parsley, chili powder, cilantro and vegetable broth, then cook for 10 more minutes. Stir constantly.
5. Pour them in a baking pan, then mix in the beans and sprinkle with salt and ground black pepper.
6. Transfer the pan in the air fryer. Bake at 350ºF (177ºC) for 10 minutes or until the vegetables are tender and the beef is well browned.
7. Remove the baking pan from the air fryer and serve immediately.

Lush Vegetable Frittata

Prep time: 15 minutes | Cook time: 20 minutes | Serves 2

4 eggs
1/3 cup milk
2 teaspoons olive oil
1 large zucchini, sliced
2 asparagus, sliced thinly
1/3 cup sliced mushrooms
1 cup baby spinach
1 small red onion, sliced
1/3 cup crumbled feta cheese
1/3 cup grated Cheddar cheese
¼ cup chopped chives
Salt and ground black pepper, to taste

1. Line a baking pan basket with parchment paper.
2. Whisk together the eggs, milk, salt, and ground black pepper in a large bowl. Set aside.
3. Heat the olive oil in a nonstick skillet over medium heat until shimmering.
4. Add the zucchini, asparagus, mushrooms, spinach, and onion to the skillet and sauté for 5 minutes or until tender.
5. Pour the sautéed vegetables into the prepared baking pan, then spread the egg mixture over and scatter with cheeses.
6. Place the baking pan in the air fryer. Bake at 380ºF (193ºC) for 15 minutes or until the eggs are set the edges are lightly browned.
7. Remove the frittata from the air fryer and sprinkle with chives before serving.

Golden Western Prosciutto Casserole

Prep time: 5 minutes | Cook time: 10 minutes | Serves 2

1 cup day-old whole grain bread, cubed
3 large eggs, beaten
2 tablespoons water
⅛ teaspoon kosher salt
1 ounce (28 g) prosciutto, roughly

chopped
1 ounce (28 g) Pepper Jack cheese, roughly chopped
1 tablespoon chopped fresh chives
Nonstick cooking spray

1. Spray a baking pan with nonstick cooking spray, then place the bread cubes in the pan. Transfer the baking pan to the air fryer.
2. In a medium bowl, stir together the beaten eggs and water, then stir in the kosher salt, prosciutto, cheese, and chives.
3. Pour the egg mixture over the bread cubes and bake at 360ºF (182ºC) for 10 minutes, or until the eggs are set and the top is golden brown.
4. Serve warm.

Cheesy Shrimp Spinach Frittata

Prep time: 6 minutes | Cook time: 14 minutes | Serves 4

4 whole eggs
1 teaspoon dried basil
½ cup shrimp, cooked and chopped
½ cup baby spinach

½ cup rice, cooked
½ cup Monterey Jack cheese, grated
Salt, to taste
Cooking spray

1. Spritz a baking pan with cooking spray.
2. Whisk the eggs with basil and salt in a large bowl until bubbly, then mix in the shrimp, spinach, rice, and cheese.
3. Pour the mixture into the baking pan, then place the pan in the air fryer.
4. Bake at 360ºF (182ºC) for 14 minutes or until the eggs are set and the frittata is golden brown.
5. Slice to serve.

Baked Mediterranean Quiche

Prep time: 10 minutes | Cook time: 30 minutes | Serves 4

4 eggs
¼ cup chopped Kalamata olives
½ cup chopped tomatoes
¼ cup chopped onion
½ cup milk
1 cup crumbled feta

cheese
½ tablespoon chopped oregano
½ tablespoon chopped basil
Salt and ground black pepper, to taste
Cooking spray

1. Spritz a baking pan with cooking spray.
2. Whisk the eggs with remaining ingredients in a large bowl. Stir to mix well.
3. Pour the mixture into the prepared baking pan, then place the pan in the air fryer.
4. Bake at 340ºF (171ºC) for 30 minutes or until the eggs are set and a toothpick inserted in the center comes out clean. Check the doneness of the quiche during the last 10 minutes of baking.
5. Serve immediately.

Baked Trout and Crème Fraiche Frittata

Prep time: 8 minutes | Cook time: 17 minutes | Serves 4

2 tablespoons olive oil
1 onion, sliced
1 egg, beaten
½ tablespoon horseradish sauce
6 tablespoons crème

fraiche
1 cup diced smoked trout
2 tablespoons chopped fresh dill
Cooking spray

1. pritz a baking pan with cooking spray.
2. Heat the olive oil in a nonstick skillet over medium heat until shimmering.
3. Add the onion and sauté for 3 minutes or until translucent.
4. Combine the egg, horseradish sauce, and crème fraiche in a large bowl. Stir to mix well, then mix in the sautéed onion, smoked trout, and dill.
5. Pour the mixture in the prepared baking pan, then set the pan in the air fryer.
6. Bake at 350ºF (177ºC) for 14 minutes or until the egg is set and the edges are lightly browned.
7. Serve immediately.

Super Cheesy Macaroni

Prep time: 10 minutes | Cook time: 10 minutes | Serves 2

1 cup cooked macaroni
1 cup grated Cheddar cheese
½ cup warm milk
Salt and ground black pepper, to taste
1 tablespoon grated Parmesan cheese

1. In a baking dish, mix all the ingredients, except for Parmesan.
2. Put the dish inside the air fryer and bake at 350ºF (177ºC) for 10 minutes.
3. Add the Parmesan cheese on top and serve.

Goat Cheese and Asparagus Spears Frittata

Prep time: 5 minutes | Cook time: 25 minutes | Serves 2 to 4

1 cup asparagus spears, cut into 1-inch pieces
1 teaspoon vegetable oil
1 tablespoon milk
6 eggs, beaten
2 ounces (57 g) goat cheese, crumbled
1 tablespoon minced chives, optional
Kosher salt and pepper, to taste

1. Add the asparagus spears to a small bowl and drizzle with the vegetable oil. Toss until well coated and transfer to a cake pan.
2. Place the pan in the air fryer. Bake at 400ºF (204ºC) for 5 minutes, or until the asparagus become tender and slightly wilted. Remove then pan from the air fryer.
3. Stir together the milk and eggs in a medium bowl. Pour the mixture over the asparagus in the pan. Sprinkle with the goat cheese and the chives (if using) over the eggs. Season with a pinch of salt and pepper.
4. Place the pan back to the air fryer and bake at 320ºF (160ºC) for 20 minutes or until the top is lightly golden and the eggs are set.
5. Transfer to a serving dish. Slice and serve.

Greek Veggies Frittata

Prep time: 7 minutes | Cook time: 8 minutes | Serves 2

1 cup chopped mushrooms
2 cups spinach, chopped
4 eggs, lightly beaten
3 ounces (85 g) feta cheese, crumbled
2 tablespoons heavy cream
A handful of fresh parsley, chopped
Salt and ground black pepper, to taste
Cooking spray

1. Spritz a baking pan with cooking spray.
2. Whisk together all the ingredients in a large bowl. Stir to mix well.
3. Pour the mixture in the prepared baking pan and place the pan in the air fryer.
4. Bake at 350ºF (177ºC) for 8 minutes or until the eggs are set.
5. Serve immediately.

Mexican Beef and Green Chile Casserole

Prep time: 10 minutes | Cook time: 15 minutes | Serves 4

1 pound (454 g) 85% lean ground beef
1 tablespoon taco seasoning
1 (7-ounce / 198-g) can diced mild green chiles
½ cup milk
2 large eggs
1 cup shredded Mexican cheese blend
2 tablespoons all-purpose flour
½ teaspoon kosher salt
Cooking spray

1. Spritz a baking pan with cooking spray.
2. Toss the ground beef with taco seasoning in a large bowl to mix well. Pour the seasoned ground beef in the prepared baking pan.
3. Combing the remaining ingredients in a medium bowl. Whisk to mix well, then pour the mixture over the ground beef.
4. Arrange the pan in the air fryer. Bake at 350ºF (177ºC) for 15 minutes or until a toothpick inserted in the center comes out clean.
5. Remove the casserole from the air fryer and allow to cool for 5 minutes, then slice to serve.

Chapter 7 Vegetables

Vegan and Vegetarian

Air-Fried Winter Veggies

Prep time: 5 minutes | Cook time: 16 minutes | Serves 2

1 parsnip, sliced
1 cup sliced butternut squash
1 small red onion, cut into wedges
½ chopped celery stalk
1 tablespoon chopped fresh thyme
2 teaspoons olive oil
Salt and black pepper, to taste

1. Toss all the ingredients in a large bowl until the vegetables are well coated.
2. Transfer the vegetables to the air fryer basket and air fry at 380ºF (193ºC) for 16 minutes, shaking the basket halfway through, or until the vegetables are golden brown and tender.
3. Remove from the basket and serve warm.

Asian Spicy Broccoli

Prep time: 5 minutes | Cook time: 10 minutes | Serves 2

12 ounces (340 g) broccoli florets
2 tablespoons Asian hot chili oil
1 teaspoon ground Sichuan peppercorns (or black pepper)
2 garlic cloves, finely chopped
1 (2-inch) piece fresh ginger, peeled and finely chopped
Kosher salt and freshly ground black pepper

1. Toss the broccoli florets with the chili oil, Sichuan peppercorns, garlic, ginger, salt, and pepper in a mixing bowl until thoroughly coated.
2. Transfer the broccoli florets to the air fryer basket and roast at 375ºF (191ºC) for about 10 minutes, shaking the basket halfway through, or until the broccoli florets are lightly browned and tender.
3. Remove the broccoli from the basket and serve on a plate.

Baked Chili Black Bean and Tomato

Prep time: 15 minutes | Cook time: 23 minutes | Serves 6

1 tablespoon olive oil
1 medium onion, diced
3 garlic cloves, minced
1 cup vegetable broth
3 cans black beans, drained and rinsed
2 cans diced tomatoes
2 chipotle peppers, chopped
2 teaspoons cumin
2 teaspoons chili powder
1 teaspoon dried oregano
½ teaspoon salt

1. Over a medium heat, fry the garlic and onions in the olive oil for 3 minutes.
2. Add the remaining ingredients, stirring constantly and scraping the bottom to prevent sticking.
3. Take a dish and place the mixture inside. Put a sheet of aluminum foil on top.
4. Transfer to the air fryer and bake at 400ºF (204ºC) for 20 minutes.
5. When ready, plate up and serve immediately.

Mediterranean Air-Fried Vegetable

Prep time: 10 minutes | Cook time: 6 minutes | Serves 4

1 large zucchini, sliced
1 cup cherry tomatoes, halved
1 parsnip, sliced
1 green pepper, sliced
1 carrot, sliced
1 teaspoon mixed herbs
1 teaspoon mustard
1 teaspoon garlic purée
6 tablespoons olive oil
Salt and ground black pepper, to taste

1. Combine all the ingredients in a bowl, making sure to coat the vegetables well.
2. Transfer to the air fryer and air fry at 400ºF (204ºC) for 6 minutes, ensuring the vegetables are tender and browned.
3. Serve immediately.

Lemony Cauliflower and Chickpea

Prep time: 10 minutes | Cook time: 25 minutes | Serves 4

1 medium head cauliflower, cut into florets
1 can chickpeas, drained and rinsed
1 tablespoon extra-virgin olive oil
2 tablespoons lemon juice
Salt and ground black pepper, to taste
4 flatbreads, toasted
2 ripe avocados, mashed

1. In a bowl, mix the chickpeas, cauliflower, lemon juice and olive oil. Sprinkle salt and pepper as desired.
2. Put inside the air fryer basket and air fry at 425ºF (218ºC) for 25 minutes.
3. Spread on top of the flatbread along with the mashed avocado. Sprinkle with more pepper and salt and serve.

Fast Baked Cheesy Spinach

Prep time: 10 minutes | Cook time: 15 minutes | Serves 4

Vegetable oil spray
1 (10-ounce / 283-g) package frozen spinach, thawed and squeezed dry
½ cup chopped onion
2 cloves garlic, minced
4 ounces (113 g)
cream cheese, diced
½ teaspoon ground nutmeg
1 teaspoon kosher salt
1 teaspoon black pepper
½ cup grated Parmesan cheese

1. Spray a heatproof pan with vegetable oil spray.
2. In a medium bowl, combine the spinach, onion, garlic, cream cheese, nutmeg, salt, and pepper. Transfer to the prepared pan.
3. Put the pan in the air fryer basket. Bake at 350ºF (177ºC) for 10 minutes. Open and stir to thoroughly combine the cream cheese and spinach.
4. Sprinkle the Parmesan cheese on top. Bake for 5 minutes, or until the cheese has melted and browned.
5. Serve hot.

Shishito Peppers with Dipping Sauce

Prep time: 10 minutes | Cook time: 6 minutes | Serves 4

Dipping Sauce:
1 cup sour cream
2 tablespoons fresh lemon juice
1 clove garlic, minced
1 green onion (white and green parts), finely chopped
Peppers:
8 ounces (227 g) shishito peppers
1 tablespoon vegetable oil
1 teaspoon toasted sesame oil
Kosher salt and black pepper, to taste
¼ to ½ teaspoon red pepper flakes
½ teaspoon toasted sesame seeds

1. In a small bowl, stir all the ingredients for the dipping sauce to combine. Cover and refrigerate until serving time.
2. In a medium bowl, toss the peppers with the vegetable oil. Put the peppers in the air fryer basket. Air fry at 400ºF (204ºC) for 6 minutes, or until peppers are lightly charred in spots, stirring the peppers halfway through the cooking time.
3. Transfer the peppers to a serving bowl. Drizzle with the sesame oil and toss to coat. Season with salt and pepper. Sprinkle with the red pepper and sesame seeds and toss again.
4. Serve immediately with the dipping sauce.

Simple Honey Baby Carrots

Prep time: 5 minutes | Cook time: 12 minutes | Serves 4

1 pound (454 g) baby carrots
2 tablespoons olive oil
1 tablespoon honey
1 teaspoon dried dill
Salt and black pepper, to taste

1. Place the carrots in a large bowl. Add the olive oil, honey, dill, salt, and pepper and toss to coat well.
2. Arrange the carrots in the air fryer basket and roast at 350ºF (177ºC) for 12 minutes until crisp-tender. Shake the basket once during cooking.
3. Serve warm.

Vegan Cauliflower Fried Rice

Prep time: 15 minutes | Cook time: 40 minutes | Serves 8

1 large head cauliflower, rinsed and drained, cut into florets
½ lemon, juiced
2 garlic cloves, minced
2 (8-ounce / 227-g) cans mushrooms
1 (8-ounce / 227-g) can water chestnuts
¾ cup peas
1 egg, beaten
4 tablespoons soy sauce
1 tablespoon peanut oil
1 tablespoon sesame oil
1 tablespoon minced fresh ginger
Cooking spray

1. Mix the peanut oil, soy sauce, sesame oil, minced ginger, lemon juice, and minced garlic to combine well.
2. In a food processor, pulse the florets in small batches to break them down to resemble rice grains. Pour into the air fryer basket.
3. Drain the chestnuts and roughly chop them. Pour into the basket. Air fry at 350°F (177°C) for 20 minutes.
4. In the meantime, drain the mushrooms. Add the mushrooms and the peas to the air fryer and continue to air fry for another 15 minutes.
5. Lightly spritz a frying pan with cooking spray. Prepare an omelet with the beaten egg, ensuring it is firm. Lay on a cutting board and slice it up.
6. When the cauliflower is ready, throw in the omelet and bake for an additional 5 minutes. Serve hot.

Roasted Asparagus and Potato

Prep time: 5 minutes | Cook time: 26 to 30 minutes | Serves 5

4 medium potatoes, cut into wedges
Cooking spray
1 bunch asparagus, trimmed
2 tablespoons olive oil
Salt and pepper, to taste
Cheese Sauce:
¼ cup crumbled cottage cheese
¼ cup buttermilk
1 tablespoon whole-grain mustard
Salt and black pepper, to taste

1. Spritz the air fryer basket with cooking spray.
2. Put the potatoes in the air fryer basket and roast at 400°F (204°C) for 20 to 22 minutes until golden brown. Shake the basket halfway through the cooking time.
3. When ready, remove the potatoes from the basket to a platter. Cover the potatoes with foil to keep warm. Set aside.
4. Place the asparagus in the air fryer basket and drizzle with the olive oil. Sprinkle with salt and pepper.
5. Roast at 400°F (204°C) for 6 to 8 minutes, shaking the basket once or twice during cooking, or until the asparagus are cooked to your desired crispiness.
6. Meanwhile, make the cheese sauce by stirring together the cottage cheese, buttermilk, and mustard in a small bowl. Season as needed with salt and pepper.
7. Transfer the asparagus to the platter of potatoes and drizzle with the cheese sauce. Serve immediately.

Air-Fried Eggplant Slices

Prep time: 5 minutes | Cook time: 15 minutes | Serves 2

1 medium eggplant, quartered and cut crosswise into ½-inch-thick slices
2 tablespoons vegetable oil
Kosher salt and freshly ground black
pepper, to taste
½ cup plain yogurt (not Greek)
2 tablespoons harissa paste
1 garlic clove, grated
2 teaspoons honey

1. Toss the eggplant slices with the vegetable oil, salt, and pepper in a large bowl until well coated.
2. Arrange the eggplant slices in the air fryer basket and air fry at 400°F (204°C) for about 15 minutes until golden brown. Shake the basket two to three times during cooking.
3. Meanwhile, make the yogurt sauce by whisking together the yogurt, harissa paste, and garlic in a small bowl.
4. Spread the yogurt sauce on a platter, and pile the eggplant slices over the top. Serve drizzled with the honey.

Buttered Cheesy Cabbage Wedges

Prep time: 5 minutes | Cook time: 20 minutes | Serves 4

4 tablespoons melted butter	Parmesan cheese
1 head cabbage, cut into wedges	Salt and black pepper, to taste
1 cup shredded	½ cup shredded Mozzarella cheese

1. Brush the melted butter over the cut sides of cabbage wedges and sprinkle both sides with the Parmesan cheese. Season with salt and pepper to taste.
2. Place the cabbage wedges in the air fryer basket and air fry at 380ºF (193ºC) for 20 minutes, flipping the cabbage halfway through, or until the cabbage wedges are lightly browned.
3. Transfer the cabbage wedges to a plate and serve with the Mozzarella cheese sprinkled on top.

Honey-Glazed Roasted Vegetables

Prep time: 15 minutes | Cook time: 20 minutes | Makes 3 cups

Glaze:

2 tablespoons raw honey	⅛ teaspoon dried sage
2 teaspoons minced garlic	⅛ teaspoon dried rosemary
¼ teaspoon dried marjoram	⅛ teaspoon dried thyme
¼ teaspoon dried basil	½ teaspoon salt
¼ teaspoon dried oregano	¼ teaspoon ground black pepper

Veggies:

3 to 4 medium red potatoes, cut into 1- to 2-inch pieces	1 (10.5-ounce / 298-g) package cherry tomatoes, halved
1 small zucchini, cut into 1- to 2-inch pieces	1 cup sliced mushrooms
1 small carrot, sliced into ¼-inch rounds	3 tablespoons olive oil

1. Combine the honey, garlic, marjoram, basil, oregano, sage, rosemary, thyme, salt, and pepper in a small bowl and stir to mix well. Set aside.

2. Place the red potatoes, zucchini, carrot, cherry tomatoes, and mushroom in a large bowl. Drizzle with the olive oil and toss to coat.
3. Pour the veggies into the air fryer basket and roast at 380ºF (193ºC) for 15 minutes, shaking the basket halfway through.
4. When ready, transfer the roasted veggies to the large bowl. Pour the honey mixture over the veggies, tossing to coat.
5. Spread out the veggies in a baking pan and place in the air fryer.
6. Increase the temperature to 390ºF (199ºC) and roast for an additional 5 minutes, or until the veggies are tender and glazed. Serve warm.

Mascarpone Mushrooms with Pasta

Prep time: 10 minutes | Cook time: 15 minutes | Serves 4

Vegetable oil spray	1 teaspoon dried thyme
4 cups sliced mushrooms	1 teaspoon kosher salt
1 medium yellow onion, chopped	1 teaspoon black pepper
2 cloves garlic, minced	½ teaspoon red pepper flakes
¼ cup heavy whipping cream or half-and-half	4 cups cooked konjac noodles, for serving
8 ounces (227 g) mascarpone cheese	½ cup grated Parmesan cheese

1. Spray a heatproof pan with vegetable oil spray.
2. In a medium bowl, combine the mushrooms, onion, garlic, cream, mascarpone, thyme, salt, black pepper, and red pepper flakes. Stir to combine. Transfer the mixture to the prepared pan.
3. Put the pan in the air fryer basket. Bake at 350ºF (177ºC) for 15 minutes, stirring halfway through the baking time.
4. Divide the pasta among four shallow bowls. Spoon the mushroom mixture evenly over the pasta. Sprinkle with Parmesan cheese and serve.

Baked Potato, Carrot, Broccoli and Zucchini

Prep time: 10 minutes | Cook time: 45 minutes | Serves 4

2 potatoes, peeled and cubed
4 carrots, cut into chunks
1 head broccoli, cut into florets
4 zucchinis, sliced

thickly
Salt and ground black pepper, to taste
¼ cup olive oil
1 tablespoon dry onion powder

1. In a baking dish, add all the ingredients and combine well.
2. Bake at 400ºF (204ºC) for 45 minutes in the air fryer, ensuring the vegetables are soft and the sides have browned before serving.

Rosemary Balsamic Glazed Beet

Prep time: 5 minutes | Cook time: 10 minutes | Serves 2
Beet:

2 beets, cubed
2 tablespoons olive oil
2 springs rosemary,

chopped
Salt and black pepper, to taste

Balsamic Glaze:

⅓ cup balsamic vinegar

1 tablespoon honey

1. Combine the beets, olive oil, rosemary, salt, and pepper in a mixing bowl and toss until the beets are completely coated.
2. Place the beets in the air fryer basket and air fry at 400ºF (204ºC) for 10 minutes until the beets are crisp and browned at the edges. Shake the basket halfway through the cooking time.
3. Meanwhile, make the balsamic glaze: Place the balsamic vinegar and honey in a small saucepan and bring to a boil over medium heat. When the sauce starts to boil, reduce the heat to medium-low heat and simmer until the liquid is reduced by half.
4. When ready, remove the beets from the basket to a platter. Pour the balsamic glaze over the top and serve immediately.

Roasted Butternut Squash

Prep time: 5 minutes | Cook time: 20 minutes | Serves 2

1 pound (454 g) butternut squash, cut into wedges
2 tablespoons olive oil
1 tablespoon dried

rosemary
Salt, to salt
1 cup crumbled goat cheese
1 tablespoon maple syrup

1. Toss the squash wedges with the olive oil, rosemary, and salt in a large bowl until well coated.
2. Transfer the squash wedges to the air fryer basket, spreading them out in as even a layer as possible.
3. Roast at 350ºF (177ºC) for 10 minutes. Flip the squash and roast for another 10 minutes until golden brown.
4. Sprinkle the goat cheese on top and serve drizzled with the maple syrup.

Fast Roasted Maitake Mushrooms

Prep time: 5 minutes | Cook time: 15 minutes | Serves 2

1 tablespoon soy sauce
2 teaspoons toasted sesame oil
3 teaspoons vegetable oil, divided
1 garlic clove, minced
7 ounces (198 g) maitake (hen of the

woods) mushrooms
½ teaspoon flaky sea salt
½ teaspoon sesame seeds
½ teaspoon finely chopped fresh thyme leaves

1. Whisk together the soy sauce, sesame oil, 1 teaspoon of vegetable oil, and garlic in a small bowl.
2. Arrange the mushrooms in the air fryer basket in a single layer. Drizzle the soy sauce mixture over the mushrooms. Roast at 300ºF (149ºC) for 10 minutes.
3. Flip the mushrooms and sprinkle the sea salt, sesame seeds, and thyme leaves on top. Drizzle the remaining 2 teaspoons of vegetable oil all over. Roast for an additional 5 minutes.
4. Remove the mushrooms from the basket to a plate and serve hot.

Golden Vegetarian Meatballs

Prep time: 15 minutes | Cook time: 18 minutes | Serves 3

½ cup grated carrots
½ cup sweet onions
2 tablespoons olive oil
1 cup rolled oats
½ cup roasted cashews
2 cups cooked chickpeas

Juice of 1 lemon
2 tablespoons soy sauce
1 tablespoon flax meal
1 teaspoon garlic powder
1 teaspoon cumin
½ teaspoon turmeric

1. Mix together the carrots, onions, and olive oil in a baking dish and stir to combine.
2. Place the baking dish in the air fryer basket and roast at 350ºF (177ºC) for 6 minutes.
3. Meanwhile, put the oats and cashews in a food processor or blender and pulse until coarsely ground. Transfer the mixture to a large bowl. Add the chickpeas, lemon juice, and soy sauce to the food processor and pulse until smooth. Transfer the chickpea mixture to the bowl of oat and cashew mixture.
4. Remove the carrots and onions from the basket to the bowl of chickpea mixture. Add the flax meal, garlic powder, cumin, and turmeric and stir to incorporate.
5. Scoop tablespoon-sized portions of the veggie mixture and roll them into balls with your hands. Transfer the balls to the air fryer basket in a single layer.
6. Increase the temperature to 370ºF (188ºC) and bake for 12 minutes until golden through. Flip the balls halfway through the cooking time.
7. Serve warm.

Air-Fried Green Beans

Prep time: 10 minutes | Cook time: 10 minutes | Serves 4

1½ pounds (680 g) French green beans, stems removed and blanched
1 tablespoon salt
½ pound (227 g)

shallots, peeled and cut into quarters
½ teaspoon ground white pepper
2 tablespoons olive oil

1. Coat the vegetables with the rest of the ingredients in a bowl.
2. Transfer to the air fryer basket and air fry at 400ºF (204ºC) for 10 minutes, making sure the green beans achieve a light brown color.
3. Serve hot.

Roasted Beet with Chermoula

Prep time: 15 minutes | Cook time: 25 minutes | Serves 4

Chermoula:

1 cup packed fresh cilantro leaves
½ cup packed fresh parsley leaves
6 cloves garlic, peeled
2 teaspoons smoked paprika
2 teaspoons ground cumin

1 teaspoon ground coriander
½ to 1 teaspoon cayenne pepper
Pinch of crushed saffron (optional)
½ cup extra-virgin olive oil
Kosher salt, to taste

Beets:

3 medium beets, trimmed, peeled, and cut into 1-inch chunks
2 tablespoons

chopped fresh cilantro
2 tablespoons chopped fresh parsley

1. In a food processor, combine the cilantro, parsley, garlic, paprika, cumin, coriander, and cayenne. Pulse until coarsely chopped. Add the saffron, if using, and process until combined. With the food processor running, slowly add the olive oil in a steady stream; process until the sauce is uniform. Season with salt.
2. In a large bowl, drizzle the beets with ½ cup of the chermoula to coat. Arrange the beets in the air fryer basket. Roast at 375ºF (191ºC) for 25 to minutes, or until the beets are tender.
3. Transfer the beets to a serving platter. Sprinkle with the chopped cilantro and parsley and serve.

Cheesy Zucchini Chips

Prep time: 5 minutes | Cook time: 14 minutes | Serves 4

2 egg whites
Salt and black pepper, to taste
½ cup seasoned bread crumbs
2 tablespoons grated

Parmesan cheese
¼ teaspoon garlic powder
2 medium zucchini, sliced
Cooking spray

1. Spritz the air fryer basket with cooking spray.
2. In a bowl, beat the egg whites with salt and pepper. In a separate bowl, thoroughly combine the bread crumbs, Parmesan cheese, and garlic powder.
3. Dredge the zucchini slices in the egg white, then coat in the bread crumb mixture.
4. Arrange the zucchini slices in the air fryer basket and air fry at 400°F (204°C) for 14 minutes, flipping the zucchini halfway through.
5. Remove from the basket to a plate and serve.

Spicy Roasted Cauliflower

Prep time: 15 minutes | Cook time: 20 minutes | Serves 4

Cauliflower:
5 cups cauliflower florets
3 tablespoons vegetable oil
½ teaspoon ground
Sauce:
½ cup Greek yogurt or sour cream
¼ cup chopped fresh cilantro
1 jalapeño, coarsely chopped

cumin
½ teaspoon ground coriander
½ teaspoon kosher salt

4 cloves garlic, peeled
½ teaspoon kosher salt
2 tablespoons water

1. In a large bowl, combine the cauliflower, oil, cumin, coriander, and salt. Toss to coat.
2. Put the cauliflower in the air fryer basket. Roast at 400°F (204°C) for 20 minutes, stirring halfway through the roasting time.

3. Meanwhile, in a blender, combine the yogurt, cilantro, jalapeño, garlic, and salt. Blend, adding the water as needed to keep the blades moving and to thin the sauce.
4. At the end of roasting time, transfer the cauliflower to a large serving bowl. Pour the sauce over and toss gently to coat. Serve immediately.

Roasted Tofu, Carrot and Cauliflower Rice

Prep time: 10 minutes | Cook time: 22 minutes | Serves 4

½ block tofu, crumbled
1 cup diced carrot
½ cup diced onions
Cauliflower:
3 cups cauliflower rice
½ cup chopped broccoli
½ cup frozen peas
2 tablespoons soy sauce
1 tablespoon minced

2 tablespoons soy sauce
1 teaspoon turmeric

ginger
2 garlic cloves, minced
1 tablespoon rice vinegar
1½ teaspoons toasted sesame oil

1. Mix together the tofu, carrot, onions, soy sauce, and turmeric in a baking dish and stir until well incorporated.
2. Place the baking dish in the air fryer and roast at 370°F (188°C) for 10 minutes.
3. Meanwhile, in a large bowl, combine all the ingredients for the cauliflower and toss well.
4. Remove the basket and add the cauliflower mixture to the tofu and stir to combine.
5. Return the basket to the air fryer and continue roasting for 12 minutes, or until the vegetables are cooked to your preference.
6. Cool for 5 minutes before serving.

Thai Sweet-Sour Brussels Sprouts

Prep time: 5 minutes | Cook time: 20 minutes | Serves 2

¼ cup Thai sweet chili sauce	8 ounces (227 g) Brussels sprouts, trimmed (large sprouts halved)
2 tablespoons black vinegar or balsamic vinegar	Kosher salt and freshly ground black pepper, to taste
½ teaspoon hot sauce	2 teaspoons lightly packed fresh cilantro leaves, for garnish
2 small shallots, cut into ¼-inch-thick slices	

1. Place the chili sauce, vinegar, and hot sauce in a large bowl and whisk to combine.
2. Add the shallots and Brussels sprouts and toss to coat. Sprinkle with the salt and pepper. Transfer the Brussels sprouts and sauce to a metal cake pan.
3. Place the metal pan in the air fryer basket and roast at 400ºF (204ºC) for about 20 minutes, or until the Brussels sprouts are crisp-tender and the sauce has reduced to a sticky glaze. Shake the basket twice during cooking.
4. Sprinkle the cilantro on top for garnish and serve warm.

Crispy Tahini Kale

Prep time: 5 minutes | Cook time: 15 minutes | Serves 2 to 4

Dressing:

¼ cup tahini	seeds
¼ cup fresh lemon juice	½ teaspoon garlic powder
2 tablespoons olive oil	¼ teaspoon cayenne pepper
1 teaspoon sesame	

Kale:

4 cups packed torn kale leaves (stems and ribs removed and leaves torn into	palm-size pieces)
	Kosher salt and freshly ground black pepper, to taste

1. Make the dressing: Whisk together the tahini, lemon juice, olive oil, sesame seeds, garlic powder, and cayenne pepper in a large bowl until well mixed.

2. Add the kale and massage the dressing thoroughly all over the leaves. Sprinkle the salt and pepper to season.
3. Place the kale in the air fryer basket in a single layer and air fry at 350ºF (177ºC) for about 15 minutes, or until the leaves are slightly wilted and crispy.
4. Remove from the basket and serve on a plate.

Lush Roasted Vegetable Salad

Prep time: 5 minutes | Cook time: 20 minutes | Serves 2

1 potato, chopped	2 tablespoons olive oil, divided
1 carrot, sliced diagonally	A handful of arugula
1 cup cherry tomatoes	A handful of baby spinach
½ small beetroot, sliced	Juice of 1 lemon
¼ onion, sliced	3 tablespoons canned chickpeas, for serving
½ teaspoon turmeric	Parmesan shavings, for serving
½ teaspoon cumin	
¼ teaspoon sea salt	

1. Combine the potato, carrot, cherry tomatoes, beetroot, onion, turmeric, cumin, salt, and 1 tablespoon of olive oil in a large bowl and toss until well coated.
2. Arrange the veggies in the air fryer basket and roast at 370ºF (188ºC) for 20 minutes, shaking the basket halfway through.
3. Let the veggies cool for 5 to 10 minutes in the basket.
4. Put the arugula, baby spinach, lemon juice, and remaining 1 tablespoon of olive oil in a salad bowl and stir to combine. Mix in the roasted veggies and toss well.
5. Scatter the chickpeas and Parmesan shavings on top and serve immediately.

Panko-Crusted Ravioli

Prep time: 10 minutes | Cook time: 6 minutes | Serves 4

½ cup panko bread crumbs
2 teaspoons nutritional yeast
1 teaspoon dried basil
1 teaspoon dried oregano
1 teaspoon garlic powder
Salt and ground black pepper, to taste
¼ cup aquafaba
8 ounces (227 g) ravioli
Cooking spray

1. Cover the air fryer basket with aluminum foil and coat with a light brushing of oil.
2. Combine the panko bread crumbs, nutritional yeast, basil, oregano, and garlic powder. Sprinkle with salt and pepper to taste.
3. Put the aquafaba in a separate bowl. Dip the ravioli in the aquafaba before coating it in the panko mixture. Spritz with cooking spray and transfer to the air fryer.
4. Air fry at 400ºF (204ºC) for 6 minutes. Shake the air fryer basket halfway.
5. Serve hot.

Classic Italian Baked Tofu

Prep time: 5 minutes | Cook time: 10 minutes | Serves 2

1 tablespoon soy sauce
1 tablespoon water
⅓ teaspoon garlic powder
⅓ teaspoon onion powder
⅓ teaspoon dried oregano
⅓ teaspoon dried basil
Black pepper, to taste
6 ounces (170 g) extra firm tofu, pressed and cubed

1. In a large mixing bowl, whisk together the soy sauce, water, garlic powder, onion powder, oregano, basil, and black pepper. Add the tofu cubes, stirring to coat, and let them marinate for 10 minutes.
2. Arrange the tofu in the air fryer basket and bake at 390ºF (199ºC) for 10 minutes until crisp. Flip the tofu halfway through the cooking time.
3. Remove from the basket to a plate and serve.

Classic Ratatouille

Prep time: 15 minutes | Cook time: 16 minutes | Serves 2

2 Roma tomatoes, thinly sliced
1 zucchini, thinly sliced
2 yellow bell peppers, sliced
2 garlic cloves, minced
2 tablespoons olive oil
2 tablespoons herbes de Provence
1 tablespoon vinegar
Salt and black pepper, to taste

1. Place the tomatoes, zucchini, bell peppers, garlic, olive oil, herbes de Provence, and vinegar in a large bowl and toss until the vegetables are evenly coated. Sprinkle with salt and pepper and toss again. Pour the vegetable mixture into a baking dish.
2. Place the baking dish in the air fryer basket and roast at 390ºF (199ºC) for 8 minutes. Stir and continue roasting for 8 minutes until tender.
3. Let the vegetable mixture stand for 5 minutes in the basket before removing and serving.

Vegetable Sides

Potatoes with Olives and Chives

Prep time: 15 minutes | Cook time: 40 minutes | Serves 1

1 medium russet potato, scrubbed and peeled
1 teaspoon olive oil
¼ teaspoon onion powder
⅛ teaspoon salt
Dollop of butter
Dollop of cream cheese
1 tablespoon Kalamata olives
1 tablespoon chopped chives

1. In a bowl, coat the potatoes with the onion powder, salt, olive oil, and butter.
2. Transfer to the air fryer and air fry at 400ºF (204ºC) for 40 minutes, turning the potatoes over at the halfway point.
3. Take care when removing the potatoes from the air fryer and serve with the cream cheese, Kalamata olives and chives on top.

Crispy Cheesy Macaroni Balls

Prep time: 10 minutes | Cook time: 10 minutes | Serves 2

2 cups leftover macaroni
1 cup shredded Cheddar cheese
½ cup flour
1 cup bread crumbs
3 large eggs
1 cup milk
½ teaspoon salt
¼ teaspoon black pepper

1. In a bowl, combine the leftover macaroni and shredded cheese.
2. Pour the flour in a separate bowl. Put the bread crumbs in a third bowl. Finally, in a fourth bowl, mix the eggs and milk with a whisk.
3. With an ice-cream scoop, create balls from the macaroni mixture. Coat them the flour, then in the egg mixture, and lastly in the bread crumbs.
4. Arrange the balls in the air fryer and air fry at 365ºF (185ºC) for about 10 minutes, giving them an occasional stir. Ensure they crisp up nicely.
5. Serve hot.

Fast Spiced Acorn Squash

Prep time: 5 minutes | Cook time: 15 minutes | Serves 2

1 medium acorn squash, halved crosswise and deseeded
1 teaspoon coconut oil
1 teaspoon light brown sugar
Few dashes of ground cinnamon
Few dashes of ground nutmeg

1. On a clean work surface, rub the cut sides of the acorn squash with coconut oil. Scatter with the brown sugar, cinnamon, and nutmeg.
2. Put the squash halves in the air fryer basket, cut-side up. Air fry at 325ºF (163ºC) for 15 minutes until just tender when pierced in the center with a paring knife.
3. Rest for 5 to 10 minutes and serve warm.

Indian Corn Pakodas

Prep time: 10 minutes | Cook time: 8 minutes | Serves 5

1 cup flour
¼ teaspoon baking soda
¼ teaspoon salt
½ teaspoon curry powder
½ teaspoon red chili powder
¼ teaspoon turmeric powder
¼ cup water
10 cobs baby corn, blanched
Cooking spray

1. Cover the air fryer basket with aluminum foil and spritz with the cooking spray.
2. In a bowl, combine all the ingredients, save for the corn. Stir with a whisk until well combined.
3. Coat the corn in the batter and put inside the air fryer.
4. Air fry at 425ºF (218ºC) for 8 minutes until a golden brown color is achieved.
5. Serve hot.

Buttered Corn Casserole

Prep time: 5 minutes | Cook time: 15 minutes | Serves 4

2 cups frozen yellow corn
1 egg, beaten
3 tablespoons flour
½ cup grated Swiss or Havarti cheese
½ cup light cream
¼ cup milk
Pinch salt
Freshly ground black pepper, to taste
2 tablespoons butter, cut into cubes
Nonstick cooking spray

1. Spritz a baking pan with nonstick cooking spray.
2. Stir together the remaining ingredients except the butter in a medium bowl until well incorporated.
3. Transfer the mixture to the prepared baking pan and scatter with the butter cubes.
4. Place the baking pan in the air fryer basket and bake at 320ºF (160ºC) for 15 minutes, or until the top is golden brown and a toothpick inserted in the center comes out clean.
5. Let the casserole cool for 5 minutes before slicing into wedges and serving.

Breaded Cauliflower Tater Tots

Prep time: 15 minutes | Cook time: 16 minutes | Serves 12

1 pound (454 g) cauliflower, steamed and chopped
½ cup nutritional yeast
1 tablespoon oats
1 tablespoon desiccated coconuts
3 tablespoons flaxseed meal
3 tablespoons water
1 onion, chopped
1 teaspoon minced garlic
1 teaspoon chopped parsley
1 teaspoon chopped oregano
1 teaspoon chopped chives
Salt and ground black pepper, to taste
½ cup bread crumbs

1. Drain any excess water out of the cauliflower by wringing it with a paper towel.
2. In a bowl, combine the cauliflower with the remaining ingredients, save the bread crumbs. Using the hands, shape the mixture into several small balls.
3. Coat the balls in the bread crumbs and transfer to the air fryer basket. Air fry at 390ºF (199ºC) for 6 minutes, then raise the temperature to 400ºF (204ºC) and then air fry for an additional 10 minutes.
4. Serve immediately.

Roasted Balsamic Asparagus

Prep time: 5 minutes | Cook time: 10 minutes | Serves 4

1 pound (454 g) asparagus, woody ends trimmed
2 tablespoons olive oil
1 tablespoon
balsamic vinegar
2 teaspoons minced garlic
Salt and freshly ground black pepper, to taste

1. In a large shallow bowl, toss the asparagus with the olive oil, balsamic vinegar, garlic, salt, and pepper until thoroughly coated.
2. Arrange the asparagus in the air fryer basket and roast at 400ºF (204ºC) for 10 minutes until crispy. Flip the asparagus with tongs halfway through the cooking time.
3. Serve warm.

Roasted Rosemary Red Potatoes

Prep time: 5 minutes | Cook time: 20 to 22 minutes | Serves 4

1½ pounds (680 g) small red potatoes, cut into 1-inch cubes
2 tablespoons olive oil
2 tablespoons minced fresh rosemary
1 tablespoon minced
garlic
1 teaspoon salt, plus additional as needed
½ teaspoon freshly ground black pepper, plus additional as needed

1. Toss the potato cubes with the olive oil, rosemary, garlic, salt, and pepper in a large bowl until thoroughly coated.
2. Arrange the potato cubes in the air fryer basket in a single layer. Roast at 400ºF (204ºC) for 20 to 22 minutes until the potatoes are tender. Shake the basket a few times during cooking for even cooking.
3. Remove from the basket to a plate. Taste and add additional salt and pepper as needed.

Golden Potato Croquettes

Prep time: 15 minutes | Cook time: 15 minutes | Serves 10

¼ cup nutritional yeast
2 cups boiled potatoes, mashed
1 flax egg
1 tablespoon flour
2 tablespoons
chopped chives
Salt and ground black pepper, to taste
2 tablespoons vegetable oil
¼ cup bread crumbs

1. In a bowl, combine the nutritional yeast, potatoes, flax egg, flour, and chives. Sprinkle with salt and pepper as desired.
2. In a separate bowl, mix the vegetable oil and bread crumbs to achieve a crumbly consistency.
3. Shape the potato mixture into small balls and dip each one into the bread crumb mixture.
4. Put the croquettes inside the air fryer and air fry at 400ºF (204ºC) for 15 minutes, ensuring the croquettes turn golden brown.
5. Serve immediately.

Veggies Salad with Baby Capers

Prep time: 15 minutes | Cook time: 10 minutes | Serves 4

6 plum tomatoes, halved
2 large red onions, sliced
4 long red pepper, sliced
2 yellow pepper, sliced
6 cloves garlic,
crushed
1 tablespoon extra-virgin olive oil
1 teaspoon paprika
½ lemon, juiced
Salt and ground black pepper, to taste
1 tablespoon baby capers

1. Put the tomatoes, onions, peppers, and garlic in a large bowl and cover with the extra-virgin olive oil, paprika, and lemon juice. Sprinkle with salt and pepper as desired.
2. Line the inside of the air fryer basket with aluminum foil. Put the vegetables inside and air fry at 420ºF (216ºC) for 10 minutes, ensuring the edges turn brown.
3. Serve in a salad bowl with the baby capers.

Air-Fried Sweet-Sour Tofu

Prep time: 15 minutes | Cook time: 20 minutes | Serves 2

2 teaspoons apple cider vinegar
1 tablespoon sugar
1 tablespoon soy sauce
3 teaspoons lime juice
1 teaspoon ground ginger
1 teaspoon garlic powder
½ block firm tofu, pressed to remove excess liquid and cut into cubes
1 teaspoon cornstarch
2 green onions, chopped
Toasted sesame seeds, for garnish

1. In a bowl, thoroughly combine the apple cider vinegar, sugar, soy sauce, lime juice, ground ginger, and garlic powder.
2. Cover the tofu with this mixture and leave to marinate for at least 30 minutes.
3. Transfer the tofu to the air fryer, keeping any excess marinade for the sauce. Air fry at 400ºF (204ºC) for 20 minutes or until crispy.
4. In the meantime, thicken the sauce with the cornstarch over a medium-low heat.
5. Serve the cooked tofu with the sauce, green onions, and sesame seeds.

Panko-Crusted Dill Pickles

Prep time: 10 minutes | Cook time: 15 minutes | Serves 4

14 dill pickles, sliced
¼ cup flour
⅛ teaspoon baking powder
Pinch of salt
2 tablespoons
cornstarch plus 3 tablespoons water
6 tablespoons panko bread crumbs
½ teaspoon paprika
Cooking spray

1. Drain any excess moisture out of the dill pickles on a paper towel.
2. In a bowl, combine the flour, baking powder and salt.
3. Throw in the cornstarch and water mixture and combine well with a whisk.
4. Put the panko bread crumbs in a shallow dish along with the paprika. Mix thoroughly.
5. Dip the pickles in the flour batter, before coating in the bread crumbs. Spritz all the pickles with the cooking spray.
6. Transfer to the air fryer basket and air fry at 400ºF (204ºC) for 15 minutes, or until golden brown.
7. Serve immediately.

Homemade Parmesan Pesto Gnocchi

Prep time: 10 minutes | Cook time: 15 minutes | Serves 4

1 (1-pound / 454-g) package gnocchi
1 medium onion, chopped
3 cloves garlic, minced
1 tablespoon extra-virgin olive oil
1 (8-ounce / 227-g) jar pesto
⅓ cup grated Parmesan cheese

1. In a large bowl combine the onion, garlic, and gnocchi, and drizzle with the olive oil. Mix thoroughly.
2. Transfer the mixture to the air fryer and air fry at 340ºF (171ºC) for 15 minutes, stirring occasionally, making sure the gnocchi become light brown and crispy.
3. Add the pesto and Parmesan cheese, and give everything a good stir before serving.

Roasted Spicy Cabbage

Prep time: 5 minutes | Cook time: 7 minutes | Serves 4

1 head cabbage, sliced into 1-inch-thick ribbons
1 tablespoon olive oil
1 teaspoon garlic powder
1 teaspoon red pepper flakes
1 teaspoon salt
1 teaspoon freshly ground black pepper

1. Toss the cabbage with the olive oil, garlic powder, red pepper flakes, salt, and pepper in a large mixing bowl until well coated.
2. Arrange the cabbage in the air fryer basket and roast at 350ºF (177ºC) for 7 minutes until crisp. Flip the cabbage with tongs halfway through the cooking time.
3. Remove from the basket to a plate and serve warm.

Arugula, Fig, and Chickpea Salad

Prep time: 15 minutes | Cook time: 20 minutes | Serves 4

8 fresh figs, halved
1½ cups cooked chickpeas
1 teaspoon crushed roasted cumin seeds
4 tablespoons balsamic vinegar
2 tablespoons extra-
virgin olive oil, plus more for greasing
Salt and ground black pepper, to taste
3 cups arugula rocket, washed and dried

1. Cover the air fryer basket with aluminum foil and grease lightly with oil. Put the figs in the air fryer basket and air fry at 375ºF (191ºC) for 10 minutes.
2. In a bowl, combine the chickpeas and cumin seeds.
3. Remove the air fried figs from the air fryer and replace with the chickpeas. Air fry for 10 minutes. Leave to cool.
4. In the meantime, prepare the dressing. Mix the balsamic vinegar, olive oil, salt and pepper.
5. In a salad bowl, combine the arugula rocket with the cooled figs and chickpeas.
6. Toss with the sauce and serve.

Air-Fried Green Beans

Prep time: 5 minutes | Cook time: 8 minutes | Serves 4

1 tablespoon reduced-sodium soy sauce or tamari
½ tablespoon Sriracha sauce
4 teaspoons toasted
sesame oil, divided
12 ounces (340 g) trimmed green beans
½ tablespoon toasted sesame seeds

1. Whisk together the soy sauce, Sriracha sauce, and 1 teaspoon of sesame oil in a small bowl until smooth.
2. Toss the green beans with the remaining sesame oil in a large bowl until evenly coated.
3. Place the green beans in the air fryer basket in a single layer. You may need to work in batches to avoid overcrowding.
4. Air fry at 375ºF (191ºC) for about 8 minutes until the green beans are lightly charred and tender. Shake the basket halfway through the cooking time.
5. Remove from the basket to a platter. Repeat with the remaining green beans.
6. Pour the prepared sauce over the top of green beans and toss well. Serve sprinkled with the toasted sesame seeds.

Cheesy Buttered Broccoli

Prep time: 5 minutes | Cook time: 4 minutes | Serves 4

1 pound (454 g) broccoli florets
1 medium shallot, minced
2 tablespoons olive oil
2 tablespoons
unsalted butter, melted
2 teaspoons minced garlic
¼ cup grated Parmesan cheese

1. Combine the broccoli florets with the shallot, olive oil, butter, garlic, and Parmesan cheese in a medium bowl and toss until the broccoli florets are thoroughly coated.
2. Arrange the broccoli florets in the air fryer basket in a single layer and roast at 360ºF (182ºC) for 4 minutes until crisp-tender.
3. Serve warm.

Air-Fried Green Beans

Prep time: 5 minutes | Cook time: 8 minutes | Serves 4

1 tablespoon reduced-sodium soy sauce or tamari
½ tablespoon Sriracha sauce
4 teaspoons toasted sesame oil, divided
12 ounces (340 g) trimmed green beans
½ tablespoon toasted sesame seeds

1. Whisk together the soy sauce, Sriracha sauce, and 1 teaspoon of sesame oil in a small bowl until smooth.
2. Toss the green beans with the remaining sesame oil in a large bowl until evenly coated.
3. Place the green beans in the air fryer basket in a single layer. You may need to work in batches to avoid overcrowding.
4. Air fry at 375°F (191°C) for about 8 minutes until the green beans are lightly charred and tender. Shake the basket halfway through the cooking time.
5. Remove from the basket to a platter. Repeat with the remaining green beans.
6. Pour the prepared sauce over the top of green beans and toss well. Serve sprinkled with the toasted sesame seeds.

Panko-Crusted Parmesan Broccoli

Prep time: 5 minutes | Cook time: 12 to 14 minutes | Serves 2

⅓ cup fat-free milk
1 tablespoon all-purpose or gluten-free flour
½ tablespoon olive oil
½ teaspoon ground sage
¼ teaspoon kosher salt
⅛ teaspoon freshly ground black pepper
2 cups roughly chopped broccoli florets
6 tablespoons shredded Cheddar cheese
2 tablespoons panko bread crumbs
1 tablespoon grated Parmesan cheese
Olive oil spray

1. Spritz a baking dish with olive oil spray.
2. Mix the milk, flour, olive oil, sage, salt, and pepper in a medium bowl and whisk to combine. Stir in the broccoli florets, Cheddar cheese, bread crumbs, and Parmesan cheese and toss to coat.
3. Pour the broccoli mixture into the prepared baking dish and place in the air fryer basket.
4. Bake at 330°F (166°C) for 12 to 14 minutes until the top is golden brown and the broccoli is tender.
5. Serve immediately.

Russet Potatoes with Yogurt

Prep time: 5 minutes | Cook time: 35 minutes | Serves 4

4 (7-ounce / 198-g) russet potatoes, rinsed
Olive oil spray
½ teaspoon kosher salt, divided
½ cup 2% plain Greek yogurt
¼ cup minced fresh chives
Freshly ground black pepper, to taste

1. Pat the potatoes dry and pierce them all over with a fork. Spritz the potatoes with olive oil spray. Sprinkle with ¼ teaspoon of the salt.
2. Put the potatoes in the air fryer basket and bake at 400°F (204°C) for 35 minutes until a knife can be inserted into the center of the potatoes easily.
3. Remove from the basket and split open the potatoes. Top with the yogurt, chives, the remaining ¼ teaspoon of salt, and finish with the black pepper. Serve immediately.

Easy Roasted Lemony Broccoli

Prep time: 5 minutes | Cook time: 15 minutes | Serves 6

2 heads broccoli, cut into florets
2 teaspoons extra-virgin olive oil, plus more for coating
1 teaspoon salt
½ teaspoon black pepper
1 clove garlic, minced
½ teaspoon lemon juice

1. Cover the air fryer basket with aluminum foil and coat with a light brushing of oil.
2. In a bowl, combine all ingredients, save for the lemon juice, and transfer to the air fryer basket. Roast at 375°F (191°C) for 15 minutes.
3. Serve with the lemon juice.

Air-Fried Lemony Falafel

Prep time: 15 minutes | Cook time: 15 minutes | Serves 8

1 teaspoon cumin seeds
½ teaspoon coriander seeds
2 cups chickpeas, drained and rinsed
½ teaspoon red pepper flakes
3 cloves garlic
¼ cup chopped parsley
¼ cup chopped coriander
½ onion, diced
1 tablespoon juice from freshly squeezed lemon
3 tablespoons flour
½ teaspoon salt
Cooking spray

1. Fry the cumin and coriander seeds over medium heat until fragrant.
2. Grind using a mortar and pestle.
3. Put all of ingredients, except for the cooking spray, in a food processor and blend until a fine consistency is achieved.
4. Use the hands to mold the mixture into falafels and spritz with the cooking spray.
5. Transfer the falafels to the air fryer basket in one layer.
6. Air fry at 400ºF (204ºC) for 15 minutes, serving when they turn golden brown.

Air-Fried Asparagus Spears

Prep time: 5 minutes | Cook time: 5 minutes | Serves 4

1 pound (454 g) fresh asparagus spears, trimmed
1 tablespoon olive oil
Salt and ground black pepper, to taste

1. Combine all the ingredients and transfer to the air fryer basket.
2. Air fry at 375ºF (191ºC) for 5 minutes or until soft.
3. Serve hot.

Breaded Brussels Sprouts with Sage

Prep time: 5 minutes | Cook time: 15 minutes | Serves 4

1 pound (454 g) Brussels sprouts, halved
1 cup bread crumbs
2 tablespoons grated Grana Padano cheese
1 tablespoon paprika
2 tablespoons canola oil
1 tablespoon chopped sage

1. Line the air fryer basket with parchment paper.
2. In a small bowl, thoroughly mix the bread crumbs, cheese, and paprika. In a large bowl, place the Brussels sprouts and drizzle the canola oil over the top. Sprinkle with the bread crumb mixture and toss to coat.
3. Place the Brussels sprouts in the air fryer basket and roast at 400ºF (204ºC) for 15 minutes, or until the Brussels sprouts are lightly browned and crisp. Shake the basket a few times during cooking to ensure even cooking.
4. Transfer the Brussels sprouts to a plate and sprinkle the sage on top before serving.

Breaded Cauliflower Florets

Prep time: 5 minutes | Cook time: 17 minutes | Serves 4

¼ cup vegan butter, melted
¼ cup sriracha sauce
4 cups cauliflower florets
1 cup bread crumbs
1 teaspoon salt

1. Mix the sriracha and vegan butter in a bowl and pour this mixture over the cauliflower, taking care to cover each floret entirely.
2. In a separate bowl, combine the bread crumbs and salt.
3. Dip the cauliflower florets in the bread crumbs, coating each one well. Air fry in the air fryer at 375ºF (191ºC) for 17 minutes.
4. Serve hot.

Stuffed Vegetables

Cheesy Stuffed Bell Peppers with Beef

Prep time: 10 minutes | Cook time: 30 minutes | Serves 4

1 pound (454 g) ground beef
1 tablespoon taco seasoning mix
1 can diced tomatoes and green chilis
4 green bell peppers
1 cup shredded Monterey jack cheese, divided

1. Set a skillet over a high heat and cook the ground beef at 350ºF (177ºC) for 8 minutes. Make sure it is cooked through and browned all over. Drain the fat.
2. Stir in the taco seasoning mix, and the diced tomatoes and green chilis. Allow the mixture to cook for a further 4 minutes.
3. In the meantime, slice the tops off the green peppers and remove the seeds and membranes.
4. When the meat mixture is fully cooked, spoon equal amounts of it into the peppers and top with the Monterey jack cheese. Then place the peppers into the air fryer. Air fry for 15 minutes.
5. The peppers are ready when they are soft, and the cheese is bubbling and brown. Serve warm.

Stuffed Butternut Squash with Tomato

Prep time: 5 minutes | Cook time: 30 minutes | Serves 4

1 pound (454 g) butternut squash, ends trimmed
2 teaspoons olive oil, divided
6 grape tomatoes, halved
1 poblano pepper, cut into strips
Salt and black pepper, to taste
¼ cup grated Mozzarella cheese

1. Using a large knife, cut the squash in half lengthwise on a flat work surface. This recipe just needs half of the squash. Scoop out the flesh to make room for the stuffing. Coat the squash half with 1 teaspoon of olive oil.

2. Put the squash half in the air fryer basket and roast at 350ºF (177ºC) for 15 minutes.
3. Meanwhile, thoroughly combine the tomatoes, poblano pepper, remaining 1 teaspoon of olive oil, salt, and pepper in a bowl.
4. Remove the basket and spoon the tomato mixture into the squash. Return to the air fryer and roast for 12 minutes until the tomatoes are soft.
5. Scatter the Mozzarella cheese on top and continue cooking for about 3 minutes, or until the cheese is melted.
6. Cool for 5 minutes before serving.

Stuffed Peppers with Rice and Olives

Prep time: 5 minutes | Cook time: 16 to 17 minutes | Serves 4

4 red bell peppers, tops sliced off
2 cups cooked rice
1 cup crumbled feta cheese
1 onion, chopped
¼ cup sliced kalamata olives
¾ cup tomato sauce
1 tablespoon Greek seasoning
Salt and black pepper, to taste
2 tablespoons chopped fresh dill, for serving

1. Microwave the red bell peppers for 1 to 2 minutes until tender.
2. When ready, transfer the red bell peppers to a plate to cool.
3. Mix together the cooked rice, feta cheese, onion, kalamata olives, tomato sauce, Greek seasoning, salt, and pepper in a medium bowl and stir until well combined.
4. Divide the rice mixture among the red bell peppers and transfer to a greased baking dish.
5. Put the baking dish in the air fryer and bake at 360ºF (182ºC) for 15 minutes, or until the rice is heated through and the vegetables are soft.
6. Remove from the basket and serve with the dill sprinkled on top.

Cheesy Pepperoni and Mushroom Pizza

Prep time: 5 minutes | Cook time: 18 minutes | Serves 4

4 large portobello mushrooms, stems removed
4 teaspoons olive oil

1 cup marinara sauce
1 cup shredded Mozzarella cheese
10 slices sugar-free pepperoni

1. Brush each mushroom cap with the olive oil, one teaspoon for each cap.
2. Put on a baking sheet and bake, stem-side down, at 375ºF (191ºC) for 8 minutes.
3. Take out of the air fryer and divide the marinara sauce, Mozzarella cheese and pepperoni evenly among the caps.
4. Air fry for another 10 minutes until browned.
5. Serve hot.

Cheesy Prosciutto and Mushroom Pizza

Prep time: 10 minutes | Cook time: 5 minutes | Serves 3

3 portobello mushroom caps, cleaned and scooped
3 tablespoons olive oil
Pinch of salt

Pinch of dried Italian seasonings
3 tablespoons tomato sauce
3 tablespoons shredded Mozzarella cheese
12 slices prosciutto

1. Season both sides of the portobello mushrooms with a drizzle of olive oil, then sprinkle salt and the Italian seasonings on the insides.
2. With a knife, spread the tomato sauce evenly over the mushroom, before adding the Mozzarella on top.
3. Put the portobello in the air fryer basket and place in the air fryer.
4. Air fry at 330ºF (166ºC) for 1 minute, before taking the air fryer basket out of the air fryer and putting the prosciutto slices on top.
5. Air fry for another 4 minutes.
6. Serve warm.

Veggies and Oatmeal Stuffed Peppers

Prep time: 15 minutes | Cook time: 6 minutes | Serves 2 to 4

2 large bell peppers, halved lengthwise, deseeded
2 tablespoons cooked kidney beans
2 tablespoons cooked chick peas
2 cups cooked oatmeal

1 teaspoon ground cumin
½ teaspoon paprika
½ teaspoon salt or to taste
¼ teaspoon black pepper powder
¼ cup yogurt

1. Put the bell peppers, cut-side down, in the air fryer basket. Air fry for 2 minutes.
2. Take the peppers out of the air fryer and let cool.
3. In a bowl, combine the rest of the ingredients.
4. Divide the mixture evenly and use each portion to stuff a pepper.
5. Return the stuffed peppers to the air fryer and continue to air fry at 355ºF (179ºC) for 4 minutes.
6. Serve hot.

Lemony Stuffed Mushrooms with Cashew

Prep time: 10 minutes | Cook time: 15 minutes | Serves 6

1 cup basil
½ cup cashew, soaked overnight
½ cup nutritional yeast
1 tablespoon lemon juice
2 cloves garlic

1 tablespoon olive oil
Salt, to taste
1 pound (454 g) baby bella mushroom, stems removed

1. Prepare the pesto. In a food processor, blend the basil, cashew nuts, nutritional yeast, lemon juice, garlic and olive oil to combine well. Sprinkle with salt as desired.
2. Turn the mushrooms cap-side down and spread the pesto on the underside of each cap.
3. Transfer to the air fryer and air fry at 400ºF (204ºC) for 15 minutes.
4. Serve warm.

Stuffed Tomato with Veggies and Cheese

Prep time: 10 minutes | Cook time: 16 to 20 minutes | Serves 4

4 medium beefsteak tomatoes, rinsed
½ cup grated carrot
1 medium onion, chopped
1 garlic clove, minced

2 teaspoons olive oil
2 cups fresh baby spinach
¼ cup crumbled low-sodium feta cheese
½ teaspoon dried basil

1. On your cutting board, cut a thin slice off the top of each tomato. Scoop out a ¼- to ½-inch-thick tomato pulp and place the tomatoes upside down on paper towels to drain. Set aside.
2. Stir together the carrot, onion, garlic, and olive oil in a baking pan. Place in the air fryer basket and bake for 4 to 6 minutes, or until the carrot is crisp-tender.
3. Remove the pan from the basket and stir in the spinach, feta cheese, and basil.
4. Spoon ¼ of the vegetable mixture into each tomato and transfer the stuffed tomatoes to the basket.
5. Bake at 350ºF (177ºC) for 12 to 14 minutes until the filling is hot and the tomatoes are lightly caramelized.
6. Let the tomatoes cool for 5 minutes and serve.

Chapter 8 Appetizers and Snacks

Crispy Olives

Prep time: 5 minutes | Cook time: 8 minutes | Serves 4

1 (5½-ounce / 156-g) jar pitted green olives
½ cup all-purpose flour
Salt and pepper, to taste
½ cup bread crumbs
1 egg
Cooking spray

1. Remove the olives from the jar and dry thoroughly with paper towels.
2. In a small bowl, combine the flour with salt and pepper to taste. Place the bread crumbs in another small bowl. In a third small bowl, beat the egg.
3. Spritz the air fryer basket with cooking spray.
4. Dip the olives in the flour, then the egg, and then the bread crumbs.
5. Place the breaded olives in the air fryer. It is okay to stack them. Spray the olives with cooking spray. Air fry at 400ºF (204ºC) for 6 minutes. Flip the olives and air fry for an additional 2 minutes, or until brown and crisp.
6. Cool before serving.

Baked Bacon-Wrapped Dates

Prep time: 10 minutes | Cook time: 10 to 14 minutes | Serves 6

12 dates, pitted
6 slices high-quality
bacon, cut in half
Cooking spray

1. Wrap each date with half a bacon slice and secure with a toothpick.
2. Spray the air fryer basket with cooking spray, then place 6 bacon-wrapped dates in the basket and bake at 360ºF (182ºC) for 5 to 7 minutes or until the bacon is crispy. Repeat this process with the remaining dates.
3. Remove the dates and allow to cool on a wire rack for 5 minutes before serving.

Fast Caramelized Peaches

Prep time: 10 minutes | Cook time: 10 to 13 minutes | Serves 4

2 tablespoons sugar
¼ teaspoon ground cinnamon
4 peaches, cut into wedges
Cooking spray

1. Lightly spray the air fryer basket with cooking spray.
2. Toss the peaches with the sugar and cinnamon in a medium bowl until evenly coated.
3. Arrange the peaches in the air fryer basket in a single layer. You may need to work in batches to avoid overcrowding.
4. Lightly mist the peaches with cooking spray and air fry at 350ºF (177ºC) for 5 minutes. Flip the peaches and air fry for another 5 to 8 minutes, or until the peaches are caramelized.
5. Repeat with the remaining peaches.
6. Let the peaches cool for 5 minutes and serve warm.

Spicy Honey Chicken Wings

Prep time: 5 minutes | Cook time: 30 minutes | Serves 4

1 tablespoon Sriracha hot sauce
1 tablespoon honey
1 garlic clove, minced
½ teaspoon kosher
salt
16 chicken wings and drumettes
Cooking spray

1. In a large bowl, whisk together the Sriracha hot sauce, honey, minced garlic, and kosher salt, then add the chicken and toss to coat.
2. Spray the air fryer basket with cooking spray, then place 8 wings in the basket and air fry at 360ºF (182ºC) for 15 minutes, turning halfway through. Repeat this process with the remaining wings.
3. Remove the wings and allow to cool on a wire rack for 10 minutes before serving.

Green Tomatoes with Horseradish Sauce

Prep time: 18 minutes | Cook time: 10 to 15 minutes | Serves 4

2 eggs
¼ cup buttermilk
½ cup bread crumbs
½ cup cornmeal
¼ teaspoon salt
1½ pounds (680 g) firm green tomatoes, cut into ¼-inch slices
Cooking spray
Horseradish Sauce:
¼ cup sour cream
¼ cup mayonnaise
2 teaspoons prepared horseradish
½ teaspoon lemon juice
½ teaspoon Worcestershire sauce
⅛ teaspoon black pepper

1. Spritz the air fryer basket with cooking spray.
2. In a small bowl, whisk together all the ingredients for the horseradish sauce until smooth. Set aside.
3. In a shallow dish, beat the eggs and buttermilk.
4. In a separate shallow dish, thoroughly combine the bread crumbs, cornmeal, and salt.
5. Dredge the tomato slices, one at a time, in the egg mixture, then roll in the bread crumb mixture until evenly coated.
6. Working in batches, place the tomato slices in the air fryer basket in a single layer. Spray them with cooking spray.
7. Air fry at 390ºF (199ºC) for 10 to 15 minutes, flipping the slices halfway through, or until the tomato slices are nicely browned and crisp.
8. Remove from the basket to a platter and repeat with the remaining tomato slices.
9. Serve drizzled with the prepared horseradish sauce.

Spicy Sesame Mixed Nut

Prep time: 10 minutes | Cook time: 2 minutes | Makes 4 cups

1 tablespoon buttery spread, melted
2 teaspoons honey
¼ teaspoon cayenne pepper
2 teaspoons sesame seeds
¼ teaspoon kosher salt
¼ teaspoon freshly ground black pepper
1 cup cashews
1 cup almonds
1 cup mini pretzels
1 cup rice squares cereal
Cooking spray

1. In a large bowl, combine the buttery spread, honey, cayenne pepper, sesame seeds, kosher salt, and black pepper, then add the cashews, almonds, pretzels, and rice squares, tossing to coat.
2. Spray a baking pan with cooking spray, then pour the mixture into the pan and bake at 360ºF (182ºC) for 2 minutes.
3. Remove the sesame mix from the air fryer and allow to cool in the pan on a wire rack for 5 minutes before serving.

Panko-Crusted Marinated Chicken Wings

Prep time: 1 hour 20 minutes | Cook time: 17 to 19 minutes | Serves 4

2 pounds (907 g) chicken wings
Marinade:
1 cup buttermilk
½ teaspoon salt
½ teaspoon black pepper
Coating:
1 cup flour
1 cup panko bread crumbs
2 tablespoons poultry seasoning
2 teaspoons salt
Cooking spray

1. Whisk together all the ingredients for the marinade in a large bowl.
2. Add the chicken wings to the marinade and toss well. Transfer to the refrigerator to marinate for at least an hour.
3. Spritz the air fryer basket with cooking spray.
4. Thoroughly combine all the ingredients for the coating in a shallow bowl.
5. Remove the chicken wings from the marinade and shake off any excess. Roll them in the coating mixture.
6. Place the chicken wings in the air fryer basket in a single layer. You'll need to work in batches to avoid overcrowding.
7. Mist the wings with cooking spray and air fry at 360ºF (182ºC) for 17 to 19 minutes, or until the wings are crisp and golden brown on the outside. Flip the wings halfway through the cooking time.
8. Remove from the basket to a plate and repeat with the remaining wings.
9. Serve hot.

Cheesy Artichoke-Spinach Dip

Prep time: 10 minutes | Cook time: 10 minutes | Makes 3 cups

1 (14-ounce / 397-g) can artichoke hearts packed in water, drained and chopped
1 (10-ounce / 284-g) package frozen spinach, thawed and drained
1 teaspoon minced garlic
2 tablespoons
mayonnaise
¼ cup nonfat plain Greek yogurt
¼ cup shredded part-skim Mozzarella cheese
¼ cup grated Parmesan cheese
¼ teaspoon freshly ground black pepper
Cooking spray

1. Wrap the artichoke hearts and spinach in a paper towel and squeeze out any excess liquid, then transfer the vegetables to a large bowl.
2. Add the minced garlic, mayonnaise, plain Greek yogurt, Mozzarella, Parmesan, and black pepper to the large bowl, stirring well to combine.
3. Spray a baking pan with cooking spray, then transfer the dip mixture to the pan and air fry at 360ºF (182ºC) for 10 minutes.
4. Remove the dip from the air fryer and allow to cool in the pan on a wire rack for 10 minutes before serving.

Fast Crispy Artichoke Hearts

Prep time: 5 minutes | Cook time: 8 minutes | Serves 14

14 whole artichoke hearts, packed in water
1 egg
½ cup all-purpose flour
⅓ cup panko bread crumbs
1 teaspoon Italian seasoning
Cooking spray

1. Squeeze excess water from the artichoke hearts and place them on paper towels to dry.
2. In a small bowl, beat the egg. In another small bowl, place the flour. In a third small bowl, combine the bread crumbs and Italian seasoning, and stir.
3. Spritz the air fryer basket with cooking spray.
4. Dip the artichoke hearts in the flour, then the egg, and then the bread crumb mixture.
5. Place the breaded artichoke hearts in the air fryer basket. Spray them with cooking spray. Air fry at 380ºF (193ºC) for 8 minutes, or until the artichoke hearts have browned and are crisp, flipping once halfway through.
6. Let cool for 5 minutes before serving.

Stuffed Mushrooms with Mozzarella and Ham

Prep time: 15 minutes | Cook time: 12 minutes | Serves 8

4 ounces (113 g) Mozzarella cheese, cut into pieces
½ cup diced ham
2 green onions, chopped
2 tablespoons bread crumbs
½ teaspoon garlic powder
¼ teaspoon ground oregano
¼ teaspoon ground black pepper
1 to 2 teaspoons olive oil
16 fresh Baby Bella mushrooms, stemmed removed

1. Process the cheese, ham, green onions, bread crumbs, garlic powder, oregano, and pepper in a food processor until finely chopped.
2. With the food processor running, slowly drizzle in 1 to 2 teaspoons olive oil until a thick paste has formed. Transfer the mixture to a bowl.
3. Evenly divide the mixture into the mushroom caps and lightly press down the mixture.
4. Lay the mushrooms in the air fryer basket in a single layer. You'll need to work in batches to avoid overcrowding.
5. Roast at 390ºF (199ºC) for 12 minutes until the mushrooms are lightly browned and tender.
6. Remove from the basket to a plate and repeat with the remaining mushrooms.
7. Let the mushrooms cool for 5 minutes and serve warm.

Golden Bruschetta with Tomato and Basil

Prep time: 5 minutes | Cook time: 6 minutes | Serves 6

4 tomatoes, diced
⅓ cup shredded fresh basil
¼ cup shredded Parmesan cheese
1 tablespoon balsamic vinegar
1 tablespoon minced garlic
1 teaspoon olive oil
1 teaspoon salt
1 teaspoon freshly ground black pepper
1 loaf French bread, cut into 1-inch-thick slices
Cooking spray

1. Mix together the tomatoes and basil in a medium bowl. Add the cheese, vinegar, garlic, olive oil, salt, and pepper and stir until well incorporated. Set aside.
2. Spritz the air fryer basket with cooking spray. Working in batches, lay the bread slices in the basket in a single layer. Spray the slices with cooking spray.
3. Bake at 250°F (121°C) for 3 minutes until golden brown.
4. Remove from the basket to a plate. Repeat with the remaining bread slices.
5. Top each slice with a generous spoonful of the tomato mixture and serve.

Air-Fried Prosciutto-Wrapped Asparagus

Prep time: 5 minutes | Cook time: 16 to 24 minutes | Serves 6

12 asparagus spears, woody ends trimmed
24 pieces thinly
sliced prosciutto
Cooking spray

1. Wrap each asparagus spear with 2 slices of prosciutto, then repeat this process with the remaining asparagus and prosciutto.
2. Spray the air fryer basket with cooking spray, then place 2 to 3 bundles in the basket and air fry at 360°F (182°C) for 4 minutes. Repeat this process with the remaining asparagus bundles.
3. Remove the bundles and allow to cool on a wire rack for 5 minutes before serving.

Crunchy Cajun Zucchini Chips

Prep time: 5 minutes | Cook time: 15 to 16 minutes | Serves 4

2 large zucchinis, cut into ⅛-inch-thick slices
2 teaspoons Cajun seasoning
Cooking spray

1. Spray the air fryer basket lightly with cooking spray.
2. Put the zucchini slices in a medium bowl and spray them generously with cooking spray.
3. Sprinkle the Cajun seasoning over the zucchini and stir to make sure they are evenly coated with oil and seasoning.
4. Place the slices in a single layer in the air fryer basket, making sure not to overcrowd. You will need to cook these in several batches.
5. Air fry at 370°F (188°C) for 8 minutes. Flip the slices over and air fry for an additional 7 to 8 minutes, or until they are as crisp and brown as you prefer.
6. Serve immediately.

Crispy Cheesy Apple Rolls

Prep time: 5 minutes | Cook time: 4 to 5 minutes | Makes 8 roll-ups

8 slices whole wheat sandwich bread
4 ounces (113 g) Colby Jack cheese, grated
½ small apple, chopped
2 tablespoons butter, melted

1. Remove the crusts from the bread and flatten the slices with a rolling pin. Don't be gentle. Press hard so that bread will be very thin.
2. Top bread slices with cheese and chopped apple, dividing the ingredients evenly.
3. Roll up each slice tightly and secure each with one or two toothpicks.
4. Brush outside of rolls with melted butter.
5. Place in air fryer basket and air fry at 390°F (199°C) for 4 to 5 minutes, or until outside is crisp and nicely browned.
6. Serve hot.

Fast Cheesy Crab Toasts

Prep time: 10 minutes | Cook time: 5 minutes | Makes 15 to 18 toasts

1 (6-ounce / 170-g) can flaked crab meat, well drained
3 tablespoons light mayonnaise
¼ cup shredded Parmesan cheese
¼ cup shredded Cheddar cheese
1 teaspoon Worcestershire sauce
½ teaspoon lemon juice
1 loaf artisan bread, French bread, or baguette, cut into ⅜-inch-thick slices

1. In a large bowl, stir together all the ingredients except the bread slices.
2. On a clean work surface, lay the bread slices. Spread ½ tablespoon of crab mixture onto each slice of bread.
3. Arrange the bread slices in the air fryer basket in a single layer. You'll need to work in batches to avoid overcrowding.
4. Bake at 360ºF (182ºC) for 5 minutes until the tops are lightly browned.
5. Transfer to a plate and repeat with the remaining bread slices.
6. Serve warm.

Crispy Cheesy Hash Brown Bruschetta

Prep time: 5 minutes | Cook time: 6 to 8 minutes | Serves 4

4 frozen hash brown patties
1 tablespoon olive oil
⅓ cup chopped cherry tomatoes
3 tablespoons diced fresh Mozzarella
2 tablespoons grated Parmesan cheese
1 tablespoon balsamic vinegar
1 tablespoon minced fresh basil

1. Place the hash brown patties in the air fryer in a single layer. Air fry at 400ºF (204ºC) for 6 to 8 minutes, or until the potatoes are crisp, hot, and golden brown.
2. Meanwhile, combine the olive oil, tomatoes, Mozzarella, Parmesan, vinegar, and basil in a small bowl.
3. When the potatoes are done, carefully remove from the basket and arrange on a serving plate. Top with the tomato mixture and serve.

Fast Cheesy Jalapeño Peppers

Prep time: 5 minutes | Cook time: 10 minutes | Serves 4

8 jalapeño peppers
½ cup whipped cream cheese
¼ cup shredded Cheddar cheese

1. Use a paring knife to carefully cut off the jalapeño tops, then scoop out the ribs and seeds. Set aside.
2. In a medium bowl, combine the whipped cream cheese and shredded Cheddar cheese. Place the mixture in a sealable plastic bag, and using a pair of scissors, cut off one corner from the bag. Gently squeeze some cream cheese mixture into each pepper until almost full.
3. Place a piece of parchment paper on the bottom of the air fryer basket and place the poppers on top, distributing evenly. Air fry at 360ºF (182ºC) for 10 minutes.
4. Allow the poppers to cool for 5 to 10 minutes before serving.

Cheesy Steak Fries with Scallions

Prep time: 5 minutes | Cook time: 20 minutes | Serves 5

1 (28-ounce / 794-g) bag frozen steak fries
Cooking spray
Salt and pepper, to taste
½ cup beef gravy
1 cup shredded Mozzarella cheese
2 scallions, green parts only, chopped

1. Place the frozen steak fries in the air fryer. Air fry at 400ºF (204ºC) for 10 minutes. Shake the basket and spritz the fries with cooking spray. Sprinkle with salt and pepper. Air fry for an additional 8 minutes.
2. Pour the beef gravy into a medium, microwave-safe bowl. Microwave for 30 seconds, or until the gravy is warm.
3. Sprinkle the fries with the cheese. Air fry for an additional 2 minutes, until the cheese is melted.
4. Transfer the fries to a serving dish. Drizzle the fries with gravy and sprinkle the scallions on top for a green garnish. Serve.

Panko-Crusted Artichoke Hearts

Prep time: 10 minutes | Cook time: 8 minutes | Serves 4

14 whole artichoke hearts packed in water
½ cup all-purpose flour
1 egg
⅓ cup panko bread crumbs
1 teaspoon Italian seasoning
Cooking spray

1. Drain the artichoke hearts and dry thoroughly with paper towels.
2. Place the flour on a plate. Beat the egg in a shallow bowl until frothy. Thoroughly combine the bread crumbs and Italian seasoning in a separate shallow bowl.
3. Dredge the artichoke hearts in the flour, then in the beaten egg, and finally roll in the bread crumb mixture until evenly coated.
4. Place the artichoke hearts in the air fryer basket and mist them with cooking spray.
5. Air fry at 375ºF (191ºC) for 8 minutes, flipping the artichoke hearts halfway through, or until they begin to brown and edges are crispy.
6. Let the artichoke hearts sit for 5 minutes before serving.

Sumptuous Cheese Sandwiches

Prep time: 10 minutes | Cook time: 5 to 6 minutes | Serves 4 to 8

8 ounces (227 g) Brie
8 slices oat nut bread
1 large ripe pear, cored and cut into
½-inch-thick slices
2 tablespoons butter, melted

1. Make the sandwiches: Spread each of 4 slices of bread with ¼ of the Brie. Top the Brie with the pear slices and remaining 4 bread slices.
2. Brush the melted butter lightly on both sides of each sandwich.
3. Arrange the sandwiches in the air fryer basket. You may need to work in batches to avoid overcrowding.
4. Bake at 360ºF (182ºC) for 5 to 6 minutes until the cheese is melted. Repeat with the remaining sandwiches.
5. Serve warm.

Simple Breaded Beef Cubes

Prep time: 10 minutes | Cook time: 12 to 16 minutes | Serves 4

1 pound (454 g) sirloin tip, cut into 1-inch cubes
1 cup cheese pasta sauce
1½ cups soft bread crumbs
2 tablespoons olive oil
½ teaspoon dried marjoram

1. In a medium bowl, toss the beef with the pasta sauce to coat.
2. In a shallow bowl, combine the bread crumbs, oil, and marjoram, and mix well. Drop the beef cubes, one at a time, into the bread crumb mixture to coat thoroughly.
3. Air fry the beef in two batches at 360ºF (182ºC) for 6 to 8 minutes, shaking the basket once during cooking time, until the beef is at least 145ºF (63ºC) and the outside is crisp and brown.
4. Serve hot.

Breaded Cod Fingers

Prep time: 5 minutes | Cook time: 12 minutes | Serves 4

2 eggs
2 tablespoons milk
2 cups flour
1 cup cornmeal
1 teaspoon seafood seasoning
Salt and black pepper, to taste
1 cup bread crumbs
1 pound (454 g) cod fillets, cut into 1-inch strips

1. Beat the eggs with the milk in a shallow bowl. In another shallow bowl, combine the flour, cornmeal, seafood seasoning, salt, and pepper. On a plate, place the bread crumbs.
2. Dredge the cod strips, one at a time, in the flour mixture, then in the egg mixture, finally in the bread crumb to coat evenly.
3. Arrange the cod strips in the air fryer basket and air fry at 400ºF (204ºC) for 12 minutes until crispy.
4. Transfer the cod strips to a paper towel-lined plate and serve warm.

Golden Mozzarella Sticks

Prep time: 5 minutes | Cook time: 6 to 7 minutes | Serves 4 to 8

1 egg
1 tablespoon water
8 eggroll wraps

8 Mozzarella string cheese "sticks"

1. Beat together egg and water in a small bowl.
2. Lay out eggroll wraps and moisten edges with egg wash.
3. Place one piece of string cheese on each wrap near one end.
4. Fold in sides of eggroll wrap over ends of cheese, and then roll up.
5. Brush outside of wrap with egg wash and press gently to seal well.
6. Place in air fryer basket in a single layer and air fry at 390ºF (199ºC) for 5 minutes. Air fry for an additional 1 or 2 minutes, if necessary, or until they are golden brown and crispy.
7. Serve immediately.

Cheesy Barbecue Chicken Pizza

Prep time: 5 minutes | Cook time: 8 minutes | Serves 1

1 piece naan bread
¼ cup Barbecue sauce
¼ cup shredded Monterrey Jack cheese
¼ cup shredded Mozzarella cheese

½ chicken herby sausage, sliced
2 tablespoons red onion, thinly sliced
Chopped cilantro or parsley, for garnish
Cooking spray

1. Spritz the bottom of naan bread with cooking spray, then transfer to the air fryer basket.
2. Brush with the Barbecue sauce. Top with the cheeses, sausage, and finish with the red onion.
3. Air fry at 400ºF (204ºC) for 8 minutes until the cheese is melted.
4. Garnish with the chopped cilantro or parsley before slicing to serve.

Air-Fried Cajun Dill Pickle Chips

Prep time: 5 minutes | Cook time: 10 minutes | Makes 16 slices

¼ cup all-purpose flour
½ cup panko bread crumbs
1 large egg, beaten
2 teaspoons Cajun

seasoning
2 large dill pickles, sliced into 8 rounds each
Cooking spray

1. Place the all-purpose flour, panko bread crumbs, and egg into 3 separate shallow bowls, then stir the Cajun seasoning into the flour.
2. Dredge each pickle chip in the flour mixture, then the egg, and finally the bread crumbs. Shake off any excess, then place each coated pickle chip on a plate.
3. Spritz the air fryer basket with cooking spray, then place 8 pickle chips in the basket and air fry at 390ºF (199ºC) for 5 minutes, or until crispy and golden brown. Repeat this process with the remaining pickle chips.
4. Remove the chips and allow to slightly cool on a wire rack before serving.

Crispy Sesame Kale Chips

Prep time: 15 minutes | Cook time: 8 minutes | Serves 5

8 cups deribbed kale leaves, torn into 2-inch pieces
1½ tablespoons olive oil
¾ teaspoon chili

powder
¼ teaspoon garlic powder
½ teaspoon paprika
2 teaspoons sesame seeds

1. In a large bowl, toss the kale with the olive oil, chili powder, garlic powder, paprika, and sesame seeds until well coated.
2. Put the kale in the air fryer basket and air fry at 350ºF (177ºC) for 8 minutes, flipping the kale twice during cooking, or until the kale is crispy.
3. Serve warm.

Golden Cuban Sandwiches

Prep time: 20 minutes | Cook time: 8 minutes | Makes 4 sandwiches

8 slices ciabatta bread, about ¼-inch thick
Cooking spray
1 tablespoon brown mustard
Toppings:
6 to 8 ounces (170 to 227 g) thinly sliced
leftover roast pork
4 ounces (113 g) thinly sliced deli turkey
⅓ cup bread and butter pickle slices
2 to 3 ounces (57 to 85 g) Pepper Jack cheese slices

1. On a clean work surface, spray one side of each slice of bread with cooking spray. Spread the other side of each slice of bread evenly with brown mustard.
2. Top 4 of the bread slices with the roast pork, turkey, pickle slices, cheese, and finish with remaining bread slices. Transfer to the air fryer basket.
3. Air fry at 390°F (199°C) for about 8 minutes until golden brown.
4. Cool for 5 minutes and serve warm.

Breaded Italian Rice Balls

Prep time: 20 minutes | Cook time: 10 minutes | Makes 8 rice balls

1½ cups cooked sticky rice
½ teaspoon Italian seasoning blend
¾ teaspoon salt, divided
8 black olives, pitted
1 ounce (28 g) Mozzarella cheese,
cut into tiny pieces (small enough to stuff into olives)
2 eggs
⅓ cup Italian bread crumbs
¾ cup panko bread crumbs
Cooking spray

1. Stuff each black olive with a piece of Mozzarella cheese. Set aside.
2. In a bowl, combine the cooked sticky rice, Italian seasoning blend, and ½ teaspoon of salt and stir to mix well. Form the rice mixture into a log with your hands and divide it into 8 equal portions. Mold each portion around a black olive and roll into a ball.
3. Transfer to the freezer to chill for 10 to 15 minutes until firm.

4. In a shallow dish, place the Italian bread crumbs. In a separate shallow dish, whisk the eggs. In a third shallow dish, combine the panko bread crumbs and remaining salt.
5. One by one, roll the rice balls in the Italian bread crumbs, then dip in the whisked eggs, finally coat them with the panko bread crumbs.
6. Arrange the rice balls in the air fryer basket and spritz both sides with cooking spray.
7. Air fry at 390°F (199°C) for 10 minutes until the rice balls are golden brown. Flip the balls halfway through the cooking time.
8. Serve warm.

Smoked Sausages Roll Dough

Prep time: 5 minutes | Cook time: 14 minutes | Serves 4 to 6

24 cocktail smoked sausages
6 slices deli-sliced Cheddar cheese, each cut into 8 rectangular
pieces
1 (8-ounce / 227-g) tube refrigerated crescent roll dough

1. Unroll the crescent roll dough into one large sheet. If your crescent roll dough has perforated seams, pinch or roll all the perforated seams together. Cut the large sheet of dough into 4 rectangles. Then cut each rectangle into 6 pieces by making one slice lengthwise in the middle and 2 slices horizontally. You should have 24 pieces of dough.
2. Make a deep slit lengthwise down the center of the cocktail sausage. Stuff two pieces of cheese into the slit in the sausage. Roll one piece of crescent dough around the stuffed cocktail sausage, leaving the ends of the sausage exposed. Pinch the seam together. Repeat with the remaining sausages.
3. Air fry in 2 batches at 350°F (177°C) for 7 minutes, placing the sausages seam-side down in the basket. Serve hot.

Cheesy Muffuletta Sliders with Olives

Prep time: 10 minutes | Cook time: 5 to 7 minutes | Makes 8 sliders

¼ pound (113 g) thinly sliced deli ham
¼ pound (113 g) thinly sliced pastrami
4 ounces (113 g) low-fat Mozzarella

cheese, grated
8 slider buns, split in half
Cooking spray
1 tablespoon sesame seeds

Olive Mix:
½ cup sliced green olives with pimentos
¼ cup sliced black olives
¼ cup chopped kalamata olives

1 teaspoon red wine vinegar
¼ teaspoon basil
⅛ teaspoon garlic powder

1. Combine all the ingredients for the olive mix in a small bowl and stir well.
2. Stir together the ham, pastrami, and cheese in a medium bowl and divide the mixture into 8 equal portions.
3. Assemble the sliders: Top each bottom bun with 1 portion of meat and cheese, 2 tablespoons of olive mix, finished by the remaining buns. Lightly spritz the tops with cooking spray. Scatter the sesame seeds on top.
4. Working in batches, arrange the sliders in the air fryer basket. Bake at 360ºF (182ºC) for 5 t0 7 minutes until the cheese melts.
5. Transfer to a large plate and repeat with the remaining sliders.
6. Serve immediately.

Classic Tortilla Chips

Prep time: 5 minutes | Cook time: 3 minutes | Serves 2

8 corn tortillas
1 tablespoon olive oil

Salt, to taste

1. Slice the corn tortillas into triangles. Coat with a light brushing of olive oil.
2. Put the tortilla pieces in the air fryer basket and air fry at 390ºF (199ºC) for 3 minutes. You may need to do this in batches.
3. Season with salt before serving.

Crispy Herbed Pita Chips

Prep time: 5 minutes | Cook time: 5 to 6 minutes | Serves 4

¼ teaspoon dried basil
¼ teaspoon marjoram
¼ teaspoon ground oregano
¼ teaspoon garlic

powder
¼ teaspoon ground thyme
¼ teaspoon salt
2 whole 6-inch pitas, whole grain or white
Cooking spray

1. Mix all the seasonings together.
2. Cut each pita half into 4 wedges. Break apart wedges at the fold.
3. Mist one side of pita wedges with oil. Sprinkle with half of seasoning mix.
4. Turn pita wedges over, mist the other side with oil, and sprinkle with remaining seasonings.
5. Place pita wedges in air fryer basket and bake at 330ºF (166ºC) for 2 minutes.
6. Shake the basket and bake for 2 minutes longer. Shake again, and if needed, bake for 1 or 2 more minutes, or until crisp. Watch carefully because at this point they will cook very quickly.
7. Serve hot.

Simple Roasted Mixed Nuts

Prep time: 5 minutes | Cook time: 20 minutes | Serves 6

2 cups mixed nuts (walnuts, pecans, and almonds)
2 tablespoons egg white

2 tablespoons sugar
1 teaspoon paprika
1 teaspoon ground cinnamon
Cooking spray

1. Spray the air fryer basket with cooking spray.
2. Stir together the mixed nuts, egg white, sugar, paprika, and cinnamon in a small bowl until the nuts are fully coated.
3. Put the nuts in the air fryer basket and roast at 300ºF (149ºC) for 20 minutes. Shake the basket halfway through the cooking time for even cooking.
4. Transfer the nuts to a bowl and serve warm.

Lemony Yogurt Endive

Prep time: 5 minutes | Cook time: 10 minutes | Serves 6

6 heads endive
½ cup plain and fat-free yogurt
3 tablespoons lemon juice
1 teaspoon garlic powder
½ teaspoon curry powder
Salt and ground black pepper, to taste

1. Wash the endives, and slice them in half lengthwise.
2. In a bowl, mix together the yogurt, lemon juice, garlic powder, curry powder, salt and pepper.
3. Brush the endive halves with the marinade, coating them completely. Allow to sit for at least 30 minutes or up to 24 hours.
4. Put the endives in the air fryer basket and air fry at 320ºF (160ºC) for 10 minutes.
5. Serve hot.

Golden Mushroom and Spinach Calzones

Prep time: 15 minutes | Cook time: 26 to 27 minutes | Serves 4

2 tablespoons olive oil
1 onion, chopped
2 garlic cloves, minced
¼ cup chopped mushrooms
1 pound (454 g) spinach, chopped
1 tablespoon Italian seasoning
½ teaspoon oregano
Salt and black pepper, to taste
1½ cups marinara sauce
1 cup ricotta cheese, crumbled
1 (13-ounce / 369-g) pizza crust
Cooking spray

Make the Filling:
1. Heat the olive oil in a pan over medium heat until shimmering.
2. Add the onion, garlic, and mushrooms and sauté for 4 minutes, or until softened.
3. Stir in the spinach and sauté for 2 to 3 minutes, or until the spinach is wilted. Sprinkle with the Italian seasoning, oregano, salt, and pepper and mix well.

4. Add the marinara sauce and cook for about 5 minutes, stirring occasionally, or until the sauce is thickened.
5. Remove the pan from the heat and stir in the ricotta cheese. Set aside.

Make the Calzones:
1. Spritz the air fryer basket with cooking spray.
2. Roll the pizza crust out with a rolling pin on a lightly floured work surface, then cut it into 4 rectangles.
3. Spoon ¼ of the filling into each rectangle and fold in half. Crimp the edges with a fork to seal. Mist them with cooking spray.
4. Place the calzones in the air fryer basket and air fry at 375ºF (191ºC) for 15 minutes, flipping once, or until the calzones are golden brown and crisp.
5. Transfer the calzones to a paper towel-lined plate and serve.

Air-Fried Old Bay Chicken Wings

Prep time: 10 minutes | Cook time: 12 to 15 minutes | Serves 4

2 tablespoons Old Bay seasoning
2 teaspoons baking powder
2 teaspoons salt
2 pounds (907 g) chicken wings, patted dry
Cooking spray

1. Lightly spray the air fryer basket with cooking spray.
2. Combine the Old Bay seasoning, baking powder, and salt in a large zip-top plastic bag. Add the chicken wings, seal, and shake until the wings are thoroughly coated in the seasoning mixture.
3. Lay the chicken wings in the air fryer basket in a single layer and lightly mist with cooking spray. You may need to work in batches to avoid overcrowding.
4. Air fry at 400ºF (204ºC) for 12 to 15 minutes, flipping the wings halfway through, or until the wings are lightly browned and the internal temperature reaches at least 165ºC (74ºC) on a meat thermometer.
5. Remove from the basket to a plate and repeat with the remaining chicken wings.
6. Serve hot.

Fast Poutine with Waffle Fries

Prep time: 10 minutes | Cook time: 15 to 17 minutes | Serves 4

2 cups frozen waffle cut fries	2 green onions, sliced
2 teaspoons olive oil	1 cup shredded Swiss cheese
1 red bell pepper, chopped	½ cup bottled chicken gravy

1. Toss the waffle fries with the olive oil and place in the air fryer basket. Air fry for 10 to 12 minutes, or until the fries are crisp and light golden brown, shaking the basket halfway through the cooking time.
2. Transfer the fries to a baking pan and top with the pepper, green onions, and cheese. Air fry at 380°F (193°C) for 3 minutes, or until the vegetables are crisp and tender.
3. Remove the pan from the air fryer and drizzle the gravy over the fries. Air fry for 2 minutes, or until the gravy is hot.
4. Serve immediately.

Air-Fried Zucchini and Potato Tots

Prep time: 5 minutes | Cook time: 20 minutes | Serves 4

1 large zucchini, grated	Cheddar cheese
1 medium baked potato, skin removed and mashed	1 large egg, beaten
¼ cup shredded	½ teaspoon kosher salt
	Cooking spray

1. Wrap the grated zucchini in a paper towel and squeeze out any excess liquid, then combine the zucchini, baked potato, shredded Cheddar cheese, egg, and kosher salt in a large bowl.
2. Spray a baking pan with cooking spray, then place individual tablespoons of the zucchini mixture in the pan and air fry at 390°F (199°C) for 10 minutes. Repeat this process with the remaining mixture.
3. Remove the tots and allow to cool on a wire rack for 5 minutes before serving.

Root Vegetable Chips with Herb Salt

Prep time: 10 minutes | Cook time: 8 minutes | Serves 2

1 parsnip, washed	½ small sweet potato, washed
1 small beet, washed	
1 small turnip, washed	1 teaspoon olive oil
	Cooking spray

Herb Salt:
¼ teaspoon kosher salt
2 teaspoons finely chopped fresh parsley

1. Peel and thinly slice the parsnip, beet, turnip, and sweet potato, then place the vegetables in a large bowl, add the olive oil, and toss.
2. Spray the air fryer basket with cooking spray, then place the vegetables in the basket and air fry at 360°F (182°C) for 8 minutes, gently shaking the basket halfway through.
3. While the chips cook, make the herb salt in a small bowl by combining the kosher salt and parsley.
4. Remove the chips and place on a serving plate, then sprinkle the herb salt on top and allow to cool for 2 to 3 minutes before serving.

Rosemary Baked Whole Cashews

Prep time: 5 minutes | Cook time: 3 minutes | Makes 2 cups

2 sprigs of fresh rosemary (1 chopped and 1 whole)	½ teaspoon honey
	2 cups roasted and unsalted whole cashews
1 teaspoon olive oil	
1 teaspoon kosher salt	Cooking spray

1. In a medium bowl, whisk together the chopped rosemary, olive oil, kosher salt, and honey. Set aside.
2. Spray the air fryer basket with cooking spray, then place the cashews and the whole rosemary sprig in the basket and bake at 300°F (149°C) for 3 minutes.
3. Remove the cashews and rosemary from the air fryer, then discard the rosemary and add the cashews to the olive oil mixture, tossing to coat.
4. Allow to cool for 15 minutes before serving.

Smoked Sausage and Mushroom Empanadas

Prep time: 5 minutes | Cook time: 12 minutes | Serves 4

½ pound (227 g) Kielbasa smoked sausage, chopped
4 chopped canned mushrooms
2 tablespoons chopped onion
½ teaspoon ground cumin
¼ teaspoon paprika

Salt and black pepper, to taste
½ package puff pastry dough, at room temperature
1 egg, beaten
Cooking spray

1. Spritz the air fryer basket with cooking spray.
2. Combine the sausage, mushrooms, onion, cumin, paprika, salt, and pepper in a bowl and stir to mix well.
3. Make the empanadas: Place the puff pastry dough on a lightly floured surface. Cut circles into the dough with a glass. Place 1 tablespoon of the sausage mixture into the center of each pastry circle. Fold each in half and pinch the edges to seal. Using a fork, crimp the edges. Brush them with the beaten egg and mist with cooking spray.
4. Place the empanadas in the air fryer basket and air fry at 360ºF (182ºC) for 12 minutes until golden brown. Flip the empanadas halfway through the cooking time.
5. Allow them to cool for 5 minutes and serve hot.

Turkey Bacon-Wrapped Dates and Almonds

Prep time: 10 minutes | Cook time: 5 to 7 minutes | Makes 16 appetizers

16 whole dates, pitted
16 whole almonds

6 to 8 strips turkey bacon, cut in half

Special Equipment:
16 toothpicks, soaked in water for at least 30 minutes

1. On a flat work surface, stuff each pitted date with a whole almond.
2. Wrap half slice of bacon around each date and secure it with a toothpick.
3. Place the bacon-wrapped dates in the air fryer basket and air fry at 390ºF (199ºC) for 5 to 7 minutes, or until the bacon is cooked to your desired crispiness.
4. Transfer the dates to a paper towel-lined plate to drain. Serve hot.

Paprika Kale Chips

Prep time: 5 minutes | Cook time: 8 to 12 minutes | Serves 4

5 cups kale, large stems removed and chopped
2 teaspoons canola oil

¼ teaspoon smoked paprika
¼ teaspoon kosher salt
Cooking spray

1. In a large bowl, toss the kale, canola oil, smoked paprika, and kosher salt.
2. Spray the air fryer basket with cooking spray, then place half the kale in the basket and air fry for 2 to 3 minutes.
3. Shake the basket and air fry at 390ºF (199ºC) 2 to 3 more minutes, or until crispy. Repeat this process with the remaining kale.
4. Remove the kale and allow to cool on a wire rack for 3 to 5 minutes before serving.

Hot Chicken Bites

Prep time: 10 minutes | Cook time: 10 to 12 minutes | Makes 30 bites

8 ounces boneless and skinless chicken thighs, cut into 30 pieces
¼ teaspoon kosher salt

2 tablespoons hot sauce
Cooking spray

1. Spray the air fryer basket with cooking spray and season the chicken bites with the kosher salt, then place in the basket and air fry at 390ºF (199ºC) for 10 to 12 minutes or until crispy.
2. While the chicken bites cook, pour the hot sauce into a large bowl.
3. Remove the bites and add to the sauce bowl, tossing to coat. Serve warm.

Fast Spinach and Crab Meat Cups

Prep time: 10 minutes | Cook time: 10 minutes | Makes 30 cups

1 (6-ounce / 170-g) can crab meat, drained to yield ⅓ cup meat
¼ cup frozen spinach, thawed, drained, and chopped
1 clove garlic, minced
½ cup grated Parmesan cheese

3 tablespoons plain yogurt
¼ teaspoon lemon juice
½ teaspoon Worcestershire sauce
30 mini frozen phyllo shells, thawed
Cooking spray

1. Remove any bits of shell that might remain in the crab meat.
2. Mix the crab meat, spinach, garlic, and cheese together.
3. Stir in the yogurt, lemon juice, and Worcestershire sauce and mix well.
4. Spoon a teaspoon of filling into each phyllo shell.
5. Spray the air fryer basket with cooking spray and arrange half the shells in the basket. Air fry at 390ºF (199ºC) for 5 minutes. Repeat with the remaining shells.
6. Serve immediately.

Chapter 9 Poultry

Fried Glazed Duck with Cherry Sauce

Prep time: 20 minutes | Cook time: 32 minutes | Serves 12

1 whole duck (about 5 pounds / 2.3 kg in total), split in half, back and rib bones removed, fat trimmed
1 teaspoon olive oil
Salt and freshly ground black pepper, to taste

Cherry Sauce:
1 tablespoon butter
1 shallot, minced
½ cup sherry
1 cup chicken stock
1 teaspoon white wine vinegar
¾ cup cherry preserves
1 teaspoon fresh thyme leaves
Salt and freshly ground black pepper, to taste

1. On a clean work surface, rub the duck with olive oil, then sprinkle with salt and ground black pepper to season.
2. Place the duck in the air fryer, breast side up, and air fry at 400ºF (204ºC) for 25 minutes or until well browned. Flip the duck during the last 10 minutes.
3. Meanwhile, make the cherry sauce: Heat the butter in a nonstick skillet over medium-high heat or until melted.
4. Add the shallot and sauté for 5 minutes or until lightly browned.
5. Add the sherry and simmer for 6 minutes or until it reduces in half.
6. Add the chicken stick, white wine vinegar, and cherry preserves. Stir to combine well. Simmer for 6 more minutes or until thickened.
7. Fold in the thyme leaves and sprinkle with salt and ground black pepper. Stir to mix well.
8. When the air frying of the duck is complete, glaze the duck with a quarter of the cherry sauce, then air fry for another 4 minutes.
9. Flip the duck and glaze with another quarter of the cherry sauce. Air fry for an additional 3 minutes.
10. Transfer the duck on a large plate and serve with remaining cherry sauce.

Fast Turkey and Mushroom Meatballs

Prep time: 10 minutes | Cook time: 15 minutes | Serves 6

Sauce:
2 tablespoons tamari
2 tablespoons tomato sauce
1 tablespoon lime juice
¼ teaspoon peeled and grated fresh ginger
1 clove garlic, smashed to a paste
½ cup chicken broth
⅓ cup sugar
2 tablespoons toasted sesame oil
Cooking spray

Meatballs:
2 pounds (907 g) ground turkey
¾ cup finely chopped button mushrooms
2 large eggs, beaten
1½ teaspoons tamari
¼ cup finely chopped green onions, plus more for garnish
2 teaspoons peeled and grated fresh ginger
1 clove garlic, smashed
2 teaspoons toasted sesame oil
2 tablespoons sugar

For Serving:
Lettuce leaves, for serving
Sliced red chiles, for garnish (optional)
Toasted sesame seeds, for garnish (optional)

1. Spritz a baking pan with cooking spray.
2. Combine the ingredients for the sauce in a small bowl. Stir to mix well. Set aside.
3. Combine the ingredients for the meatballs in a large bowl. Stir to mix well, then shape the mixture in twelve 1½-inch meatballs.
4. Arrange the meatballs in a single layer on the baking pan, then baste with the sauce. You may need to work in batches to avoid overcrowding.
5. Arrange the pan in the air fryer. Air fry at 350ºF (177ºC) for 15 minutes or until the meatballs are golden brown. Flip the balls halfway through the cooking time.
6. Unfold the lettuce leaves on a large serving plate, then transfer the cooked meatballs on the leaves. Spread the red chiles and sesame seeds over the balls, then serve.

Turkey and Carrot Meatloaves

Prep time: 6 minutes | Cook time: 20 to 24 minutes | Serves 4

⅓ cup minced onion
¼ cup grated carrot
2 garlic cloves, minced
2 tablespoons ground almonds
2 teaspoons olive oil
1 teaspoon dried marjoram
1 egg white
¾ pound (340 g) ground turkey breast

1. In a medium bowl, stir together the onion, carrot, garlic, almonds, olive oil, marjoram, and egg white.
2. Add the ground turkey. With your hands, gently but thoroughly mix until combined.
3. Double 16 foil muffin cup liners to make 8 cups. Divide the turkey mixture evenly among the liners.
4. Bake at 400°F (204°C) for 20 to 24 minutes, or until the meatloaves reach an internal temperature of 165°F (74°C) on a meat thermometer. Serve immediately.

Broiled Goulash

Prep time: 5 minutes | Cook time: 17 minutes | Serves 2

2 red bell peppers, chopped
1 pound (454 g) ground chicken
2 medium tomatoes, diced
½ cup chicken broth
Salt and ground black pepper, to taste
Cooking spray

1. Spritz a baking pan with cooking spray.
2. Set the bell pepper in the baking pan and put in the air fry to broil at 365°F (185°C) for 5 minutes or until the bell pepper is tender. Shake the basket halfway through.
3. Add the ground chicken and diced tomatoes in the baking pan and stir to mix well. Broil for 6 more minutes or until the chicken is lightly browned.
4. Pour the chicken broth over and sprinkle with salt and ground black pepper. Stir to mix well. Broil for an additional 6 minutes.
5. Serve immediately.

Air-Fried Mayo Chicken Tenders

Prep time: 5 minutes | Cook time: 7 minutes | Serves 4

Seasoning:
1 teaspoon kosher salt
½ teaspoon garlic powder
½ teaspoon onion powder
½ teaspoon chili powder
¼ teaspoon sweet paprika
¼ teaspoon freshly ground black pepper

Chicken:
8 chicken breast tenders (1 pound / 454 g total)
2 tablespoons mayonnaise

1. For the seasoning: In a small bowl, combine the salt, garlic powder, onion powder, chili powder, paprika, and pepper.
2. For the chicken: Place the chicken in a medium bowl and add the mayonnaise. Mix well to coat all over, then sprinkle with the seasoning mix.
3. Working in batches, arrange a single layer of the chicken in the air fryer basket. Air fry at 375°F (191°C) for 6 to 7 minutes, flipping halfway, until cooked through in the center. Serve immediately.

Baked Garlicky Whole Chicken

Prep time: 10 minutes | Cook time: 1 hour | Serves 2 to 4

½ cup melted butter
3 tablespoons garlic, minced
Salt, to taste
1 teaspoon ground black pepper
1 (1-pound / 454-g) whole chicken

1. Combine the butter with garlic, salt, and ground black pepper in a small bowl.
2. Brush the butter mixture over the whole chicken, then place the chicken in the air fryer, skin side down.
3. Bake the chicken at 350°F (177°C) for an hour or until an instant-read thermometer inserted in the thickest part of the chicken registers at least 165°F (74°C). Flip the chicken halfway through.
4. Remove the chicken from the air fryer and allow to cool for 15 minutes before serving.

Spicy Apricot-Glazed Turkey

Prep time: 20 minutes | Cook time: 30 minutes | Serves 4

¼ cup sugar-free apricot preserves
½ tablespoon spicy brown mustard
1½ pounds (680 g) turkey breast
tenderloin
Salt and freshly ground black pepper, to taste
Olive oil spray

1. Spray the air fryer basket lightly with olive oil spray.
2. In a small bowl, combine the apricot preserves and mustard to make a paste.
3. Season the turkey with salt and pepper. Spread the apricot paste all over the turkey.
4. Place the turkey in the air fryer basket and lightly spray with olive oil spray.
5. Air fry at 370ºF (188ºC) for 15 minutes. Flip the turkey over and lightly spray with olive oil spray. Air fry until the internal temperature reaches at least 170ºF (77ºC), an additional 10 to 15 minutes.
6. Let the turkey rest for 10 minutes before slicing and serving.

Chinese Spiced Turkey Thighs

Prep time: 10 minutes | Cook time: 25 minutes | Serves 6

2 pounds (907 g) turkey thighs
1 teaspoon Chinese five-spice powder
¼ teaspoon Sichuan pepper
1 teaspoon pink Himalayan salt
1 tablespoon Chinese rice vinegar
1 tablespoon mustard
1 tablespoon chili sauce
2 tablespoons soy sauce
Cooking spray

1. Spritz the air fryer basket with cooking spray.
2. Rub the turkey thighs with five-spice powder, Sichuan pepper, and salt on a clean work surface.
3. Put the turkey thighs in the air fryer and spritz with cooking spray. You may need to work in batches to avoid overcrowding.
4. Air fry at 360ºF (182ºC) for 22 minutes or until well browned. Flip the thighs at least three times during the cooking.

5. Meanwhile, heat the remaining ingredients in a saucepan over medium-high heat. Cook for 3 minutes or until the sauce is thickened and reduces to two thirds.
6. Transfer the thighs onto a plate and baste with sauce before serving.

Crispy Israeli Chicken Schnitzel

Prep time: 5 minutes | Cook time: 10 minutes | Serves 4

2 large boneless, skinless chicken breasts, each weighing about 1 pound (454 g)
1 cup all-purpose flour
2 teaspoons garlic powder
2 teaspoons kosher salt
1 teaspoon black pepper
1 teaspoon paprika
2 eggs beaten with 2 tablespoons water
2 cups panko bread crumbs
Vegetable oil spray
Lemon juice, for serving

1. Place 1 chicken breast between 2 pieces of plastic wrap. Use a mallet or a rolling pin to pound the chicken until it is ¼ inch thick. Set aside. Repeat with the second breast. Whisk together the flour, garlic powder, salt, pepper, and paprika on a large plate. Place the panko in a separate shallow bowl or pie plate.
2. Dredge 1 chicken breast in the flour, shaking off any excess, then dip it in the egg mixture. Dredge the chicken breast in the panko, making sure to coat it completely. Shake off any excess panko. Place the battered chicken breast on a plate. Repeat with the second chicken breast.
3. Spray the air fryer basket with oil spray. Place 1 of the battered chicken breasts in the basket and spray the top with oil spray. Air fry at 375ºF (191ºC) until the top is browned, about 5 minutes. Flip the chicken and spray the second side with oil spray. Air fry until the second side is browned and crispy and the internal temperature reaches 165ºF (74ºC). Remove the first chicken breast from the air fryer and repeat with the second chicken breast.
4. Serve hot with lemon juice.

Stuffed Bell Peppers with Turkey

Prep time: 20 minutes | Cook time: 15 minutes | Serves 4

½ pound (227 g) lean ground turkey
4 medium bell peppers
1 (15-ounce / 425-g) can black beans, drained and rinsed
1 cup shredded reduced-fat Cheddar cheese
1 cup cooked long-grain brown rice
1 cup mild salsa
1¼ teaspoons chili powder
1 teaspoon salt
½ teaspoon ground cumin
½ teaspoon freshly ground black pepper
Olive oil spray
Chopped fresh cilantro, for garnish

1. In a large skillet over medium-high heat, cook the turkey, breaking it up with a spoon, until browned, about 5 minutes. Drain off any excess fat.
2. Cut about ½ inch off the tops of the peppers and then cut in half lengthwise. Remove and discard the seeds and set the peppers aside.
3. In a large bowl, combine the browned turkey, black beans, Cheddar cheese, rice, salsa, chili powder, salt, cumin, and black pepper. Spoon the mixture into the bell peppers.
4. Lightly spray the air fryer basket with olive oil spray.
5. Place the stuffed peppers in the air fryer basket. Air fry at 360ºF (182ºC) until heated through, 10 to 15 minutes. Garnish with cilantro and serve.

Blackened Naked Chicken Breasts

Prep time: 10 minutes | Cook time: 20 minutes | Serves 4

1 large egg, beaten
¾ cup Blackened seasoning
2 whole boneless, skinless chicken
breasts (about 1 pound / 454 g each), halved
Cooking spray

1. Line the air fryer basket with parchment paper.
2. Place the beaten egg in one shallow bowl and the Blackened seasoning in another shallow bowl.
3. One at a time, dip the chicken pieces in the beaten egg and the Blackened seasoning, coating thoroughly.
4. Place the chicken pieces on the parchment and spritz with cooking spray.
5. Air fry at 360ºF (182ºC) for 10 minutes. Flip the chicken, spritz it with cooking spray, and air fry for 10 minutes more until the internal temperature reaches 165ºF (74ºC) and the chicken is no longer pink inside. Let sit for 5 minutes before serving.

Chicken Thighs with Colantro

Prep time: 10 minutes | Cook time: 10 minutes | Serves 4

¼ cup julienned peeled fresh ginger
2 tablespoons vegetable oil
1 tablespoon honey
1 tablespoon soy sauce
1 tablespoon ketchup
1 teaspoon garam masala
1 teaspoon ground turmeric
¼ teaspoon kosher salt
½ teaspoon cayenne pepper
Vegetable oil spray
1 pound (454 g) boneless, skinless chicken thighs, cut crosswise into thirds
¼ cup chopped fresh cilantro, for garnish

1. In a small bowl, combine the ginger, oil, honey, soy sauce, ketchup, garam masala, turmeric, salt, and cayenne. Whisk until well combined. Place the chicken in a resealable plastic bag and pour the marinade over. Seal the bag and massage to cover all of the chicken with the marinade. Marinate at room temperature for 30 minutes or in the refrigerator for up to 24 hours.
2. Spray the air fryer basket with vegetable oil spray and add the chicken and as much of the marinade and julienned ginger as possible. Bake at 350ºF (177ºC) for 10 minutes. Use a meat thermometer to ensure the chicken has reached an internal temperature of 165ºF (74ºC).
3. To serve, garnish with cilantro.

Air-Fried Pomegranate-Glazed Chicken

Prep time: 25 minutes | Cook time: 20 minutes | Serves 4

3 tablespoons plus 2 teaspoons pomegranate molasses
½ teaspoon ground cinnamon
1 teaspoon minced fresh thyme
Salt and ground black pepper, to taste
2 (12-ounce / 340-g) bone-in split chicken breasts, trimmed
¼ cup chicken broth
¼ cup water
½ cup couscous
1 tablespoon minced fresh parsley
2 ounces (57 g) cherry tomatoes, quartered
1 scallion, white part minced, green part sliced thin on bias
1 tablespoon extra-virgin olive oil
1 ounce (28 g) feta cheese, crumbled
Cooking spray

1. Spritz the air fryer basket with cooking spray.
2. Combine 3 tablespoons of pomegranate molasses, cinnamon, thyme, and ⅛ teaspoon of salt in a small bowl. Stir to mix well. Set aside.
3. Place the chicken breasts in the air fryer, skin side down, and spritz with cooking spray. Sprinkle with salt and ground black pepper.
4. Air fry the chicken at 350ºF (177ºC) for 10 minutes, then brush the chicken with half of pomegranate molasses mixture and flip. Air fry for 5 more minutes.
5. Brush the chicken with remaining pomegranate molasses mixture and flip. Air fry for another 5 minutes or until the internal temperature of the chicken breasts reaches at least 165ºF (74ºC).
6. Meanwhile, pour the broth and water in a pot and bring to a boil over medium-high heat. Add the couscous and sprinkle with salt. Cover and simmer for 7 minutes or until the liquid is almost absorbed.
7. Combine the remaining ingredients, except for the cheese, with cooked couscous in a large bowl. Toss to mix well. Scatter with the feta cheese.
8. When the air frying is complete, remove the chicken from the air fryer and allow to cool for 10 minutes. Serve with vegetable and couscous salad.

Potato Flake-Crusted Chicken

Prep time: 15 minutes | Cook time: 22 to 25 minutes | Serves 4

¼ cup buttermilk
1 large egg, beaten
1 cup instant potato flakes
¼ cup grated Parmesan cheese
1 teaspoon salt
½ teaspoon freshly
ground black pepper
2 whole boneless, skinless chicken breasts (about 1 pound / 454 g each), halved
Cooking spray

1. Line the air fryer basket with parchment paper.
2. In a shallow bowl, whisk the buttermilk and egg until blended. In another shallow bowl, stir together the potato flakes, cheese, salt, and pepper.
3. One at a time, dip the chicken pieces in the buttermilk mixture and the potato flake mixture, coating thoroughly.
4. Place the coated chicken on the parchment and spritz with cooking spray.
5. Bake at 325ºF (163ºC) for 15 minutes. Flip the chicken, spritz it with cooking spray, and bake for 7 to 10 minutes more until the outside is crispy and the inside is no longer pink. Serve immediately.

Roasted Cajun Turkey Thigh

Prep time: 10 minutes | Cook time: 30 minutes | Serves 4

2 pounds (907 g) turkey thighs, skinless and boneless
1 red onion, sliced
2 bell peppers, sliced
1 habanero pepper, minced
1 carrot, sliced
1 tablespoon Cajun seasoning mix
1 tablespoon fish sauce
2 cups chicken broth
Nonstick cooking spray

1. Spritz the bottom and sides of a baking dish with nonstick cooking spray.
2. Arrange the turkey thighs in the baking dish. Add the onion, peppers, and carrot. Sprinkle with Cajun seasoning. Add the fish sauce and chicken broth.
3. Roast in the air fryer at 360ºF (182ºC) for 30 minutes until cooked through. Serve warm.

Air-Fried Duck Leg Quarters

Prep time: 5 minutes | Cook time: 45 minutes | Serves 4

4 (½-pound / 227-g) skin-on duck leg quarters
2 medium garlic
cloves, minced
½ teaspoon salt
½ teaspoon ground black pepper

1. Spritz the air fryer basket with cooking spray.
2. On a clean work surface, rub the duck leg quarters with garlic, salt, and black pepper.
3. Arrange the leg quarters in the air fryer and spritz with cooking spray.
4. Air fry at 300ºF (149ºC) for 30 minutes, then flip the leg quarters and increase the temperature to 375ºF (191ºC). Air fry for 15 more minutes or until well browned and crispy.
5. Remove the duck leg quarters from the air fryer and allow to cool for 10 minutes before serving.

Marmalade-Glazed Duck Breasts

Prep time: 5 minutes | Cook time: 13 minutes | Serves 4

4 (6-ounce / 170-g) skin-on duck breasts
1 teaspoon salt
¼ cup orange marmalade
1 tablespoon white balsamic vinegar
¾ teaspoon ground black pepper

1. Cut 10 slits into the skin of the duck breasts, then sprinkle with salt on both sides.
2. Place the breasts in the air fryer, skin side up, and air fry at 400ºF (204ºC) for 10 minutes.
3. Meanwhile, combine the remaining ingredients in a small bowl. Stir to mix well.
4. When the frying is complete, brush the duck skin with the marmalade mixture. Flip the breast and air fry for 3 more minutes or until the skin is crispy and the breast is well browned.
5. Serve immediately.

Fajita Chicken Strips and Bell Pepper

Prep time: 10 minutes | Cook time: 15 minutes | Serves 4

1 pound (454 g) boneless, skinless chicken tenderloins, cut into strips
3 bell peppers, any color, cut into chunks
1 onion, cut into chunks
1 tablespoon olive oil
1 tablespoon fajita seasoning mix
Cooking spray

1. In a large bowl, mix together the chicken, bell peppers, onion, olive oil, and fajita seasoning mix until completely coated.
2. Spray the air fryer basket lightly with cooking spray.
3. Place the chicken and vegetables in the air fryer basket and lightly spray with cooking spray.
4. Air fry at 370ºF (188ºC) for 7 minutes. Shake the basket and air fry for an additional 5 to 8 minutes, until the chicken is cooked through and the veggies are starting to char.
5. Serve warm.

Air-Fried Buffalo Chicken Tortillas

Prep time: 15 minutes | Cook time: 5 to 10 minutes | Serves 6

8 ounces (227 g) fat-free cream cheese, softened
⅛ cup Buffalo sauce
2 cups shredded
cooked chicken
12 (7-inch) low-carb flour tortillas
Olive oil spray

1. Spray the air fryer basket lightly with olive oil spray.
2. In a large bowl, mix together the cream cheese and Buffalo sauce until well combined. Add the chicken and stir until combined.
3. Place the tortillas on a clean workspace. Spoon 2 to 3 tablespoons of the chicken mixture in a thin line down the center of each tortilla. Roll up the tortillas.
4. Place the tortillas in the air fryer basket, seam-side down. Spray each tortilla lightly with olive oil spray. You may need to cook the tortillas in batches.
5. Air fry at 360ºF (182ºC) until golden brown, 5 to 10 minutes. Serve hot.

Strawberry-Glazed Turkey Breast

Prep time: 15 minutes | Cook time: 37 minutes | Serves 2

2 pounds (907 g) turkey breast
1 tablespoon olive oil
Salt and ground black
pepper, to taste
1 cup fresh strawberries

1. Rub the turkey bread with olive oil on a clean work surface, then sprinkle with salt and ground black pepper.
2. Transfer the turkey in the air fryer and air fry at 375ºF (191ºC) for 30 minutes or until the internal temperature of the turkey reaches at least 165ºF (74ºC). flip the turkey breast halfway through.
3. Meanwhile, put the strawberries in a food processor and pulse until smooth.
4. When the frying of the turkey is complete, spread the puréed strawberries over the turkey and fry for 7 more minutes.
5. Serve immediately.

Air-Fried Chicken Drumsticks

Prep time: 5 minutes | Cook time: 22 minutes | Serves 2

2 teaspoons paprika
1 teaspoon packed brown sugar
1 teaspoon garlic powder
½ teaspoon dry mustard
½ teaspoon salt
Pinch pepper
4 (5-ounce / 142-g) chicken drumsticks, trimmed
1 teaspoon vegetable oil
1 scallion, green part only, sliced thin on bias

1. Combine paprika, sugar, garlic powder, mustard, salt, and pepper in a bowl. Pat drumsticks dry with paper towels. Using metal skewer, poke 10 to 15 holes in skin of each drumstick. Rub with oil and sprinkle evenly with spice mixture.
2. Arrange drumsticks in air fryer basket, spaced evenly apart, alternating ends. Air fry at 400ºF (204ºC) until chicken is crisp and registers 195ºF (91ºC), 22 to 25 minutes, flipping chicken halfway through cooking.

3. Transfer chicken to serving platter, tent loosely with aluminum foil, and let rest for 5 minutes. Sprinkle with scallion and serve.

Tangy Honey-Glazed Duck

Prep time: 5 minutes | Cook time: 15 minutes | Serves 2 to 3

1 pound (454 g) duck breasts (2 to 3 breasts)
Kosher salt and pepper, to taste
Juice and zest of 1 orange
¼ cup honey
2 sprigs thyme, plus more for garnish
2 firm tart apples, such as Fuji

1. Pat the duck breasts dry and, using a sharp knife, make 3 to 4 shallow, diagonal slashes in the skin. Turn the breasts and score the skin on the diagonal in the opposite direction to create a cross-hatch pattern. Season well with salt and pepper.
2. Place the duck breasts skin-side up in the air fryer basket. Roast at 400ºF (204ºC) for 8 minutes, then flip and roast for 4 more minutes on the second side.
3. While the duck is cooking, prepare the sauce. Combine the orange juice and zest, honey, and thyme in a small saucepan. Bring to a boil, stirring to dissolve the honey, then reduce the heat and simmer until thickened. Core the apples and cut into quarters. Cut each quarter into 3 or 4 slices depending on the size.
4. After the duck has cooked on both sides, turn it and brush the skin with the orange-honey glaze. Roast for 1 more minute. Remove the duck breasts to a cutting board and allow to rest.
5. Toss the apple slices with the remaining orange-honey sauce in a medium bowl. Arrange the apples in a single layer in the air fryer basket. Air fry for 10 minutes while the duck breast rests. Slice the duck breasts on the bias and divide them and the apples among 2 or 3 plates.
6. Serve warm, garnished with additional thyme.

Celery Chicken Tenderloins

Prep time: 10 minutes | Cook time: 15 minutes | Serves 4

½ cup soy sauce
2 tablespoons hoisin sauce
4 teaspoons minced garlic
1 teaspoon freshly ground black pepper
8 boneless, skinless chicken tenderloins
1 cup chopped celery
1 medium red bell pepper, diced
Olive oil spray

1. Spray the air fryer basket lightly with olive oil spray.
2. In a large bowl, mix together the soy sauce, hoisin sauce, garlic, and black pepper to make a marinade. Add the chicken, celery, and bell pepper and toss to coat.
3. Shake the excess marinade off the chicken, place it and the vegetables in the air fryer basket, and lightly spray with olive oil spray. You may need to cook them in batches. Reserve the remaining marinade.
4. Air fry at 375ºF (191ºC) for 8 minutes. Turn the chicken over and brush with some of the remaining marinade. Air fry for an additional 5 to 7 minutes, or until the chicken reaches an internal temperature of at least 165ºF (74ºC). Serve.

Crispy Dill Chicken Strips

Prep time: 15 minutes | Cook time: 10 minutes | Serves 4

2 whole boneless, skinless chicken breasts, halved lengthwise
1 cup Italian dressing
3 cups finely crushed potato chips
1 tablespoon dried dill weed
1 tablespoon garlic powder
1 large egg, beaten
Cooking spray

1. In a large resealable bag, combine the chicken and Italian dressing. Seal the bag and refrigerate to marinate at least 1 hour.
2. In a shallow dish, stir together the potato chips, dill, and garlic powder. Place the beaten egg in a second shallow dish.

3. Remove the chicken from the marinade. Roll the chicken pieces in the egg and the potato chip mixture, coating thoroughly.
4. Line the air fryer basket with parchment paper.
5. Place the coated chicken on the parchment and spritz with cooking spray.
6. Bake at 325ºF (163ºC) for 5 minutes. Flip the chicken, spritz it with cooking spray, and bake for 5 minutes more until the outsides are crispy and the insides are no longer pink. Serve immediately.

Maple Turkey Breast

Prep time: 2 hours 20 minutes | Cook time: 30 minutes | Serves 6

½ teaspoon dried rosemary
2 minced garlic cloves
2 teaspoons salt
1 teaspoon ground black pepper
¼ cup olive oil
2½ pounds (1.1 kg)
turkey breast
¼ cup pure maple syrup
1 tablespoon stone-ground brown mustard
1 tablespoon melted vegan butter

1. Combine the rosemary, garlic, salt, ground black pepper, and olive oil in a large bowl. Stir to mix well.
2. Dunk the turkey breast in the mixture and wrap the bowl in plastic. Refrigerate for 2 hours to marinate.
3. Remove the bowl from the refrigerator and let sit for half an hour before cooking.
4. Spritz the air fryer basket with cooking spray.
5. Remove the turkey from the marinade and place in the air fry and air fry at 400ºF (204ºC) for 20 minutes or until well browned. Flip the breast halfway through.
6. Meanwhile, combine the remaining ingredients in a small bowl. Stir to mix well.
7. Pour half of the butter mixture over the turkey breast in the air fryer and air fry for 10 more minutes. Flip the breast and pour the remaining half of butter mixture over halfway through.
8. Transfer the turkey on a plate and slice to serve.

Lemony Chicken Skewer

Prep time: 12 minutes | Cook time: 12 to 18 minutes | Serves 4

½ cup crunchy peanut butter
⅓ cup chicken broth
3 tablespoons low-sodium soy sauce
2 tablespoons lemon juice
2 cloves garlic, minced
2 tablespoons olive oil
1 teaspoon curry powder
1 pound (454 g) chicken tenders

1. In a medium bowl, combine the peanut butter, chicken broth, soy sauce, lemon juice, garlic, olive oil, and curry powder, and mix well with a wire whisk until smooth. Remove 2 tablespoons of this mixture to a small bowl. Put remaining sauce into a serving bowl and set aside.
2. Add the chicken tenders to the bowl with the 2 tablespoons sauce and stir to coat. Let stand for a few minutes to marinate, then run a bamboo skewer through each chicken tender lengthwise.
3. Put the chicken in the air fryer basket and air fry in batches at 390ºF (199ºC) for 6 to 9 minutes or until the chicken reaches 165ºF (74ºC) on a meat thermometer. Serve the chicken with the reserved sauce.

Golden Chicken Strips

Prep time: 15 minutes | Cook time: 20 minutes | Serves 4

1 tablespoon olive oil
1 pound (454 g) boneless, skinless chicken tenderloins
1 teaspoon salt
½ teaspoon freshly ground black pepper
½ teaspoon paprika
½ teaspoon garlic powder
½ cup whole-wheat seasoned bread crumbs
1 teaspoon dried parsley
Cooking spray

1. Spray the air fryer basket lightly with cooking spray.
2. In a medium bowl, toss the chicken with the salt, pepper, paprika, and garlic powder until evenly coated.
3. Add the olive oil and toss to coat the chicken evenly.

4. In a separate, shallow bowl, mix together the bread crumbs and parsley.
5. Coat each piece of chicken evenly in the bread crumb mixture.
6. Place the chicken in the air fryer basket in a single layer and spray it lightly with cooking spray. You may need to cook them in batches.
7. Air fry at 370ºF (188ºC) for 10 minutes. Flip the chicken over, lightly spray it with cooking spray, and air fry for an additional 8 to 10 minutes, until golden brown. Serve.

Air-Fried Herbed Turkey Breast

Prep time: 20 minutes | Cook time: 45 minutes | Serves 6

1 tablespoon olive oil
Cooking spray
2 garlic cloves, minced
2 teaspoons Dijon mustard
1½ teaspoons rosemary
1½ teaspoons sage
1½ teaspoons thyme
1 teaspoon salt
½ teaspoon freshly ground black pepper
3 pounds (1.4 kg) turkey breast, thawed if frozen

1. Spray the air fryer basket lightly with cooking spray.
2. In a small bowl, mix together the garlic, olive oil, Dijon mustard, rosemary, sage, thyme, salt, and pepper to make a paste. Smear the paste all over the turkey breast.
3. Place the turkey breast in the air fryer basket. Air fry at 370ºF (188ºC) for 20 minutes. Flip turkey breast over and baste it with any drippings that have collected in the bottom drawer of the air fryer. Air fry until the internal temperature of the meat reaches at least 170ºF (77ºC), 20 more minutes.
4. If desired, increase the temperature to 400ºF (204ºC), flip the turkey breast over one last time, and air fry for 5 minutes to get a crispy exterior.
5. Let the turkey rest for 10 minutes before slicing and serving.

Tangy Chicken Breast

Prep time: 35 minutes | Cook time: 20 minutes | Serves 4

4 (4-ounce / 113-g) boneless, skinless chicken breasts	Chicken seasoning or rub, to taste
½ cup chopped fresh cilantro	Salt and ground black pepper, to taste
Juice of 1 lime	Cooking spray

1. Put the chicken breasts in the large bowl, then add the cilantro, lime juice, chicken seasoning, salt, and black pepper. Toss to coat well.
2. Wrap the bowl in plastic and refrigerate to marinate for at least 30 minutes.
3. Spritz the air fryer basket with cooking spray.
4. Remove the marinated chicken breasts from the bowl and place in the air fryer. Spritz with cooking spray. You may need to work in batches to avoid overcrowding.
5. Air fry at 400ºF (204ºC) for 10 minutes or until the internal temperature of the chicken reaches at least 165ºF (74ºC). Flip the breasts halfway through.
6. Serve immediately.

Honey Balsamic Chicken Breast

Prep time: 10 minutes | Cook time: 20 minutes | Serves 4

¼ cup balsamic vinegar	½ teaspoon freshly ground black pepper
¼ cup honey	2 whole boneless, skinless chicken breasts (about 1 pound / 454 g each), halved
2 tablespoons olive oil	
1 tablespoon dried rosemary leaves	
1 teaspoon salt	Cooking spray

1. In a large resealable bag, combine the vinegar, honey, olive oil, rosemary, salt, and pepper. Add the chicken pieces, seal the bag, and refrigerate to marinate for at least 2 hours.
2. Line the air fryer basket with parchment paper.
3. Remove the chicken from the marinade and place it on the parchment. Spritz with cooking spray.

4. Bake at 325ºF (163ºC) for 10 minutes. Flip the chicken, spritz it with cooking spray, and bake for 10 minutes more until the internal temperature reaches 165ºF (74ºC) and the chicken is no longer pink inside. Let sit for 5 minutes before serving.

Fast Spicy Chicken Skewers

Prep time: 5 minutes | Cook time: 10 minutes | Serves 4

4 (6-ounce / 170-g) boneless, skinless chicken breasts, sliced into strips	1 teaspoon sea salt
	1 teaspoon paprika
	Cooking spray
Satay Sauce:	
¼ cup creamy almond butter	chicken broth
½ teaspoon hot sauce	1 teaspoon peeled and minced fresh ginger
1½ tablespoons coconut vinegar	1 clove garlic, minced
2 tablespoons	1 teaspoon sugar
For Serving:	
¼ cup chopped cilantro leaves	Thinly sliced red, orange, or / and yellow bell peppers
Red pepper flakes, to taste	

Special Equipment:
16 wooden or bamboo skewers, soaked in water for 15 minutes

1. Spritz the air fryer basket with cooking spray.
2. Run the bamboo skewers through the chicken strips, then arrange the chicken skewers in the air fryer and sprinkle with salt and paprika.
3. Air fry at 400ºF (204ºC) for 10 minutes or until lightly browned on all sides. Flip the chicken skewers halfway during the cooking.
4. Meanwhile, combine the ingredients for the sauce in a small bowl. Stir to mix well.
5. Transfer the cooked chicken skewers on a large plate, then top with cilantro, sliced bell peppers, red pepper flakes. Serve with the sauce or just baste the sauce over before serving.

Golden Rosemary Turkey

Prep time: 15 minutes | Cook time: 12 minutes | Serves 4

1 egg
1 cup panko breadcrumbs
½ teaspoon rosemary
1 pound (454 g) ground turkey
4 hard-boiled eggs, peeled
Salt and ground black pepper, to taste
Cooking spray

1. Spritz the air fryer basket with cooking spray.
2. Whisk the egg with salt in a bowl. Combine the breadcrumbs with rosemary in a shallow dish.
3. Stir the ground turkey with salt and ground black pepper in a separate large bowl, then divide the ground turkey into four portions.
4. Wrap each hard-boiled egg with a portion of ground turkey. Dredge in the whisked egg, then roll over the breadcrumb mixture.
5. Place the wrapped eggs in the air fryer and spritz with cooking spray. Air fry at 400°F (204°C) for 12 minutes or until golden brown and crunchy. Flip the eggs halfway through.
6. Serve immediately.

Herbed Turkey Slices

Prep time: 5 minutes | Cook time: 30 minutes | Serves 4

1 teaspoon chopped fresh sage
1 teaspoon chopped fresh tarragon
1 teaspoon chopped fresh thyme leaves
1 teaspoon chopped fresh rosemary leaves
1½ teaspoons sea
salt
1 teaspoon ground black pepper
1 (2-pound / 907-g) turkey breast
3 tablespoons Dijon mustard
3 tablespoons butter, melted
Cooking spray

1. Spritz the air fryer basket with cooking spray.
2. Combine the herbs, salt, and black pepper in a small bowl. Stir to mix well. Set aside.

3. Combine the Dijon mustard and butter in a separate bowl. Stir to mix well.
4. Rub the turkey with the herb mixture on a clean work surface, then brush the turkey with Dijon mixture.
5. Arrange the turkey in the air fryer basket. Air fry at 390°F (199°C) for 30 minutes or until an instant-read thermometer inserted in the thickest part of the turkey breast reaches at least 165°F (74°C).
6. Transfer the cooked turkey breast on a large plate and slice to serve.

Peanut Buttered Chicken with Lettuce

Prep time: 10 minutes | Cook time: 6 minutes | Serves 4

1 pound (454 g) ground chicken
2 cloves garlic, minced
¼ cup diced onions
¼ teaspoon sea salt
Cooking spray

Peanut Sauce:
¼ cup creamy peanut butter, at room temperature
2 tablespoons tamari
1½ teaspoons hot sauce
2 tablespoons lime
juice
2 tablespoons grated fresh ginger
2 tablespoons chicken broth
2 teaspoons sugar

For Serving:
2 small heads butter lettuce, leaves
separated
Lime slices (optional)

1. Spritz a baking pan with cooking spray.
2. Combine the ground chicken, garlic, and onions in the baking pan, then sprinkle with salt. Use a fork to break the ground chicken and combine them well.
3. Place the pan in the air fryer. Bake in the air fryer at 350°F (177°C) for 5 minutes or until the chicken is lightly browned. Stir them halfway through the cooking time.
4. Meanwhile, combine the ingredients for the sauce in a small bowl. Stir to mix well.
5. Pour the sauce in the pan of chicken, then cook for 1 more minute or until heated through.
6. Unfold the lettuce leaves on a large serving plate, then divide the chicken mixture on the lettuce leaves. Drizzle with lime juice and serve immediately.

Air-Fried Chicken Wings

Prep time: 10 minutes | Cook time: 15 minutes | Serves 4

1 tablespoon olive oil
8 whole chicken wings
Chicken seasoning or rub, to taste
1 teaspoon garlic powder
Freshly ground black pepper, to taste

1. Grease the air fryer basket with olive oil.
2. On a clean work surface, rub the chicken wings with chicken seasoning and rub, garlic powder, and ground black pepper.
3. Arrange the well-coated chicken wings in the air fryer. Air fry at 400ºF (204ºC) for 15 minutes or until the internal temperature of the chicken wings reaches at least 165ºF (74ºC). Flip the chicken wings halfway through.
4. Remove the chicken wings from the air fryer. Serve immediately.

Brown Sugar-Glazed Chicken Thighs

Prep time: 5 minutes | Cook time: 25 minutes | Serves 4

¼ cup piri-piri sauce
1 tablespoon freshly squeezed lemon juice
2 tablespoons brown sugar, divided
2 cloves garlic, minced
1 tablespoon extra-virgin olive oil
4 bone-in, skin-on chicken thighs, each weighing approximately 7 to 8 ounces (198 to 227 g)
½ teaspoon cornstarch

1. To make the marinade, whisk together the piri-piri sauce, lemon juice, 1 tablespoon of brown sugar, and the garlic in a small bowl. While whisking, slowly pour in the oil in a steady stream and continue to whisk until emulsified. Using a skewer, poke holes in the chicken thighs and place them in a small glass dish. Pour the marinade over the chicken and turn the thighs to coat them with the sauce. Cover the dish and refrigerate for at least 15 minutes and up to 1 hour.
2. Remove the chicken thighs from the dish, reserving the marinade, and place them skin-side down in the air fryer basket. Air fry at 375ºF (191ºC) until the internal temperature reaches 165ºF (74ºC), 15 to 20 minutes.
3. Meanwhile, whisk the remaining brown sugar and the cornstarch into the marinade and microwave it on high power for 1 minute until it is bubbling and thickened to a glaze.
4. Once the chicken is cooked, turn the thighs over and brush them with the glaze. Air fry for a few additional minutes until the glaze browns and begins to char in spots.
5. Remove the chicken to a platter and serve with additional piri-piri sauce, if desired.

Panko-Crusted Turkey Cutlets

Prep time: 10 minutes | Cook time: 10 to 12 minutes | Serves 4

¾ cup panko bread crumbs
¼ teaspoon salt
¼ teaspoon pepper
¼ teaspoon dry mustard
¼ teaspoon poultry seasoning
½ cup pecans
¼ cup cornstarch
1 egg, beaten
1 pound (454 g) turkey cutlets, ½-inch thick
Salt and pepper, to taste
Cooking spray

1. Place the panko crumbs, salt, pepper, mustard, and poultry seasoning in a food processor. Process until crumbs are finely crushed. Add pecans and process just until nuts are finely chopped.
2. Place cornstarch in a shallow dish and beaten egg in another. Transfer coating mixture from food processor into a third shallow dish.
3. Sprinkle turkey cutlets with salt and pepper to taste.
4. Dip cutlets in cornstarch and shake off excess, then dip in beaten egg and finally roll in crumbs, pressing to coat well. Spray both sides with cooking spray.
5. Place 2 cutlets in air fryer basket in a single layer and air fry at 360ºF (182ºC) for 10 to 12 minutes. Repeat with the remaining cutlets.
6. Serve warm.

Baked Asian Turkey Meatballs

Prep time: 10 minutes | Cook time: 11 to 14 minutes | Serves 4

2 tablespoons peanut oil, divided
1 small onion, minced
¼ cup water chestnuts, finely chopped
½ teaspoon ground ginger
2 tablespoons low-sodium soy sauce
¼ cup panko bread crumbs
1 egg, beaten
1 pound (454 g) ground turkey

1. In a round metal pan, combine 1 tablespoon of peanut oil and onion. Air fry for 1 to 2 minutes or until crisp and tender. Transfer the onion to a medium bowl.
2. Add the water chestnuts, ground ginger, soy sauce, and bread crumbs to the onion and mix well. Add egg and stir well. Mix in the ground turkey until combined.
3. Form the mixture into 1-inch meatballs. Drizzle the remaining 1 tablespoon of oil over the meatballs.
4. Bake the meatballs in the pan in batches at 400°F (204°C) for 10 to 12 minutes or until they are 165°F (74°C) on a meat thermometer. Rest for 5 minutes before serving.

Cheesy Turkey and Veggies Wraps

Prep time: 10 minutes | Cook time: 3 to 4 minutes | Serves 4

4 large whole wheat wraps
½ cup hummus
16 thin slices deli turkey
8 slices provolone cheese
1 cup fresh baby spinach, or more to taste

1. To assemble, place 2 tablespoons of hummus on each wrap and spread to within about a half inch from edges. Top with 4 slices of turkey and 2 slices of provolone. Finish with ¼ cup of baby spinach, or pile on as much as you like.
2. Roll up each wrap. You don't need to fold or seal the ends.
3. Place 2 wraps in air fryer basket, seam-side down.

4. Air fry at 360°F (182°C) for 3 to 4 minutes to warm filling and melt cheese. Repeat step 4 to air fry the remaining wraps. Serve immediately.

Air-Fried Korean Chicken Wings

Prep time: 10 minutes | Cook time: 25 minutes | Serves 4

Wings:
2 pounds (907 g) chicken wings
1 teaspoon salt
1 teaspoon ground black pepper
Sauce:
2 tablespoons gochujang
1 tablespoon mayonnaise
1 tablespoon minced ginger
1 tablespoon minced
garlic
1 teaspoon agave nectar
2 packets Splenda
1 tablespoon sesame oil
For Garnish:
2 teaspoons sesame seeds
¼ cup chopped green onions

1. Line a baking pan with aluminum foil, then arrange the rack on the pan.
2. On a clean work surface, rub the chicken wings with salt and ground black pepper, then arrange the seasoned wings on the rack.
3. Air fry for 20 minutes or until the wings are well browned. Flip the wings halfway through. You may need to work in batches to avoid overcrowding.
4. Meanwhile, combine the ingredients for the sauce in a small bowl. Stir to mix well. Reserve half of the sauce in a separate bowl until ready to serve.
5. Remove the air fried chicken wings from the air fryer and toss with remaining half of the sauce to coat well.
6. Place the wings back to the air fryer and air fry at 400°F (204°C) for 5 more minutes or until the internal temperature of the wings reaches at least 165°F (74°C).
7. Remove the wings from the air fryer and place on a large plate. Sprinkle with sesame seeds and green onions. Serve with reserved sauce.

Chicken Nuggets with Sweet-Sour Sauce

Prep time: 15 minutes | Cook time: 15 minutes | Serves 4

1 cup cornstarch
Chicken seasoning or rub, to taste
Salt and ground black pepper, to taste
2 eggs
2 (4-ounce/ 113-g)
boneless, skinless chicken breasts, cut into 1-inch pieces
1½ cups sweet-and-sour sauce
Cooking spray

1. Spritz the air fryer basket with cooking spray.
2. Combine the cornstarch, chicken seasoning, salt, and pepper in a large bowl. Stir to mix well. Whisk the eggs in a separate bowl.
3. Dredge the chicken pieces in the bowl of cornstarch mixture first, then in the bowl of whisked eggs, and then in the cornstarch mixture again.
4. Arrange the well-coated chicken pieces in the air fryer basket. Spritz with cooking spray.
5. Air fry at 360°F (182°C) for 15 minutes or until golden brown and crispy. Shake the basket halfway through the cooking time.
6. Transfer the chicken pieces on a large serving plate, then baste with sweet-and-sour sauce before serving.

Spicy Hoisin Turkey Meatballs

Prep time: 15 minutes | Cook time: 15 minutes | Serves 6

1 pound (454 g) lean ground turkey
½ cup whole-wheat panko bread crumbs
1 egg, beaten
1 tablespoon soy sauce
¼ cup plus 1 tablespoon hoisin
sauce, divided
2 teaspoons minced garlic
⅛ teaspoon salt
⅛ teaspoon freshly ground black pepper
1 teaspoon sriracha
Olive oil spray

1. Spray the air fryer basket lightly with olive oil spray.
2. In a large bowl, mix together the turkey, panko bread crumbs, egg, soy sauce, 1 tablespoon of hoisin sauce, garlic, salt, and black pepper.
3. Using a tablespoon, form the mixture into 24 meatballs.
4. In a small bowl, combine the remaining ¼ cup of hoisin sauce and sriracha to make a glaze and set aside.
5. Place the meatballs in the air fryer basket in a single layer. You may need to cook them in batches.
6. Air fry at 350°F (177°C) for 8 minutes. Brush the meatballs generously with the glaze and air fry until cooked through, an additional 4 to 7 minutes. Serve warm.

Spicy Tandoori Naked Drumsticks

Prep time: 70 minutes | Cook time: 14 minutes | Serves 4

8 (4- to 5-ounce / 113- to 142-g) skinless bone-in chicken drumsticks
½ cup plain full-fat or low-fat yogurt
¼ cup buttermilk
2 teaspoons minced garlic
2 teaspoons minced
fresh ginger
2 teaspoons ground cinnamon
2 teaspoons ground coriander
2 teaspoons mild paprika
1 teaspoon salt
1 teaspoon Tabasco hot red pepper sauce

1. In a large bowl, stir together all the ingredients except for chicken drumsticks until well combined. Add the chicken drumsticks to the bowl and toss until well coated. Cover in plastic and set in the refrigerator to marinate for 1 hour, tossing once.
2. Arrange the marinated drumsticks in a single layer in the air fryer basket, leaving enough space between them. Air fry at 375°F (191°C) for 14 minutes, or until the internal temperature of the chicken drumsticks reaches 160°F (71°C) on a meat thermometer. Flip the drumsticks once halfway through to ensure even cooking.
3. Transfer the drumsticks to plates. Rest for 5 minutes before serving.

Lemony Parmesan Chicken Breast

Prep time: 10 minutes | Cook time: 20 minutes | Serves 4

1 egg
2 tablespoons lemon juice
2 teaspoons minced garlic
½ teaspoon salt
½ teaspoon freshly ground black pepper
4 boneless, skinless chicken breasts, thin cut
Olive oil spray
½ cup whole-wheat bread crumbs
¼ cup grated Parmesan cheese

1. In a medium bowl, whisk together the egg, lemon juice, garlic, salt, and pepper. Add the chicken breasts, cover, and refrigerate for up to 1 hour.
2. In a shallow bowl, combine the bread crumbs and Parmesan cheese.
3. Spray the air fryer basket lightly with olive oil spray.
4. Remove the chicken breasts from the egg mixture, then dredge them in the bread crumb mixture, and place in the air fryer basket in a single layer. Lightly spray the chicken breasts with olive oil spray. You may need to cook the chicken in batches.
5. Air fry at 360ºF (182ºC) for 8 minutes. Flip the chicken over, lightly spray with olive oil spray, and air fry until the chicken reaches an internal temperature of 165ºF (74ºC), for an additional 7 to 12 minutes.
6. Serve warm.

Air-Fried Spiced Turkey Tenderloin

Prep time: 20 minutes | Cook time: 30 minutes | Serves 4

½ teaspoon paprika
½ teaspoon garlic powder
½ teaspoon salt
½ teaspoon freshly ground black pepper
Pinch cayenne pepper
1½ pounds (680 g) turkey breast tenderloin
Olive oil spray

1. Spray the air fryer basket lightly with olive oil spray.
2. In a small bowl, combine the paprika, garlic powder, salt, black pepper, and cayenne pepper. Rub the mixture all over the turkey.

3. Place the turkey in the air fryer basket and lightly spray with olive oil spray.
4. Air fry at 370ºF (188ºC) for 15 minutes. Flip the turkey over and lightly spray with olive oil spray. Air fry until the internal temperature reaches at least 170ºF (77ºC) for an additional 10 to 15 minutes.
5. Let the turkey rest for 10 minutes before slicing and serving.

Air-Fried Brazilian Chicken Drumstick

Prep time: 5 minutes | Cook time: 20 minutes | Serves 4

1 teaspoon cumin seeds
1 teaspoon dried oregano
1 teaspoon dried parsley
1 teaspoon ground turmeric
½ teaspoon coriander seeds
1 teaspoon kosher salt
½ teaspoon black peppercorns
½ teaspoon cayenne pepper
¼ cup fresh lime juice
2 tablespoons olive oil
1½ pounds (680 g) chicken drumsticks

1. In a clean coffee grinder or spice mill, combine the cumin, oregano, parsley, turmeric, coriander seeds, salt, peppercorns, and cayenne. Process until finely ground.
2. In a small bowl, combine the ground spices with the lime juice and oil. Place the chicken in a resealable plastic bag. Add the marinade, seal, and massage until the chicken is well coated. Marinate at room temperature for 30 minutes or in the refrigerator for up to 24 hours.
3. Place the drumsticks skin-side up in the air fryer basket and air fry at 400ºF (204ºC) for 20 to 25 minutes, turning the drumsticks halfway through the cooking time. Use a meat thermometer to ensure that the chicken has reached an internal temperature of 165ºF (74ºC). Serve immediately.

Mayo-Mustard Chicken Tender

Prep time: 10 minutes | Cook time: 15 minutes | Serves 4

6 tablespoons mayonnaise
2 tablespoons coarse-ground mustard
2 teaspoons honey (optional)
2 teaspoons curry powder

1 teaspoon kosher salt
1 teaspoon cayenne pepper
1 pound (454 g) chicken tenders

1. In a large bowl, whisk together the mayonnaise, mustard, honey (if using), curry powder, salt, and cayenne. Transfer half of the mixture to a serving bowl to serve as a dipping sauce. Add the chicken tenders to the large bowl and toss until well coated.
2. Place the tenders in the air fryer basket and bake at 350ºF (177ºC) for 15 minutes. Use a meat thermometer to ensure the chicken has reached an internal temperature of 165ºF (74ºC).
3. Serve the chicken with the dipping sauce.

Garlicky Turkey and Cauliflower Meatloaf

Prep time: 15 minutes | Cook time: 50 minutes | Serves 6

2 pounds (907 g) lean ground turkey
1⅓ cups riced cauliflower
2 large eggs, lightly beaten
¼ cup almond flour
⅔ cup chopped yellow or white onion
1 teaspoon ground dried turmeric

1 teaspoon ground cumin
1 teaspoon ground coriander
1 tablespoon minced garlic
1 teaspoon salt
1 teaspoon ground black pepper
Cooking spray

1. Spritz a loaf pan with cooking spray.
2. Combine all the ingredients in a large bowl. Stir to mix well. Pour half of the mixture in the prepared loaf pan and press with a spatula to coat the bottom evenly. Spritz the mixture with cooking spray.
3. Arrange the loaf pan in the air fryer and bake at 350ºF (177ºC) for 25 minutes or until the meat is well browned and the internal temperature reaches at least 165ºF (74ºC). Repeat with remaining mixture.
4. Remove the loaf pan from the air fryer and serve immediately.

Cheesy Turkey and Cranberry Quesadillas

Prep time: 7 minutes | Cook time: 4 to 8 minutes | Serves 4

6 low-sodium whole-wheat tortillas
⅓ cup shredded low-sodium low-fat Swiss cheese
¾ cup shredded cooked low-sodium turkey breast

2 tablespoons cranberry sauce
2 tablespoons dried cranberries
½ teaspoon dried basil
Olive oil spray, for spraying the tortillas

1. Put 3 tortillas on a work surface.
2. Evenly divide the Swiss cheese, turkey, cranberry sauce, and dried cranberries among the tortillas. Sprinkle with the basil and top with the remaining tortillas.
3. Spray the outsides of the tortillas with olive oil spray.
4. One at a time, air fry the quesadillas in the air fryer at 400ºF (204ºC) for 4 to 8 minutes, or until crisp and the cheese is melted. Cut into quarters and serve.

Honey Chicken Tenders with Veggies

Prep time: 10 minutes | Cook time: 18 to 20 minutes | Serves 4

1 pound (454 g) chicken tenders
1 tablespoon honey
Pinch salt
Freshly ground black pepper, to taste
½ cup soft fresh bread crumbs

½ teaspoon dried thyme
1 tablespoon olive oil
2 carrots, sliced
12 small red potatoes

1. In a medium bowl, toss the chicken tenders with the honey, salt, and pepper.
2. In a shallow bowl, combine the bread crumbs, thyme, and olive oil, and mix.
3. Coat the tenders in the bread crumbs, pressing firmly onto the meat.
4. Place the carrots and potatoes in the air fryer basket and top with the chicken tenders.
5. Roast at 380ºF (193ºC) for 18 to 20 minutes or until the chicken is cooked to 165ºF (74ºC) and the vegetables are tender, shaking the basket halfway during the cooking time.
6. Serve warm.

Thai Game Hens with Vegetable Salad

Prep time: 25 minutes | Cook time: 25 minutes | Serves 6

2 (1¼-pound / 567-g) Cornish game hens, giblets discarded
1 tablespoon fish sauce
6 tablespoons chopped fresh cilantro
2 teaspoons lime zest
1 teaspoon ground coriander
2 garlic cloves, minced
2 tablespoons packed light brown sugar
2 teaspoons vegetable oil
Salt and ground black pepper, to taste

1 English cucumber, halved lengthwise and sliced thin
1 Thai chile, stemmed, deseeded, and minced
2 tablespoons chopped dry-roasted peanuts
1 small shallot, sliced thinly
1 tablespoon lime juice
Lime wedges, for serving
Cooking spray

1. Arrange a game hen on a clean work surface, remove the backbone with kitchen shears, then pound the hen breast to flat. Cut the breast in half. Repeat with the remaining game hen.
2. Loose the breast and thigh skin with your fingers, then pat the game hens dry and pierce about 10 holes into the fat deposits of the hens. Tuck the wings under the hens.
3. Combine 2 teaspoons of fish sauce, ¼ cup of cilantro, lime zest, coriander, garlic, 4 teaspoons of sugar, 1 teaspoon of vegetable oil, ½ teaspoon of salt, and ⅛ teaspoon of ground black pepper in a small bowl. Stir to mix well.
4. Rub the fish sauce mixture under the breast and thigh skin of the game hens, then let sit for 10 minutes to marinate.
5. Spritz the air fryer basket with cooking spray.
6. Arrange the marinated game hens in the air fryer, skin side down.
7. Air fry at 400ºF (204ºC) for 15 minutes, then gently turn the game hens over and air fry for 10 more minutes or until the skin is golden brown and the internal temperature of the hens reads at least 165ºF (74ºC).
8. Meanwhile, combine all the remaining ingredients, except for the lime wedges, in a large bowl and sprinkle with salt and black pepper. Toss to mix well.
9. Transfer the fried hens on a large plate, then sit the salad aside and squeeze the lime wedges over before serving.

Panko-Crusted Chicken Nuggets

Prep time: 10 minutes | Cook time: 20 minutes | Serves 4

1 pound (454 g) boneless, skinless chicken breasts, cut into 1-inch pieces
2 tablespoons panko breadcrumbs
6 tablespoons breadcrumbs

Chicken seasoning or rub, to taste
Salt and ground black pepper, to taste
2 eggs
Cooking spray

1. Spritz the air fryer basket with cooking spray.
2. Combine the breadcrumbs, chicken seasoning, salt, and black pepper in a large bowl. Stir to mix well. Whisk the eggs in a separate bowl.
3. Dunk the chicken pieces in the egg mixture, then in the breadcrumb mixture. Shake the excess off.
4. Arrange the well-coated chicken pieces in the air fryer. Spritz with cooking spray and air fry at 400°F (204°C) for 8 minutes or until crispy and golden brown. Shake the basket halfway through. You may need to work in batches to avoid overcrowding.
5. Serve immediately.

Peanut-Coated Chicken Tenders

Prep time: 5 minutes | Cook time: 12 minutes | Serves 4

1 pound (454 g) chicken tenders
1 teaspoon kosher salt
1 teaspoon black pepper
½ teaspoon smoked paprika

¼ cup coarse mustard
2 tablespoons honey
1 cup finely crushed pecans

1. Place the chicken in a large bowl. Sprinkle with the salt, pepper, and paprika. Toss until the chicken is coated with the spices. Add the mustard and honey and toss until the chicken is coated.
2. Place the pecans on a plate. Working with one piece of chicken at a time, roll the chicken in the pecans until both sides are coated. Lightly brush off any loose pecans. Place the chicken in the air fryer basket.
3. Bake at 350°F (177°C) for 12 minutes, or until the chicken is cooked through and the pecans are golden brown.
4. Serve warm.

Lemony Honey Chicken Drumsticks

Prep time: 5 minutes | Cook time: 23 to 25 minutes | Serves 4

6 chicken drumsticks
3 tablespoons lemon juice, divided
3 tablespoons low-sodium soy sauce, divided
1 tablespoon peanut oil

3 tablespoons honey
3 tablespoons brown sugar
2 tablespoons ketchup
¼ cup pineapple juice

1. Sprinkle the drumsticks with 1 tablespoon of lemon juice and 1 tablespoon of soy sauce. Place in the air fryer basket and drizzle with the peanut oil. Toss to coat. Bake at 350ºF (177ºC) for 18 minutes or until the chicken is almost done.
2. Meanwhile, in a metal bowl, combine the remaining 2 tablespoons of lemon juice, the remaining 2 tablespoons of soy sauce, honey, brown sugar, ketchup, and pineapple juice.
3. Add the cooked chicken to the bowl and stir to coat the chicken well with the sauce.
4. Place the metal bowl in the basket. Bake for 5 to 7 minutes or until the chicken is glazed and registers 165ºF (74ºC) on a meat thermometer. Serve warm.

Simple Tex-Mex Turkey Burgers

Prep time: 10 minutes | Cook time: 14 to 16 minutes | Serves 4

¹/₃ cup finely crushed corn tortilla chips
1 egg, beaten
¼ cup salsa
¹/₃ cup shredded pepper Jack cheese
Pinch salt

Freshly ground black pepper, to taste
1 pound (454 g) ground turkey
1 tablespoon olive oil
1 teaspoon paprika

1. In a medium bowl, combine the tortilla chips, egg, salsa, cheese, salt, and pepper, and mix well.
2. Add the turkey and mix gently but thoroughly with clean hands.
3. Form the meat mixture into patties about ½ inch thick. Make an indentation in the center of each patty with your thumb so the burgers don't puff up while cooking.
4. Brush the patties on both sides with the olive oil and sprinkle with paprika.
5. Put in the air fryer basket and air fry at 330ºF (166ºC) for 14 to 16 minutes or until the meat registers at least 165ºF (74ºC).
6. Let sit for 5 minutes before serving.

Spanish Chicken with Mayo Sauce

Prep time: 10 minutes | Cook time: 20 minutes | Serves 2

1¼ pounds (567 g) assorted small chicken parts, breasts cut into halves
¼ teaspoon salt
¼ teaspoon ground black pepper
2 teaspoons olive oil
½ pound (227 g) mini sweet peppers
¼ cup light mayonnaise
¼ teaspoon smoked paprika
½ clove garlic, crushed
Baguette, for serving
Cooking spray

1. Spritz the air fryer basket with cooking spray.
2. Toss the chicken with salt, ground black pepper, and olive oil in a large bowl.
3. Arrange the sweet peppers and chicken in the air fryer and air fry at 375ºF (191ºC) for 10 minutes, then transfer the peppers on a plate.
4. Flip the chicken and air fry for 10 more minutes or until well browned.
5. Meanwhile, combine the mayo, paprika, and garlic in a small bowl. Stir to mix well.
6. Assemble the baguette with chicken and sweet pepper, then spread with mayo mixture and serve.

Japanese Chicken Skewers

Prep time: 10 minutes | Cook time: 15 minutes | Serves 4

½ cup mirin
¼ cup dry white wine
½ cup soy sauce
1 tablespoon light brown sugar
1½ pounds (680 g) boneless, skinless
chicken thighs, cut into 1½-inch pieces, fat trimmed
4 medium scallions, trimmed, cut into 1½-inch pieces
Cooking spray

Special Equipment:
4 (4-inch) bamboo skewers, soaked in water for at least 30 minutes

1. Combine the mirin, dry white wine, soy sauce, and brown sugar in a saucepan. Bring to a boil over medium heat. Keep stirring.
2. Boil for another 2 minutes or until it has a thick consistency. Turn off the heat.
3. Spritz the air fryer basket with cooking spray.
4. Run the bamboo skewers through the chicken pieces and scallions alternatively.
5. Arrange the skewers in the air fryer, then brush with mirin mixture on both sides. Spritz with cooking spray.
6. Air fry at 400ºF (204ºC) for 10 minutes or until the chicken and scallions are glossy. Flip the skewers halfway through.
7. Serve immediately.

Easy Hoisin Turkey Burgers

Prep time: 10 minutes | Cook time: 20 minutes | Serves 4

1 pound (454 g) lean ground turkey
¼ cup whole-wheat bread crumbs
¼ cup hoisin sauce

2 tablespoons soy sauce
4 whole-wheat buns
Olive oil spray

1. In a large bowl, mix together the turkey, bread crumbs, hoisin sauce, and soy sauce.
2. Form the mixture into 4 equal patties. Cover with plastic wrap and refrigerate the patties for 30 minutes.
3. Spray the air fryer basket lightly with olive oil spray.
4. Place the patties in the air fryer basket in a single layer. Spray the patties lightly with olive oil spray.
5. Air fry at 370ºF (188ºC) for 10 minutes. Flip the patties over, lightly spray with olive oil spray, and air fry for an additional 5 to 10 minutes, until golden brown.
6. Place the patties on buns and top with your choice of low-calorie burger toppings like sliced tomatoes, onions, and cabbage slaw. Serve immediately.

Air-Fried Teriyaki Chicken Thighs

Prep time: 30 minutes | Cook time: 34 minutes | Serves 4

¼ cup chicken broth
½ teaspoon grated fresh ginger
⅛ teaspoon red pepper flakes
1½ tablespoons soy sauce
4 (5-ounce / 142-g) bone-in chicken thighs, trimmed
1 tablespoon mirin
½ teaspoon cornstarch

1 tablespoon sugar
6 ounces (170 g) snow peas, strings removed
⅛ teaspoon lemon zest
1 garlic clove, minced
¼ teaspoon salt
Ground black pepper, to taste
½ teaspoon lemon juice

1. Combine the broth, ginger, pepper flakes, and soy sauce in a large bowl. Stir to mix well.
2. Pierce 10 to 15 holes into the chicken skin. Put the chicken in the broth mixture and toss to coat well. Let sit for 10 minutes to marinate.
3. Transfer the marinated chicken on a plate and pat dry with paper towels.
4. Scoop 2 tablespoons of marinade in a microwave-safe bowl and combine with mirin, cornstarch and sugar. Stir to mix well. Microwave for 1 minute or until frothy and has a thick consistency. Set aside.
5. Arrange the chicken in the air fryer, skin side up, and air fry at 400ºF (205ºC) for 25 minutes or until the internal temperature of the chicken reaches at least 165ºF (74ºC). Gently turn the chicken over halfway through.
6. When the frying is complete, brush the chicken skin with marinade mixture. Air fryer the chicken for 5 more minutes or until glazed.
7. Remove the chicken from the air fryer and reserve ½ teaspoon of chicken fat remains in the air fryer. Allow the chicken to cool for 10 minutes.
8. Meanwhile, combine the reserved chicken fat, snow peas, lemon zest, garlic, salt, and ground black pepper in a small bowl. Toss to coat well.
9. Transfer the snow peas in the air fryer and air fry for 3 minutes or until soft. Remove the peas from the air fryer and toss with lemon juice.
10. Serve the chicken with lemony snow peas.

Chapter 10 Red Meats

Panko-Crusted Wasabi Spam

Prep time: 5 minutes | Cook time: 12 minutes | Serves 3

⅔ cup all-purpose flour
2 large eggs
1½ tablespoons wasabi paste

2 cups panko breadcrumbs
6 ½-inch-thick spam slices
Cooking spray

1. Pour the flour in a shallow plate. Whisk the eggs with wasabi in a large bowl. Pour the panko in a separate shallow plate.
2. Dredge the spam slices in the flour first, then dunk in the egg mixture, and then roll the spam over the panko to coat well. Shake the excess off.
3. Arrange the spam slices in a single layer in the air fryer and spritz with cooking spray.
4. Air fry at 400ºF (204ºC) for 12 minutes or until the spam slices are golden and crispy. Flip the spam slices halfway through.
5. Serve immediately.

Air-Fried Mustard Lamb Ribs

Prep time: 5 minutes | Cook time: 18 minutes | Serves 4

2 tablespoons mustard
1 pound (454 g) lamb ribs
1 teaspoon rosemary, chopped

Salt and ground black pepper, to taste
¼ cup mint leaves, chopped
1 cup Greek yogurt

1. Use a brush to apply the mustard to the lamb ribs, and season with rosemary, salt, and pepper.
2. Air fry the ribs in the air fryer at 350ºF (177ºC) for 18 minutes.
3. Meanwhile, combine the mint leaves and yogurt in a bowl.
4. Remove the lamb ribs from the air fryer when cooked and serve with the mint yogurt.

Air-Fried Marinated London Broil

Prep time: 15 minutes | Cook time: 25 minutes | Serves 8

2 pounds (907 g) London broil
3 large garlic cloves, minced
3 tablespoons balsamic vinegar
3 tablespoons whole-

grain mustard
2 tablespoons olive oil
Sea salt and ground black pepper, to taste
½ teaspoons dried hot red pepper flakes

1. Wash and dry the London broil. Score its sides with a knife.
2. Mix the remaining ingredients. Rub this mixture into the broil, coating it well. Allow to marinate for a minimum of 3 hours.
3. Air fry the meat at 400ºF (204ºC) for 15 minutes. Turn it over and air fry for an additional 10 minutes before serving.

Tangy Pork Ribs

Prep time: 1 hour 10 minutes | Cook time: 25 minutes | Serves 6

2½ pounds (1.1 kg) boneless country-style pork ribs, cut into 2-inch pieces
3 tablespoons olive brine
1 tablespoon minced fresh oregano leaves
⅓ cup orange juice

1 teaspoon ground cumin
1 tablespoon minced garlic
1 teaspoon salt
1 teaspoon ground black pepper
Cooking spray

1. Combine all the ingredients in a large bowl. Toss to coat the pork ribs well. Wrap the bowl in plastic and refrigerate for at least an hour to marinate.
2. Arrange the marinated pork ribs in a single layer in the air fryer and spritz with cooking spray.
3. Air fry at 400ºF (204ºC) for 25 minutes or until well browned. Flip the ribs halfway through.
4. Serve immediately.

Air-Fried Citrus Pork Loin

Prep time: 10 minutes | Cook time: 45 minutes | Serves 8

1 tablespoon lime juice
1 tablespoon orange marmalade
1 teaspoon coarse brown mustard
1 teaspoon curry powder
1 teaspoon dried lemongrass
2 pound (907 g) boneless pork loin roast
Salt and ground black pepper, to taste
Cooking spray

1. Mix the lime juice, marmalade, mustard, curry powder, and lemongrass.
2. Rub mixture all over the surface of the pork loin. Season with salt and pepper.
3. Spray air fryer basket with cooking spray and place pork roast diagonally in the basket.
4. Air fry at 360ºF (182ºC) for approximately 45 minutes, until the internal temperature reaches at least 145ºF (63ºC).
5. Wrap roast in foil and let rest for 10 minutes before slicing.
6. Serve immediately.

Apple-Glazed Pork Chop

Prep time: 15 minutes | Cook time: 19 minutes | Serves 4

1 sliced apple
1 small onion, sliced
2 tablespoons apple cider vinegar, divided
½ teaspoon thyme
½ teaspoon rosemary
¼ teaspoon brown sugar
3 tablespoons olive oil, divided
¼ teaspoon smoked paprika
4 pork chops
Salt and ground black pepper, to taste

1. Combine the apple slices, onion, 1 tablespoon of vinegar, thyme, rosemary, brown sugar, and 2 tablespoons of olive oil in a baking pan. Stir to mix well.
2. Arrange the pan in the air fryer and bake at 350ºF (177ºC) for 4 minutes.
3. Meanwhile, combine the remaining vinegar and olive oil, and paprika in a large bowl. Sprinkle with salt and ground black pepper. Stir to mix well. Dredge the pork in the mixture and toss to coat well.

4. Remove the baking pan from the air fryer and put in the pork. Air fry for 10 minutes to lightly brown the pork. Flip the pork chops halfway through.
5. Remove the pork from the air fryer and baste with baked apple mixture on both sides. Put the pork back to the air fryer and air fry for an additional 5 minutes. Flip halfway through.
6. Serve immediately.

Beef Cube and Veggies

Prep time: 15 minutes | Cook time: 17 minutes | Serves 4

2 tablespoons olive oil
1 tablespoon apple cider vinegar
1 teaspoon fine sea salt
½ teaspoons ground black pepper
1 teaspoon shallot powder
¾ teaspoon smoked cayenne pepper
½ teaspoons garlic powder
¼ teaspoon ground cumin
1 pound (454 g) top round steak, cut into cubes
4 ounces (113 g) broccoli, cut into florets
4 ounces (113 g) mushrooms, sliced
1 teaspoon dried basil
1 teaspoon celery seeds

1. Massage the olive oil, vinegar, salt, black pepper, shallot powder, cayenne pepper, garlic powder, and cumin into the cubed steak, ensuring to coat each piece evenly.
2. Allow to marinate for a minimum of 3 hours.
3. Put the beef cubes in the air fryer basket and air fry at 365ºF (185ºC) for 12 minutes.
4. When the steak is cooked through, place it in a bowl.
5. Wipe the grease from the basket and pour in the vegetables. Season them with basil and celery seeds.
6. Increase the temperature of the air fryer to 400ºF (204ºC) and air fry for 5 to 6 minutes. When the vegetables are hot, serve them with the steak.

Fast Bacon-Wrapped Hot Dogs

Prep time: 5 minutes | Cook time: 10 to 12 minutes | Serves 5

10 thin slices of bacon
5 pork hot dogs, halved
Sauce:
¼ cup mayonnaise
4 tablespoons low-carb ketchup
1 teaspoon rice vinegar
1 teaspoon cayenne pepper
1 teaspoon chili powder

1. Arrange the slices of bacon on a clean work surface. One by one, place the halved hot dog on one end of each slice, season with cayenne pepper and wrap the hot dog with the bacon slices and secure with toothpicks as needed.
2. Work in batches, place half the wrapped hot dogs in the air fryer basket and air fry at 390ºF (199ºC) for 10 to 12 minutes or until the bacon becomes browned and crispy.
3. Make the sauce: Stir all the ingredients for the sauce in a small bowl. Wrap the bowl in plastic and set in the refrigerator until ready to serve.
4. Transfer the hot dogs to a platter and serve hot with the sauce.

Bacon-Wrapped Sausage with Relish

Prep time: 1 hour 15 minutes | Cook time: 32 minutes | Serves 4

8 pork sausages
Relish:
8 large tomatoes, chopped
1 small onion, peeled
1 clove garlic, peeled
1 tablespoon white wine vinegar
3 tablespoons
8 bacon strips
chopped parsley
1 teaspoon smoked paprika
2 tablespoons sugar
Salt and ground black pepper, to taste

1. Purée the tomatoes, onion, and garlic in a food processor until well mixed and smooth.
2. Pour the purée in a saucepan and drizzle with white wine vinegar. Sprinkle with salt and ground black pepper. Simmer over medium heat for 10 minutes.

3. Add the parsley, paprika, and sugar to the saucepan and cook for 10 more minutes or until it has a thick consistency. Keep stirring during the cooking. Refrigerate for an hour to chill.
4. Wrap the sausage with bacon strips and secure with toothpicks, then place them in the air fryer.
5. Air fry at 350ºF (177ºC) for 12 minutes or until the bacon is crispy and browned. Flip the bacon-wrapped sausage halfway through.
6. Transfer the bacon-wrapped sausage on a plate and baste with the relish or just serve with the relish alongside.

Air-Fried Pork Butt

Prep time: 1 hour 15 minutes | Cook time: 30 minutes | Serves 4

1 teaspoon golden flaxseed meal
1 egg white, well whisked
1 tablespoon soy sauce
1 teaspoon lemon juice, preferably freshly squeezed
1 tablespoon olive oil
1 pound (454 g) pork butt, cut into pieces 2-inches long
Salt and ground black pepper, to taste
Garlicky Coriander-Parsley Sauce:
3 garlic cloves, minced
1/3 cup fresh coriander leaves
1/3 cup fresh parsley leaves
1 teaspoon lemon juice
½ tablespoon salt
1/3 cup extra-virgin olive oil

1. Combine the flaxseed meal, egg white, soy sauce, lemon juice, salt, black pepper, and olive oil in a large bowl. Dunk the pork strips in and press to submerge.
2. Wrap the bowl in plastic and refrigerate to marinate for at least an hour.
3. Arrange the marinated pork strips in the air fryer and air fry at 380ºF (193ºC) for 30 minutes or until cooked through and well browned. Flip the strips halfway through.
4. Meanwhile, combine the ingredients for the sauce in a small bowl. Stir to mix well. Arrange the bowl in the refrigerator to chill until ready to serve.
5. Serve the air fried pork strips with the chilled sauce.

Air-Fried Barbecue Pork Ribs

Prep time: 5 minutes | Cook time: 30 minutes | Serves 4

1 tablespoon barbecue dry rub
1 teaspoon mustard
1 tablespoon apple cider vinegar
1 teaspoon sesame oil
1 pound (454 g) pork ribs, chopped

1. Combine the dry rub, mustard, apple cider vinegar, and sesame oil, then coat the ribs with this mixture. Refrigerate the ribs for 20 minutes.
2. When the ribs are ready, place them in the air fryer and air fry at 360ºF (182ºC) for 15 minutes. Flip them and air fry on the other side for a further 15 minutes.
3. Serve immediately.

Crispy Walliser Schnitzel

Prep time: 5 minutes | Cook time: 14 minutes | Serves 2

½ cup pork rinds
½ tablespoon fresh parsley
½ teaspoon fennel seed
½ teaspoon mustard
⅓ tablespoon cider vinegar
1 teaspoon garlic salt
⅓ teaspoon ground black pepper
2 eggs
2 pork schnitzel, halved
Cooking spray

1. Put the pork rinds, parsley, fennel seeds, and mustard in a food processor. Pour in the vinegar and sprinkle with salt and ground black pepper. Pulse until well combined and smooth.
2. Pour the pork rind mixture in a large bowl. Whisk the eggs in a separate bowl.
3. Dunk the pork schnitzel in the whisked eggs, then dunk in the pork rind mixture to coat well. Shake the excess off.
4. Arrange the schnitzel in the air fryer and spritz with cooking spray. Air fry at 350ºF (177ºC) for 14 minutes or until golden and crispy. Flip the schnitzel halfway through.
5. Serve immediately.

Easy Beef Steak Fingers

Prep time: 5 minutes | Cook time: 8 minutes | Serves 4

4 small beef cube steaks
Salt and ground black
pepper, to taste
½ cup flour
Cooking spray

1. Cut cube steaks into 1-inch-wide strips.
2. Sprinkle lightly with salt and pepper to taste.
3. Roll in flour to coat all sides.
4. Spritz air fryer basket with cooking spray.
5. Put steak strips in air fryer basket in a single layer. Spritz top of steak strips with cooking spray.
6. Air fry at 390ºF (199ºC) for 4 minutes, turn strips over, and spritz with cooking spray.
7. Air fry 4 more minutes and test with fork for doneness. Steak fingers should be crispy outside with no red juices inside.
8. Repeat steps 5 through 7 to air fry remaining strips.
9. Serve immediately.

BBQ Sausage, Pineapple and Peppers

Prep time: 15 minutes | Cook time: 10 minutes | Serves 2 to 4

¾ pound (340 g) kielbasa sausage, cut into ½-inch slices
1 (8-ounce / 227-g) can pineapple chunks in juice, drained
1 cup bell pepper
chunks
1 tablespoon barbecue seasoning
1 tablespoon soy sauce
Cooking spray

1. Spritz the air fryer basket with cooking spray.
2. Combine all the ingredients in a large bowl. Toss to mix well.
3. Pour the sausage mixture in the air fryer.
4. Air fry at 390ºF (199ºC) for 10 minutes or until the sausage is lightly browned and the bell pepper and pineapple are soft. Shake the basket halfway through.
5. Serve immediately.

China Char Siew

Prep time: 10 minutes | Cook time: 20 minutes | Serves 4 to 6

1 strip of pork shoulder butt with a good amount of fat marbling
Olive oil, for brushing the pan
Marinade:
1 teaspoon sesame oil
4 tablespoons raw

honey
1 teaspoon low-sodium dark soy sauce
1 teaspoon light soy sauce
1 tablespoon rose wine
2 tablespoons Hoisin sauce

1. Combine all the marinade ingredients together in a Ziploc bag. Put pork in bag, making sure all sections of pork strip are engulfed in the marinade. Chill for 3 to 24 hours.
2. Take out the strip 30 minutes before planning to roast.
3. Put foil on small pan and brush with olive oil. Put marinated pork strip onto prepared pan.
4. Roast in the air fryer at 350ºF (177ºC) for 20 minutes.
5. Glaze with marinade every 5 to 10 minutes.
6. Remove strip and leave to cool a few minutes before slicing.
7. Serve immediately.

Char Siu (Cantonese Roasted Pork)

Prep time: 8 hours 10 minutes | Cook time: 15 minutes | Serves 4

¼ cup honey
1 teaspoon Chinese five-spice powder
1 tablespoon Shaoxing wine (rice cooking wine)
1 tablespoon hoisin sauce
2 teaspoons minced garlic

2 teaspoons minced fresh ginger
2 tablespoons soy sauce
1 tablespoon sugar
1 pound (454 g) fatty pork shoulder, cut into long, 1-inch-thick pieces
Cooking spray

1. Combine all the ingredients, except for the pork should, in a microwave-safe bowl. Stir to mix well. Microwave until the honey has dissolved. Stir periodically.

2. Pierce the pork pieces generously with a fork, then put the pork in a large bowl. Pour in half of the honey mixture. Set the remaining sauce aside until ready to serve.
3. Press the pork pieces into the mixture to coat and wrap the bowl in plastic and refrigerate to marinate for at least 8 hours.
4. Spritz the air fryer basket with cooking spray.
5. Discard the marinade and transfer the pork pieces in the air fryer basket.
6. Air fry at 400ºF (204ºC) for 15 minutes or until well browned. Flip the pork pieces halfway through the cooking time.
7. Meanwhile, microwave the remaining marinade on high for a minute or until it has a thick consistency. Stir periodically.
8. Remove the pork from the air fryer and allow to cool for 10 minutes before serving with the thickened marinade.

Dijon Pork Tenderloin

Prep time: 5 minutes | Cook time: 10 minutes | Serves 6

2 large egg whites
1½ tablespoons Dijon mustard
2 cups crushed pretzel crumbs

1½ pounds (680 g) pork tenderloin, cut into ¼-pound (113-g) sections
Cooking spray

1. Spritz the air fryer basket with cooking spray.
2. Whisk the egg whites with Dijon mustard in a bowl until bubbly. Pour the pretzel crumbs in a separate bowl.
3. Dredge the pork tenderloin in the egg white mixture and press to coat. Shake the excess off and roll the tenderloin over the pretzel crumbs.
4. Arrange the well-coated pork tenderloin in batches in a single layer in the air fryer basket and spritz with cooking spray.
5. Air fry at 350ºF (177ºC) for 10 minutes or until the pork is golden brown and crispy. Flip the pork halfway through. Repeat with remaining pork sections.
6. Serve immediately.

Garlicky Parmesan Beef Meatballs

Prep time: 5 minutes | Cook time: 18 minutes | Serves 6

1 pound (454 g) ground beef	garlic
½ cup grated Parmesan cheese	½ cup Mozzarella cheese
1 tablespoon minced	1 teaspoon freshly ground pepper

1. In a bowl, mix all the ingredients together.
2. Roll the meat mixture into 5 generous meatballs.
3. Air fry inside the air fryer at 165ºF (74ºC) for about 18 minutes.
4. Serve immediately.

Easy Classic Spring Rolls

Prep time: 10 minutes | Cook time: 8 minutes | Serves 20

¹/₃ cup noodles	1 small onion, diced
1 cup ground beef	1 tablespoon sesame oil
1 teaspoon soy sauce	
1 cup fresh mix vegetables	1 packet spring roll sheets
3 garlic cloves, minced	2 tablespoons cold water

1. Cook the noodle in enough hot water to soften them up, drain them and snip them to make them shorter.
2. In a frying pan over medium heat, cook the beef, soy sauce, mixed vegetables, garlic, and onion in sesame oil until the beef is cooked through. Take the pan off the heat and throw in the noodles. Mix well to incorporate everything.
3. Unroll a spring roll sheet and lay it flat. Scatter the filling diagonally across it and roll it up, brushing the edges lightly with water to act as an adhesive. Repeat until you have used up all the sheets and the filling.
4. Coat each spring roll with a light brushing of oil and transfer to the air fryer.
5. Air fry at 350ºF (177ºC) for 8 minutes and serve hot.

Breaded Beef Schnitzel

Prep time: 5 minutes | Cook time: 12 minutes | Serves 1

½ cup friendly bread crumbs	Pepper and salt, to taste
2 tablespoons olive oil	1 egg, beaten
	1 thin beef schnitzel

1. In a shallow dish, combine the bread crumbs, oil, pepper, and salt.
2. In a second shallow dish, place the beaten egg.
3. Dredge the schnitzel in the egg before rolling it in the bread crumbs.
4. Put the coated schnitzel in the air fryer basket and air fry at 350ºF (177ºC) for 12 minutes. Flip the schnitzel halfway through.
5. Serve immediately.

Spiced Lamb Kofta

Prep time: 25 minutes | Cook time: 10 minutes | Serves 4

1 pound (454 g) ground lamb	powder
1 tablespoon ras el hanout (North African spice)	1 teaspoon garlic powder
½ teaspoon ground coriander	1 teaspoon cumin
	2 tablespoons mint, chopped
1 teaspoon onion	Salt and ground black pepper, to taste

Special Equipment:
4 bamboo skewers

1. Combine the ground lamb, ras el hanout, coriander, onion powder, garlic powder, cumin, mint, salt, and ground black pepper in a large bowl. Stir to mix well.
2. Transfer the mixture into sausage molds and sit the bamboo skewers in the mixture. Refrigerate for 15 minutes.
3. Spritz the basket with cooking spray.
4. Place the lamb skewers in the air fryer and spritz with cooking spray.
5. Air fry at 380ºF (193ºC) for 10 minutes or until the lamb is well browned. Flip the lamb skewers halfway through.
6. Serve immediately.

Fast Lamb Skewers

Prep time: 5 minutes | Cook time: 8 minutes | Serves 2

¼ teaspoon cumin
1 teaspoon ginger
½ teaspoons nutmeg
Salt and ground black

pepper, to taste
2 boneless lamb
steaks
Cooking spray

1. Combine the cumin, ginger, nutmeg, salt and pepper in a bowl.
2. Cube the lamb steaks and massage the spice mixture into each one.
3. Leave to marinate for 10 minutes, then transfer onto metal skewers.
4. Spritz the skewers with the cooking spray, then air fry them in the air fryer at 400ºF (204ºC) for 8 minutes.
5. Take care when removing them from the air fryer and serve.

Homemade Sweet-Sour Pork

Prep time: 20 minutes | Cook time: 14 minutes | Serves 2 to 4

$^1/_3$ cup all-purpose
flour
$^1/_3$ cup cornstarch
2 teaspoons Chinese
five-spice powder
1 teaspoon salt
Freshly ground black
pepper, to taste
1 egg
2 tablespoons milk
¾ pound (340 g)
boneless pork, cut
into 1-inch cubes
Vegetable or canola
oil
1½ cups large chunks

of red and green
peppers
½ cup ketchup
2 tablespoons rice
wine vinegar or apple
cider vinegar
2 tablespoons brown
sugar
¼ cup orange juice
1 tablespoon soy
sauce
1 clove garlic, minced
1 cup cubed
pineapple
Chopped scallions,
for garnish

1. Set up a dredging station with two bowls. Combine the flour, cornstarch, Chinese five-spice powder, salt and pepper in one large bowl. Whisk the egg and milk together in a second bowl. Dredge the pork cubes in the flour mixture first, then dip them into the egg and then back into the flour to coat on all sides. Spray the coated pork cubes with vegetable or canola oil.

2. Toss the pepper chunks with a little oil and air fry for 5 minutes, shaking the basket halfway through the cooking time.
3. While the peppers are cooking, start making the sauce. Combine the ketchup, rice wine vinegar, brown sugar, orange juice, soy sauce, and garlic in a medium saucepan and bring the mixture to a boil on the stovetop. Reduce the heat and simmer for 5 minutes. When the peppers have finished air frying, add them to the saucepan along with the pineapple chunks. Simmer the peppers and pineapple in the sauce for an additional 2 minutes. Set aside and keep warm.
4. Add the dredged pork cubes to the air fryer basket and air fry at 400ºF (204ºC) for 6 minutes, shaking the basket to turn the cubes over for the last minute of the cooking process.
5. When ready to serve, toss the cooked pork with the pineapple, peppers and sauce. Serve garnished with chopped scallions.

Classic Teriyaki Pork Ribs

Prep time: 5 minutes | Cook time: 30 minutes | Serves 4

¼ cup soy sauce
¼ cup honey
1 teaspoon garlic
powder
1 teaspoon ground

dried ginger
4 (8-ounce / 227-
g) boneless country-
style pork ribs
Cooking spray

1. Spritz the air fryer basket with cooking spray.
2. Make the teriyaki sauce: combine the soy sauce, honey, garlic powder, and ginger in a bowl. Stir to mix well.
3. Brush the ribs with half of the teriyaki sauce, then arrange the ribs in the air fryer. Spritz with cooking spray. You may need to work in batches to avoid overcrowding.
4. Air fry at 350ºF (177ºC) for 30 minutes or until the internal temperature of the ribs reaches at least 145ºF (63ºC). Brush the ribs with remaining teriyaki sauce and flip halfway through.
5. Serve immediately.

Classic Mongolian Flank Steak

Prep time: 20 minutes | Cook time: 15 minutes | Serves 4

1½ pounds (680 g) flank steak, thinly sliced on the bias into ¼-inch strips
Marinade:
2 tablespoons soy
Sauce:
1 tablespoon vegetable oil
2 cloves garlic, minced
1 tablespoon finely grated fresh ginger
3 dried red chili peppers
¾ cup soy sauce
sauce
1 clove garlic, smashed
Pinch crushed red pepper flakes

¾ cup chicken stock
5 to 6 tablespoons brown sugar
½ cup cornstarch, divided
1 bunch scallions, sliced into 2-inch pieces

1. Marinate the beef in the soy sauce, garlic and red pepper flakes for one hour.
2. In the meantime, make the sauce. Add the oil, garlic, ginger and dried chili peppers and sauté for just a minute or two. Add the soy sauce, chicken stock and brown sugar and continue to simmer for a few minutes. Dissolve 3 tablespoons of cornstarch in 3 tablespoons of water and stir this into the saucepan. Stir the sauce over medium heat until it thickens. Set this aside.
3. Remove the beef from the marinade and transfer it to a zipper sealable plastic bag with the remaining cornstarch. Shake it around to completely coat the beef and transfer the coated strips of beef to a baking sheet or plate, shaking off any excess cornstarch. Spray the strips with vegetable oil on all sides and transfer them to the air fryer basket.
4. Air fry at 400°F (204°C) for 15 minutes, shaking the basket to toss the beef strips throughout the cooking process. Add the scallions for the last 4 minutes of the cooking. Transfer the hot beef strips and scallions to a bowl and toss with the sauce, coating all the beef strips with the sauce. Serve warm.

Pistachios-Crusted Lamb Rack

Prep time: 10 minutes | Cook time: 20 minutes | Serves 2

½ cup finely chopped pistachios
1 teaspoon chopped fresh rosemary
3 tablespoons panko breadcrumbs
2 teaspoons chopped fresh oregano
1 tablespoon olive oil
Salt and freshly ground black pepper, to taste
1 lamb rack, bones fat trimmed and frenched
1 tablespoon Dijon mustard

1. Put the pistachios, rosemary, breadcrumbs, oregano, olive oil, salt, and black pepper in a food processor. Pulse to combine until smooth.
2. Rub the lamb rack with salt and black pepper on a clean work surface, then place it in the air fryer.
3. Air fry at 380°F (193°C) for 12 minutes or until lightly browned. Flip the lamb halfway through the cooking time.
4. Transfer the lamb on a plate and brush with Dijon mustard on the fat side, then sprinkle with the pistachios mixture over the lamb rack to coat well.
5. Put the lamb rack back to the air fryer and air fry for 8 more minutes or until the internal temperature of the rack reaches at least 145°F (63°C).
6. Remove the lamb rack from the air fryer with tongs and allow to cool for 5 minutes before sling to serve.

Beef and Mushroom Meatloaf

Prep time: 10 minutes | Cook time: 25 minutes | Serves 4

1 pound (454 g) ground beef
1 egg, beaten
1 cup mushroom, sliced
1 tablespoon thyme
1 small onion, chopped
3 tablespoons bread crumbs
Ground black pepper, to taste

1. Put all the ingredients into a large bowl and combine entirely.
2. Transfer the meatloaf mixture into the loaf pan and move it to the air fryer basket.
3. Bake at 400°F (204°C) for 25 minutes. Slice up before serving.

Crispy Lechon Kawali

Prep time: 10 minutes | Cook time: 30 minutes | Serves 4

1 pound (454 g) pork belly, cut into three thick chunks	1 teaspoon kosher salt
6 garlic cloves	1 teaspoon ground black pepper
2 bay leaves	3 cups water
2 tablespoons soy sauce	Cooking spray

1. Put all the ingredients in a pressure cooker, then put the lid on and cook on high for 15 minutes.
2. Natural release the pressure and release any remaining pressure, transfer the tender pork belly on a clean work surface. Allow to cool under room temperature until you can handle.
3. Generously spritz the air fryer basket with cooking spray.
4. Cut each chunk into two slices, then put the pork slices in the air fryer.
5. Air fry at 400ºF (204ºC) for 15 minutes or until the pork fat is crispy. Spritz the pork with more cooking spray, if necessary.
6. Serve immediately.

Golden Lemony Pork Chop

Prep time: 15 minutes | Cook time: 15 minutes | Serves 4

4 thin boneless pork loin chops	1 teaspoon salt
2 tablespoons lemon juice	1 cup panko breadcrumbs
½ cup flour	2 eggs
¼ teaspoon marjoram	Lemon wedges, for serving
	Cooking spray

1. On a clean work surface, drizzle the pork chops with lemon juice on both sides.
2. Combine the flour with marjoram and salt on a shallow plate. Pour the breadcrumbs on a separate shallow dish. Beat the eggs in a large bowl.
3. Dredge the pork chops in the flour, then dunk in the beaten eggs to coat well. Shake the excess off and roll over the breadcrumbs.

4. Arrange the chops in the air fryer and spritz with cooking spray. Air fry at 390ºF (199ºC) for 15 minutes or until the chops are golden and crispy. Flip the chops halfway through.
5. Squeeze the lemon wedges over the fried chops and serve immediately.

Lamb with Horseradish Cream Sauce

Prep time: 10 minutes | Cook time: 13 minutes | Serves 4

For the Lamb:

4 lamb loin chops	½ teaspoon kosher salt
2 tablespoons vegetable oil	½ teaspoon black pepper
1 clove garlic, minced	

For the Horseradish Cream Sauce:

1 to 1½ tablespoons prepared horseradish	½ cup mayonnaise
1 tablespoon Dijon mustard	2 teaspoons sugar
	Cooking spray

1. Spritz the air fryer basket with cooking spray.
2. Place the lamb chops on a plate. Rub with the oil and sprinkle with the garlic, salt and black pepper. Let sit to marinate for 30 minutes at room temperature.
3. Make the horseradish cream sauce: Mix the horseradish, mustard, mayonnaise, and sugar in a bowl until well combined. Set half of the sauce aside until ready to serve.
4. Arrange the marinated chops in the prepared basket. Set the time to 10 minutes, flipping the chops halfway through..
5. Transfer the chops from the air fryer to the bowl of the horseradish sauce. Roll to coat well.
6. Put the coated chops in the air fryer basket again. Set the temperature to 400ºF (204ºC) and the time to 3 minutes. Air fry until the internal temperature reaches 145ºF (63ºC) on a meat thermometer (for medium-rare).
7. Serve hot with the horseradish cream sauce.

Nut-Crusted Rosemary Pork Rack

Prep time: 5 minutes | Cook time: 35 minutes | Serves 2

1 clove garlic, minced
2 tablespoons olive oil
1 pound (454 g) rack of pork
1 cup chopped macadamia nuts
1 tablespoon breadcrumbs
1 tablespoon rosemary, chopped
1 egg
Salt and ground black pepper, to taste

1. Combine the garlic and olive oil in a small bowl. Stir to mix well.
2. On a clean work surface, rub the pork rack with the garlic oil and sprinkle with salt and black pepper on both sides.
3. Combine the macadamia nuts, breadcrumbs, and rosemary in a shallow dish. Whisk the egg in a large bowl.
4. Dredge the pork in the egg, then roll the pork over the macadamia nut mixture to coat well. Shake the excess off.
5. Arrange the pork in the air fryer and air fry at 350ºF (177ºC) for 30 minutes on both sides. Increase to 390ºF (199ºC) and fry for 5 more minutes or until the pork is well browned.
6. Serve immediately.

Air-Fried Miso Marinated Steak

Prep time: 5 minutes | Cook time: 12 minutes | Serves 4

¾ pound (340 g) flank steak
1½ tablespoons sake
1 tablespoon brown miso paste
1 teaspoon honey
2 cloves garlic, pressed
1 tablespoon olive oil

1. Put all the ingredients in a Ziploc bag. Shake to cover the steak well with the seasonings and refrigerate for at least 1 hour.
2. Coat all sides of the steak with cooking spray. Put the steak in the baking pan.
3. Air fry at 400ºF (204ºC) for 12 minutes, turning the steak twice during the cooking time, then serve immediately.

Paprika Pork Chops

Prep time: 5 minutes | Cook time: 24 minutes | Serves 4 to 6

½ cup flour
1½ teaspoons salt
Freshly ground black pepper, to taste
2 eggs
½ cup milk
1½ cups toasted breadcrumbs
1 teaspoon paprika
6 boneless, center cut pork chops (about 1½ pounds / 680 g), fat trimmed, pound to ½-inch thick
2 tablespoons olive oil
3 tablespoons melted butter
Lemon wedges, for serving
Sour Cream and Dill Sauce:
1 cup chicken stock
1½ tablespoons cornstarch
⅓ cup sour cream
1½ tablespoons chopped fresh dill
Salt and ground black pepper, to taste

1. Combine the flour with salt and black pepper in a large bowl. Stir to mix well. Whisk the egg with milk in a second bowl. Stir the breadcrumbs and paprika in a third bowl.
2. Dredge the pork chops in the flour bowl, then in the egg milk, and then into the breadcrumbs bowl. Press to coat well. Shake the excess off.
3. Arrange one pork chop in the air fryer each time, then brush with olive oil and butter on all sides.
4. Air fry each pork chop at 400ºF (204ºC) for 4 minutes or until golden brown and crispy. Flip the chop halfway through the cooking time.
5. Transfer the cooked pork chop (schnitzel) to a baking pan in the oven and keep warm over low heat while air frying the remaining pork chops.
6. Meanwhile, combine the chicken stock and cornstarch in a small saucepan and bring to a boil over medium-high heat. Simmer for 2 more minutes.
7. Turn off the heat, then mix in the sour cream, fresh dill, salt, and black pepper.
8. Remove the schnitzels from the air fryer to a plate and baste with sour cream and dill sauce. Squeeze the lemon wedges over and slice to serve.

Tangy Pork Tenderloin

Prep time: 15 minutes | Cook time: 23 minutes | Serves 3 to 4

2 tablespoons brown sugar
2 teaspoons cornstarch
2 teaspoons Dijon mustard
½ cup orange juice
½ teaspoon soy sauce
2 teaspoons grated fresh ginger
¼ cup white wine
Zest of 1 orange
1 pound (454 g) pork tenderloin
Salt and freshly ground black pepper, to taste
Oranges, halved, for garnish
Fresh parsley, for garnish

1. Combine the brown sugar, cornstarch, Dijon mustard, orange juice, soy sauce, ginger, white wine and orange zest in a small saucepan and bring the mixture to a boil on the stovetop. Lower the heat and simmer while you air fry the pork tenderloin or until the sauce has thickened.
2. Season all sides of the pork tenderloin with salt and freshly ground black pepper. Transfer the tenderloin to the air fryer basket.
3. Air fry at 370ºF (188ºC) for 20 to 23 minutes, or until the internal temperature reaches 145ºF (63ºC). Flip the tenderloin over halfway through the cooking process and baste with the sauce.
4. Transfer the tenderloin to a cutting board and let it rest for 5 minutes. Slice the pork at a slight angle and serve immediately with orange halves and fresh parsley.

Stuffed Bell Pepper with Pepperoni

Prep time: 5 minutes | Cook time: 8 minutes | Serves 4

4 bread slices, 1-inch thick
Olive oil, for misting
24 slices pepperoni
1 ounce (28 g) roasted red peppers,
drained and patted dry
1 ounce (28 g) Pepper Jack cheese, cut into 4 slices

1. Spray both sides of bread slices with olive oil.
2. Stand slices upright and cut a deep slit in the top to create a pocket (almost to the bottom crust, but not all the way through).
3. Stuff each bread pocket with 6 slices of pepperoni, a large strip of roasted red pepper, and a slice of cheese.
4. Put bread pockets in air fryer basket, standing up. Air fry at 360ºF (182ºC) for 8 minutes, until filling is heated through and bread is lightly browned.
5. Serve hot.

Cheesy Beef and Pork Meatballs

Prep time: 15 minutes | Cook time: 12 minutes | Serves 4 to 6

1 tablespoon olive oil
1 small onion, finely chopped
1 to 2 cloves garlic, minced
¾ pound (340 g) ground beef
¾ pound (340 g) ground pork
¾ cup bread crumbs
¼ cup grated Parmesan cheese
¼ cup finely chopped fresh parsley
½ teaspoon dried oregano
1½ teaspoons salt
Freshly ground black pepper, to taste
2 eggs, lightly beaten
5 ounces (142 g) sharp or aged provolone cheese, cut into 1-inch cubes

1. Add the oil and cook the onion and garlic until tender, but not browned.
2. Transfer the onion and garlic to a large bowl and add the beef, pork, bread crumbs, Parmesan cheese, parsley, oregano, salt, pepper and eggs. Mix well until all the ingredients are combined. Divide the mixture into 12 evenly sized balls. Make one meatball at a time, by pressing a hole in the meatball mixture with the finger and pushing a piece of provolone cheese into the hole. Mold the meat back into a ball, enclosing the cheese.
3. Working in two batches, transfer six of the meatballs to the air fryer basket and air fry at 380ºF (193ºC) for 12 minutes, shaking the basket and turning the meatballs twice during the cooking process. Repeat with the remaining 6 meatballs. Serve warm.

Cheesy Pork and Pinto Bean Gorditas

Prep time: 20 minutes | Cook time: 21 minutes | Serves 4

1 pound (454 g) lean ground pork
2 tablespoons chili powder
2 tablespoons ground cumin
1 teaspoon dried oregano
2 teaspoons paprika
1 teaspoon garlic powder
½ cup water
1 (15-ounce / 425-g) can pinto beans, drained and rinsed
½ cup taco sauce
Salt and freshly ground black pepper,
to taste
2 cups grated Cheddar cheese
5 (12-inch) flour tortillas
4 (8-inch) crispy corn tortilla shells
4 cups shredded lettuce
1 tomato, diced
⅓ cup sliced black olives
Sour cream, for serving
Tomato salsa, for serving
Cooking spray

1. Spritz the air fryer basket with cooking spray.
2. Put the ground pork in the air fryer basket and air fry at 400ºF (204ºC) for 10 minutes, stirring a few times to gently break up the meat. Combine the chili powder, cumin, oregano, paprika, garlic powder and water in a small bowl. Stir the spice mixture into the browned pork. Stir in the beans and taco sauce and air fry for an additional minute. Transfer the pork mixture to a bowl. Season with salt and freshly ground black pepper.
3. Sprinkle ½ cup of the grated cheese in the center of the flour tortillas, leaving a 2-inch border around the edge free of cheese and filling. Divide the pork mixture among the four tortillas, placing it on top of the cheese. Put a crunchy corn tortilla on top of the pork and top with shredded lettuce, diced tomatoes, and black olives. Cut the remaining flour tortilla into 4 quarters. These quarters of tortilla will serve as the bottom of the gordita. Put one quarter tortilla on top of each gordita and fold the edges of the bottom flour tortilla up over the sides, enclosing the filling. While holding the seams down, brush the bottom of the gordita with olive oil and place the seam side down on the countertop while you finish the remaining three gorditas.
4. Adjust the temperature to 380ºF (193ºC).
5. Air fry one gordita at a time. Transfer the gordita carefully to the air fryer basket, seam side down. Brush or spray the top tortilla with oil and air fry for 5 minutes. Carefully turn the gordita over and air fry for an additional 4 to 5 minutes until both sides are browned. When finished air frying all four gorditas, layer them back into the air fryer for an additional minute to make sure they are all warm before serving with sour cream and salsa.

Spicy Pork Chops with Veggies

Prep time: 10 minutes | Cook time: 15 to 18 minutes | Serves 4

2 carrots, cut into sticks
1 cup mushrooms, sliced
2 garlic cloves, minced
2 tablespoons olive oil
1 pound (454 g) boneless pork chops
1 teaspoon dried oregano
1 teaspoon dried thyme
1 teaspoon cayenne pepper
Salt and ground black pepper, to taste
Cooking spray

1. Spritz the air fryer basket with cooking spray.
2. In a mixing bowl, toss together the carrots, mushrooms, garlic, olive oil and salt until well combined.
3. Add the pork chops to a different bowl and season with oregano, thyme, cayenne pepper, salt and black pepper.
4. Lower the vegetable mixture in the prepared air fryer basket. Place the seasoned pork chops on top. Air fry at 360ºF (182ºC) for 15 to 18 minutes, or until the pork is well browned and the vegetables are tender, flipping the pork and shaking the basket once halfway through.
5. Transfer the pork chops to the serving dishes and let cool for 5 minutes. Serve warm with vegetable on the side.

Bangers and Cauliflower Mash

Prep time: 5 minutes | Cook time: 27 minutes | Serves 6

1 pound (454 g) cauliflower, chopped
6 pork sausages, chopped
½ onion, sliced
3 eggs, beaten
⅓ cup Colby cheese
1 teaspoon cumin powder
½ teaspoon tarragon
½ teaspoon sea salt
½ teaspoon ground black pepper
Cooking spray

1. Spritz a baking pan with cooking spray.
2. In a saucepan over medium heat, boil the cauliflower until tender. Place the boiled cauliflower in a food processor and pulse until puréed. Transfer to a large bowl and combine with remaining ingredients until well blended.
3. Pour the cauliflower and sausage mixture into the baking pan. Bake in the air fryer at 365ºF (185ºC) for 27 minutes, or until lightly browned.
4. Divide the mixture among six serving dishes and serve warm.

Rosemary Lamb Chops

Prep time: 15 minutes | Cook time: 7 minutes | Serves 4

½ small clove garlic
¼ cup packed fresh parsley
¾ cup packed fresh mint
½ teaspoon lemon juice
¼ cup grated Parmesan cheese
⅓ cup shelled pistachios
¼ teaspoon salt
½ cup olive oil
8 lamb chops (1 rack)
2 tablespoons vegetable oil
Salt and freshly ground black pepper, to taste
1 tablespoon dried rosemary, chopped
1 tablespoon dried thyme

1. Make the pesto by combining the garlic, parsley and mint in a food processor and process until finely chopped. Add the lemon juice, Parmesan cheese, pistachios and salt. Process until all the ingredients have turned into a paste. With the processor running, slowly pour the olive oil in. Scrape the sides of the processor with a spatula and process for another 30 seconds.
2. Rub both sides of the lamb chops with vegetable oil and season with salt, pepper, rosemary and thyme, pressing the herbs into the meat gently with the fingers. Transfer the lamb chops to the air fryer basket.
3. Air fry the lamb chops at 400ºF (204ºC) for 5 minutes. Flip the chops over and air fry for an additional 2 minutes.
4. Serve the lamb chops with mint pesto drizzled on top.

Pork Cutlets with Aloha Salsa

Prep time: 20 minutes | Cook time: 8 minutes | Serves 4

2 eggs
2 tablespoons milk
¼ cup flour
¼ cup panko bread crumbs
4 teaspoons sesame seeds
1 pound (454 g)
boneless, thin pork cutlets (⅜- to ½-inch thick)
Lemon pepper and salt, to taste
¼ cup cornstarch
Cooking spray

Aloha Salsa:

1 cup fresh pineapple, chopped in small pieces
¼ cup red onion, finely chopped
¼ cup green or red bell pepper, chopped
½ teaspoon ground
cinnamon
1 teaspoon low-sodium soy sauce
⅛ teaspoon crushed red pepper
⅛ teaspoon ground black pepper

1. In a medium bowl, stir together all ingredients for salsa. Cover and refrigerate while cooking the pork.
2. Beat the eggs and milk in a shallow dish.
3. In another shallow dish, mix the flour, panko, and sesame seeds.
4. Sprinkle pork cutlets with lemon pepper and salt.
5. Dip pork cutlets in cornstarch, egg mixture, and then panko coating. Spray both sides with cooking spray.
6. Air fry the cutlets at 390ºF (199ºC) for 3 minutes. Turn cutlets over, spraying both sides, and continue air frying for 5 minutes or until well done.
7. Serve fried cutlets with salsa on the side.

Cheesy Prosciutto and Potato Salad

Prep time: 10 minutes | Cook time: 7 minutes | Serves 8

Salad:

4 pounds (1.8 kg) potatoes, boiled and cubed	diced
	2 cups shredded Cheddar cheese
15 slices prosciutto,	

Dressing:

15 ounces (425 g) sour cream	1 teaspoon black pepper
2 tablespoons mayonnaise	1 teaspoon dried basil
1 teaspoon salt	

1. Put the potatoes, prosciutto, and Cheddar in a baking dish. Put it in the air fryer and air fry at 350ºF (177ºC) for 7 minutes.
2. In a separate bowl, mix the sour cream, mayonnaise, salt, pepper, and basil using a whisk.
3. Coat the salad with the dressing and serve.

Rosemary Balsamic Ribeye Steaks

Prep time: 10 minutes | Cook time: 15 minutes | Serves 2

¼ cup butter	balsamic vinegar
1 clove garlic, minced	¼ cup rosemary, chopped
Salt and ground black pepper, to taste	2 ribeye steaks
1½ tablespoons	

1. Melt the butter in a skillet over medium heat. Add the garlic and fry until fragrant.
2. Remove the skillet from the heat and add the salt, pepper, and vinegar. Allow it to cool.
3. Add the rosemary, then pour the mixture into a Ziploc bag.
4. Put the ribeye steaks in the bag and shake well, coating the meat well. Refrigerate for an hour, then allow to sit for a further twenty minutes.
5. Air fry the ribeye steaks at 400ºF (204ºC) for 15 minutes.
6. Take care when removing the steaks from the air fryer and plate up.
7. Serve immediately.

Air-Fried Meatballs with Red Chili

Prep time: 5 minutes | Cook time: 15 minutes | Serves 4

1 pound (454 g) ground pork	grated ginger root
2 cloves garlic, finely minced	1 teaspoon turmeric powder
1 cup scallions, finely chopped	1 tablespoon oyster sauce
1½ tablespoons Worcestershire sauce	1 small sliced red chili, for garnish
½ teaspoon freshly	Cooking spray

1. Spritz the air fryer basket with cooking spray.
2. Combine all the ingredients, except for the red chili in a large bowl. Toss to mix well.
3. Shape the mixture into equally sized balls, then arrange them in the air fryer and spritz with cooking spray.
4. Air fry at 350ºF (177ºC) for 15 minutes or until the balls are lightly browned. Flip the balls halfway through.
5. Serve the pork meatballs with red chili on top.

Spicy Smoked Beef

Prep time: 10 minutes | Cook time: 45 minutes | Serves 8

2 pounds (907 g) roast beef, at room temperature	black pepper
	1 teaspoon smoked paprika
2 tablespoons extra-virgin olive oil	Few dashes of liquid smoke
1 teaspoon sea salt flakes	2 jalapeño peppers, thinly sliced
1 teaspoon ground	

1. With kitchen towels, pat the beef dry.
2. Massage the extra-virgin olive oil, salt, black pepper, and paprika into the meat. Cover with liquid smoke.
3. Put the beef in the air fryer and roast at 330ºF (166ºC) for 30 minutes. Flip the roast over and allow to roast for another 15 minutes.
4. When cooked through, serve topped with sliced jalapeños.

Air-Fried Skirt Steak Fajitas

Prep time: 15 minutes | Cook time: 30 minutes | Serves 4

2 tablespoons olive oil	1 pound (454 g) skirt steak
¼ cup lime juice	1 onion, sliced
1 clove garlic, minced	1 teaspoon chili powder
½ teaspoon ground cumin	1 red pepper, sliced
½ teaspoon hot sauce	1 green pepper, sliced
½ teaspoon salt	Salt and freshly ground black pepper, to taste
2 tablespoons chopped fresh cilantro	8 flour tortillas

Toppings:

Shredded lettuce	Sliced black olives
Crumbled Queso Fresco (or grated Cheddar cheese)	Diced tomatoes
	Sour cream
	Guacamole

1. Combine the olive oil, lime juice, garlic, cumin, hot sauce, salt and cilantro in a shallow dish. Add the skirt steak and turn it over several times to coat all sides. Pierce the steak with a needle-style meat tenderizer or paring knife. Marinate the steak in the refrigerator for at least 3 hours, or overnight. When you are ready to cook, remove the steak from the refrigerator and let it sit at room temperature for 30 minutes.
2. Toss the onion slices with the chili powder and a little olive oil and transfer them to the air fryer basket. Air fry for 5 minutes. Add the red and green peppers to the air fryer basket with the onions, season with salt and pepper and air fry at 400ºF (204ºC) for 8 more minutes, until the onions and peppers are soft. Transfer the vegetables to a dish and cover with aluminum foil to keep warm.
3. Put the skirt steak in the air fryer basket and pour the marinade over the top. Air fry at 400ºF (204ºC) for 12 minutes. Flip the steak over and air fry for an additional 5 minutes. Transfer the cooked steak to a cutting board and let the steak rest for a few minutes. If the peppers and onions need to be heated, return them to the air fryer for just 1 to 2 minutes.
4. Thinly slice the steak at an angle, cutting against the grain of the steak. Serve the steak with the onions and peppers, the warm tortillas and the fajita toppings on the side.

Polish Kielbasa Sausage and Pierogies

Prep time: 15 minutes | Cook time: 30 minutes | Serves 3 to 4

1 sweet onion, sliced	sausage, cut into 2-inch chunks
1 teaspoon olive oil	1 (13-ounce / 369-g) package frozen mini pierogies
Salt and freshly ground black pepper, to taste	2 teaspoons vegetable or olive oil
2 tablespoons butter, cut into small cubes	Chopped scallions, for garnish
1 teaspoon sugar	
1 pound (454 g) light Polish kielbasa	

1. Toss the sliced onions with olive oil, salt and pepper and transfer them to the air fryer basket. Dot the onions with pieces of butter and air fry at 400ºF (204ºC) for 2 minutes. Then sprinkle the sugar over the onions and stir. Pour any melted butter from the bottom of the air fryer drawer over the onions. Continue to air fry for another 13 minutes, stirring or shaking the basket every few minutes to air fry the onions evenly.
2. Add the kielbasa chunks to the onions and toss. Air fry for another 5 minutes, shaking the basket halfway through the cooking time. Transfer the kielbasa and onions to a bowl and cover with aluminum foil to keep warm.
3. Toss the frozen pierogies with the vegetable or olive oil and transfer them to the air fryer basket. Air fry at 400ºF (204ºC) for 8 minutes, shaking the basket twice during the cooking time.
4. When the pierogies have finished cooking, return the kielbasa and onions to the air fryer and gently toss with the pierogies. Air fry for 2 more minutes and then transfer everything to a serving platter. Garnish with the chopped scallions and serve hot.

Pork Sausage and Ratatouille

Prep time: 10 minutes | Cook time: 25 minutes | Serves 4

4 pork sausages
Ratatouille:

2 zucchinis, sliced	1 tablespoon balsamic vinegar
1 eggplant, sliced	2 garlic cloves, minced
15 ounces (425 g) tomatoes, sliced	1 red chili, chopped
1 red bell pepper, sliced	2 tablespoons fresh thyme, chopped
1 medium red onion, sliced	2 tablespoons olive oil
1 cup canned butter beans, drained	

1. Place the sausages in the air fryer and air fry at 390ºF (199ºC) for 10 minutes or until the sausage is lightly browned. Flip the sausages halfway through.
2. Meanwhile, make the ratatouille: arrange the vegetable slices on the prepared baking pan alternatively, then add the remaining ingredients on top.
3. Transfer the air fried sausage to a plate, then arrange the baking pan in the air fryer and bake for 15 minutes or until the vegetables are tender.
4. Serve the ratatouille with the sausage on top.

Paprika Pork and Veggies Kabobs

Prep time: 25 minutes | Cook time: 15 minutes | Serves 4

1 pound (454 g) pork tenderloin, cubed	cut into chunks
1 teaspoon smoked paprika	1 zucchini, cut into chunks
Salt and ground black pepper, to taste	1 red onion, sliced
1 green bell pepper,	1 tablespoon oregano
	Cooking spray

Special Equipment:
Small bamboo skewers, soaked in water for 20 minutes to keep them from burning while cooking

1. Spritz the air fryer basket with cooking spray.

2. Add the pork to a bowl and season with the smoked paprika, salt and black pepper. Thread the seasoned pork cubes and vegetables alternately onto the soaked skewers.
3. Arrange the skewers in the prepared air fryer basket and spray with cooking spray. Air fry at 350ºF (177ºC) for 15 minutes, or until the pork is well browned and the vegetables are tender, flipping once halfway through.
4. Transfer the skewers to the serving dishes and sprinkle with oregano. Serve hot.

Cheesy Ham and Pepperoni Rolls

Prep time: 10 minutes | Cook time: 6 minutes | Serves 4

1 teaspoon butter	½ cup pizza sauce
½ medium onion, slivered	8 flour tortillas
½ red or green bell pepper, julienned	8 thin slices deli ham
4 ounces (113 g) fresh white mushrooms, chopped	24 pepperoni slices
	1 cup shredded Mozzarella cheese
	Cooking spray

1. Put butter, onions, bell pepper, and mushrooms in a baking pan. Bake in the air fryer for 3 minutes. Stir and cook 3 to 4 minutes longer until just crisp and tender. Remove pan and set aside.
2. To assemble rolls, spread about 2 teaspoons of pizza sauce on one half of each tortilla. Top with a slice of ham and 3 slices of pepperoni. Divide sautéed vegetables among tortillas and top with cheese.
3. Roll up tortillas, secure with toothpicks if needed, and spray with oil.
4. Put 4 rolls in air fryer basket and air fry at 390ºF (199ºC) for 4 minutes. Turn and air fry 4 minutes, until heated through and lightly browned.
5. Repeat step 4 to air fry remaining pizza rolls.
6. Serve immediately.

Spicy Pork Leg with Candy Onions

Prep time: 10 minutes | Cook time: 52 minutes | Serves 4

2 teaspoons sesame oil
1 teaspoon dried sage, crushed
1 teaspoon cayenne pepper
1 rosemary sprig, chopped
1 thyme sprig, chopped

Sea salt and ground black pepper, to taste
2 pounds (907 g) pork leg roast, scored
½ pound (227 g) candy onions, sliced
4 cloves garlic, finely chopped
2 chili peppers, minced

1. In a mixing bowl, combine the sesame oil, sage, cayenne pepper, rosemary, thyme, salt and black pepper until well mixed. In another bowl, place the pork leg and brush with the seasoning mixture.
2. Place the seasoned pork leg in a baking pan and air fry at 400ºF (204ºC) for 40 minutes, or until lightly browned, flipping halfway through. Add the candy onions, garlic and chili peppers to the pan and air fry for another 12 minutes.
3. Transfer the pork leg to a plate. Let cool for 5 minutes and slice. Spread the juices left in the pan over the pork and serve warm with the candy onions.

Homemade Lahmacun (Turkish Pizza)

Prep time: 20 minutes | Cook time: 10 minutes per batch | Serves 4

4 (6-inch) flour tortillas
For the Meat Topping:
4 ounces (113 g) ground lamb or 85% lean ground beef
¼ cup finely chopped green bell pepper
¼ cup chopped fresh parsley
1 small plum tomato, deseeded and chopped
2 tablespoons chopped yellow onion
1 garlic clove, minced
2 teaspoons tomato

paste
¼ teaspoon sweet paprika
¼ teaspoon ground cumin
⅛ to ¼ teaspoon red pepper flakes
⅛ teaspoon ground allspice
⅛ teaspoon kosher salt
⅛ teaspoon black pepper

For Serving:
¼ cup chopped fresh mint
1 teaspoon extra-

virgin olive oil
1 lemon, cut into wedges

1. Combine all the ingredients for the meat topping in a medium bowl until well mixed.
2. Lay the tortillas on a clean work surface. Spoon the meat mixture on the tortillas and spread all over.
3. Place the tortillas in the air fryer basket. Air fry in batches, one at a time, at 400ºF (204ºC) for 10 minutes, or until the edge of the tortilla is golden and the meat is lightly browned.
4. Transfer them to a serving dish. Top with chopped fresh mint and drizzle with olive oil. Squeeze the lemon wedges on top and serve.

Beef and Squash Lasagna

Prep time: 5 minutes | Cook time: 1 hour 15 minutes | Serves 6

2 large spaghetti squash, cooked (about 2¾ pounds / 1.2 kg)
4 pounds (1.8 kg) ground beef
1 (2½-pound / 1.1-

kg) large jar Marinara sauce
25 slices Mozzarella cheese
30 ounces whole-milk ricotta cheese

1. Slice the spaghetti squash and place it face down inside a baking dish. Fill with water until covered.
2. Bake in the air fryer at 375ºF (191ºC) for 45 minutes until skin is soft.
3. Sear the ground beef in a skillet over medium-high heat for 5 minutes or until browned, then add the marinara sauce and heat until warm. Set aside.
4. Scrape the flesh off the cooked squash to resemble strands of spaghetti.
5. Layer the lasagna in a large greased pan in alternating layers of spaghetti squash, beef sauce, Mozzarella, ricotta. Repeat until all the ingredients have been used.
6. Bake for 30 minutes and serve!

Easy Teriyaki Pork and Mushroom Rolls

Prep time: 10 minutes | Cook time: 8 minutes | Serves 6

4 tablespoons brown sugar	2-inch ginger, chopped
4 tablespoons mirin	6 (4-ounce / 113-g) pork belly slices
4 tablespoons soy sauce	6 ounces (170 g) Enoki mushrooms
1 teaspoon almond flour	

1. Mix the brown sugar, mirin, soy sauce, almond flour, and ginger together until brown sugar dissolves.
2. Take pork belly slices and wrap around a bundle of mushrooms. Brush each roll with teriyaki sauce. Chill for half an hour.
3. Add marinated pork rolls into the air fryer basket.
4. Air fry at 350ºF (177ºC) for 8 minutes. Flip the rolls halfway through.
5. Serve immediately.

Lamb Meatballs with Tomato Sauce

Prep time: 20 minutes | Cook time: 8 minutes | Serves 4

Meatballs:

½ small onion, finely diced	oregano, finely chopped
1 clove garlic, minced	2 tablespoons milk
1 pound (454 g) ground lamb	1 egg yolk
2 tablespoons fresh parsley, finely chopped (plus more for garnish)	Salt and freshly ground black pepper, to taste
2 teaspoons fresh	½ cup crumbled feta cheese, for garnish

Tomato Sauce:

2 tablespoons butter	cinnamon
1 clove garlic, smashed	1 (28-ounce / 794-g) can crushed tomatoes
Pinch crushed red pepper flakes	Salt, to taste
¼ teaspoon ground	Olive oil, for greasing

1. Combine all ingredients for the meatballs in a large bowl and mix just until everything is combined. Shape the mixture into 1½-inch balls or shape the meat between two spoons to make quenelles.

2. Start the quick tomato sauce. Put the butter, garlic and red pepper flakes in a sauté pan and heat over medium heat on the stovetop. Let the garlic sizzle a little, but before the butter browns, add the cinnamon and tomatoes. Bring to a simmer and simmer for 15 minutes. Season with salt.
3. Grease the bottom of the air fryer basket with olive oil and transfer the meatballs to the air fryer basket in one layer, air frying in batches if necessary.
4. Air fry at 400ºF (204ºC) for 8 minutes, giving the basket a shake once during the cooking process to turn the meatballs over.
5. To serve, spoon a pool of the tomato sauce onto plates and add the meatballs. Sprinkle the feta cheese on top and garnish with more fresh parsley.

Crunchy Tonkatsu

Prep time: 5 minutes | Cook time: 10 minutes per batch | Serves 4

⅔ cup all-purpose flour	4 (4-ounce / 113-g) center-cut boneless pork loin chops (about ½ inch thick)
2 large egg whites	
1 cup panko breadcrumbs	Cooking spray

1. Spritz the air fryer basket with cooking spray.
2. Pour the flour in a bowl. Whisk the egg whites in a separate bowl. Spread the breadcrumbs on a large plate.
3. Dredge the pork loin chops in the flour first, press to coat well, then shake the excess off and dunk the chops in the eggs whites, and then roll the chops over the breadcrumbs. Shake the excess off.
4. Arrange the pork chops in batches in a single layer in the air fryer and spritz with cooking spray.
5. Air fry at 375ºF (191ºC) for 10 minutes or until the pork chops are lightly browned and crunchy. Flip the chops halfway through. Repeat with remaining chops.
6. Serve immediately.

Air-Fried Swedish Beef Meatballs

Prep time: 10 minutes | Cook time: 12 minutes | Serves 8

1 pound (454 g) ground beef
1 egg, beaten
2 carrots, shredded
2 bread slices, crumbled
1 small onion, minced

½ teaspoons garlic salt
Pepper and salt, to taste
1 cup tomato sauce
2 cups pasta sauce

1. In a bowl, combine the ground beef, egg, carrots, crumbled bread, onion, garlic salt, pepper and salt.
2. Divide the mixture into equal amounts and shape each one into a small meatball.
3. Put them in the air fryer basket and air fry at 400ºF (204ºC) for 7 minutes.
4. Transfer the meatballs to an oven-safe dish and top with the tomato sauce and pasta sauce.
5. Set the dish into the air fryer basket and allow to air fry at 320ºF (160ºC) for 5 more minutes. Serve hot.

Pork and Veggies Kebabs

Prep time: 1 hour 20 minutes | Cook time: 8 minutes per batch | Serves 4

For the Pork:
1 pound (454 g) pork steak, cut in cubes
1 tablespoon white wine vinegar
3 tablespoons steak sauce
¼ cup soy sauce

1 teaspoon powdered chili
1 teaspoon red chili flakes
2 teaspoons smoked paprika
1 teaspoon garlic salt

For the Vegetable:
1 green squash, deseeded and cut in cubes
1 yellow squash, deseeded and cut in cubes
1 red pepper, cut in cubes

1 green pepper, cut in cubes
Salt and ground black pepper, to taste
Cooking spray

Special Equipment:
4 bamboo skewers, soaked in water for at least 30 minutes

1. Combine the ingredients for the pork in a large bowl. Press the pork to dunk in the marinade. Wrap the bowl in plastic and refrigerate for at least an hour.
2. Remove the pork from the marinade and run the skewers through the pork and vegetables alternatively. Sprinkle with salt and pepper to taste.
3. Arrange the skewers in the air fryer and spritz with cooking spray. Air fry at 370ºF (188ºC) for 8 minutes or until the pork is browned and the vegetables are lightly charred and tender. Flip the skewers halfway through. You may need to work in batches to avoid overcrowding.
4. Serve immediately.

Classic Vietnamese Pork Chops

Prep time: 15 minutes | Cook time: 12 minutes | Serves 2

1 tablespoon chopped shallot
1 tablespoon chopped garlic
1 tablespoon fish sauce
3 tablespoons lemongrass
1 teaspoon soy sauce

1 tablespoon brown sugar
1 tablespoon olive oil
1 teaspoon ground black pepper
2 pork chops

1. Combine shallot, garlic, fish sauce, lemongrass, soy sauce, brown sugar, olive oil, and pepper in a bowl. Stir to mix well.
2. Put the pork chops in the bowl. Toss to coat well. Place the bowl in the refrigerator to marinate for 2 hours.
3. Remove the pork chops from the bowl and discard the marinade. Transfer the chops into the air fryer.
4. Air fry at 400ºF (204ºC) for 12 minutes or until lightly browned. Flip the pork chops halfway through the cooking time.
5. Remove the pork chops from the basket and serve hot.

Air-Fried Lamb Burger

Prep time: 15 minutes | Cook time: 16 minutes | Serves 3 to 4

2 teaspoons olive oil
⅓ onion, finely chopped
1 clove garlic, minced
1 pound (454 g) ground lamb
2 tablespoons fresh parsley, finely chopped
1½ teaspoons fresh oregano, finely chopped

½ cup black olives, finely chopped
⅓ cup crumbled feta cheese
½ teaspoon salt
Freshly ground black pepper, to taste
4 thick pita breads

1. Add the olive oil and cook the onion until tender, but not browned about 4 to 5 minutes. Add the garlic and cook for another minute. Transfer the onion and garlic to a mixing bowl and add the ground lamb, parsley, oregano, olives, feta cheese, salt and pepper. Gently mix the ingredients together.
2. Divide the mixture into 3 or 4 equal portions and then form the hamburgers, being careful not to over-handle the meat. One good way to do this is to throw the meat back and forth between the hands like a baseball, packing the meat each time you catch it. Flatten the balls into patties, making an indentation in the center of each patty. Flatten the sides of the patties as well to make it easier to fit them into the air fryer basket.
3. If you don't have room for all four burgers, air fry two or three burgers at a time at 370ºF (188ºC) for 8 minutes. Flip the burgers over and air fry for another 8 minutes. If you cooked the burgers in batches, return the first batch of burgers to the air fryer for the last two minutes of cooking to re-heat. This should give you a medium-well burger. If you'd prefer a medium-rare burger, shorten the cooking time to about 13 minutes. Remove the burgers to a resting plate and let the burgers rest for a few minutes before dressing and serving.
4. While the burgers are resting, bake the pita breads in the air fryer for 2 minutes. Tuck the burgers into the toasted pita breads, or wrap the pitas around the burgers and serve with a tzatziki sauce or some mayonnaise.

Chapter 11 Fish and Seafood

Air-Fried Shrimp Spring Rolls

Prep time: 10 minutes | Cook time: 17 to 22 minutes | Serves 4

2 teaspoons minced garlic
2 cups finely sliced cabbage
1 cup matchstick cut carrots
2 (4-ounce / 113-g) cans tiny shrimp, drained
4 teaspoons soy sauce
Salt and freshly ground black pepper, to taste
16 square spring roll wrappers
Cooking spray

1. Spray the air fryer basket lightly with cooking spray. Spray a medium sauté pan with cooking spray.
2. Add the garlic to the sauté pan and cook over medium heat until fragrant, 30 to 45 seconds. Add the cabbage and carrots and sauté until the vegetables are slightly tender, about 5 minutes.
3. Add the shrimp and soy sauce and season with salt and pepper, then stir to combine. Sauté until the moisture has evaporated, 2 more minutes. Set aside to cool.
4. Place a spring roll wrapper on a work surface so it looks like a diamond. Place 1 tablespoon of the shrimp mixture on the lower end of the wrapper.
5. Roll the wrapper away from you halfway, then fold in the right and left sides, like an envelope. Continue to roll to the very end, using a little water to seal the edge. Repeat with the remaining wrappers and filling.
6. Place the spring rolls in the air fryer basket in a single layer, leaving room between each roll. Lightly spray with cooking spray. You may need to cook them in batches.
7. Air fry at 370ºF (188ºC) for 5 minutes. Turn the rolls over, lightly spray with cooking spray, and air fry until heated through and the rolls start to brown, 5 to 10 more minutes. Cool for 5 minutes before serving.

Crab Cakes with Remoulade

Prep time: 15 minutes | Cook time: 10 minutes | Serves 4

Remoulade:
¾ cup mayonnaise
2 teaspoons Dijon mustard
1½ teaspoons yellow mustard
1 teaspoon vinegar
¼ teaspoon hot sauce
1 teaspoon tiny capers, drained and chopped
¼ teaspoon salt
⅛ teaspoon ground black pepper

Crab Cakes:
1 cup bread crumbs, divided
2 tablespoons mayonnaise
1 scallion, finely chopped
6 ounces (170 g) crab meat
2 tablespoons pasteurized egg
product (liquid eggs in a carton)
2 teaspoons lemon juice
½ teaspoon red pepper flakes
½ teaspoon Old Bay seasoning
Cooking spray

1. In a small bowl, whisk to combine the mayonnaise, Dijon mustard, yellow mustard, vinegar, hot sauce, capers, salt, and pepper.
2. Refrigerate for at least 1 hour before serving.
3. Place a parchment liner in the air fryer basket.
4. In a large bowl, mix to combine ½ cup of bread crumbs with the mayonnaise and scallion. Set the other ½ cup of bread crumbs aside in a small bowl.
5. Add the crab meat, egg product, lemon juice, red pepper flakes, and Old Bay seasoning to the large bowl, and stir to combine.
6. Divide the crab mixture into 4 portions, and form into patties.
7. Dredge each patty in the remaining bread crumbs to coat.
8. Place the prepared patties on the liner in the air fryer in a single layer.
9. Spray lightly with cooking spray and air fry at 400ºF (204ºC) for 5 minutes. Flip the crab cakes over, air fry for another 5 minutes, until golden, and serve.

Blackened Salmon with Salsa

Prep time: 10 minutes | Cook time: 5 to 7 minutes | Serves 4

Salmon:

1 tablespoon sweet paprika	thyme
½ teaspoon cayenne pepper	¾ teaspoon kosher salt
1 teaspoon garlic powder	⅛ teaspoon freshly ground black pepper
1 teaspoon dried oregano	Cooking spray
1 teaspoon dried	4 (6 ounces / 170 g each) wild salmon fillets

Cucumber-Avocado Salsa:

2 tablespoons chopped red onion	teaspoon kosher salt
1½ tablespoons fresh lemon juice	Freshly ground black pepper, to taste
1 teaspoon extra-virgin olive oil	4 Persian cucumbers, diced
¼ teaspoon plus ⅛	6 ounces (170 g) Hass avocado, diced

1. For the salmon: In a small bowl, combine the paprika, cayenne, garlic powder, oregano, thyme, salt, and black pepper. Spray both sides of the fish with oil and rub all over. Coat the fish all over with the spices.
2. For the cucumber-avocado salsa: In a medium bowl, combine the red onion, lemon juice, olive oil, salt, and pepper. Let stand for 5 minutes, then add the cucumbers and avocado.
3. Working in batches, arrange the salmon fillets skin side down in the air fryer basket. Air fry at 400°F (204°C) for 5 to 7 minutes, or until the fish flakes easily with a fork, depending on the thickness of the fish.
4. Serve topped with the salsa.

Breaded Calamari Rings

Prep time: 5 minutes | Cook time: 12 minutes | Serves 4

2 large eggs	1 pound (454 g) calamari rings
2 garlic cloves, minced	Cooking spray
½ cup cornstarch	1 lemon, sliced
1 cup bread crumbs	

1. In a small bowl, whisk the eggs with minced garlic. Place the cornstarch and bread crumbs into separate shallow dishes.
2. Dredge the calamari rings in the cornstarch, then dip in the egg mixture, shaking off any excess, finally roll them in the bread crumbs to coat well. Let the calamari rings sit for 10 minutes in the refrigerator.
3. Spritz the air fryer basket with cooking spray.
4. Put the calamari rings in the basket and air fry at 390°F (199°C) for 12 minutes until cooked through. Shake the basket halfway through the cooking time.
5. Serve the calamari rings with the lemon slices sprinkled on top.

Scallops with Belgian Endive

Prep time: 10 minutes | Cook time: 12 minutes | Serves 2

⅓ cup shallots, chopped	balsamic vinegar
1½ tablespoons olive oil	½ teaspoon ginger, grated
1½ tablespoons coconut aminos	1 clove garlic, chopped
1 tablespoon Mediterranean seasoning mix	1 pound (454 g) scallops, cleaned
½ tablespoon	Cooking spray
	Belgian endive, for garnish

1. Place all the ingredients except the scallops and Belgian endive in a small skillet over medium heat and stir to combine. Let this mixture simmer for about 2 minutes.
2. Remove the mixture from the skillet to a large bowl and set aside to cool.
3. Add the scallops, coating them all over, then transfer to the refrigerator to marinate for at least 2 hours.
4. Arrange the scallops in the air fryer basket in a single layer and spray with cooking spray.
5. Air fry at 345°F (174°C) for 10 minutes, flipping the scallops halfway through, or until the scallops are tender and opaque.
6. Serve garnished with the Belgian endive.

Air-Fried Bacon-Wrapped Scallops

Prep time: 5 minutes | Cook time: 10 minutes | Serves 4

8 slices bacon, cut in half
16 sea scallops, patted dry
Cooking spray
Salt and freshly
ground black pepper, to taste
16 toothpicks, soaked in water for at least 30 minutes

1. On a clean work surface, wrap half of a slice of bacon around each scallop and secure with a toothpick.
2. Lay the bacon-wrapped scallops in the air fryer basket in a single layer. You may need to work in batches to avoid overcrowding.
3. Spritz the scallops with cooking spray and sprinkle the salt and pepper to season.
4. Air fry at 370ºF (188ºC) for 10 minutes, flipping the scallops halfway through, or until the bacon is cooked through and the scallops are firm.
5. Remove the scallops from the basket to a plate and repeat with the remaining scallops. Serve warm.

Fast Baked Flounder Fillets

Prep time: 8 minutes | Cook time: 12 minutes | Serves 2

2 flounder fillets, patted dry
1 egg
½ teaspoon Worcestershire sauce
¼ cup almond flour
¼ cup coconut flour
½ teaspoon coarse sea salt
½ teaspoon lemon pepper
¼ teaspoon chili powder
Cooking spray

1. Spritz the air fryer basket with cooking spray.
2. In a shallow bowl, beat together the egg with Worcestershire sauce until well incorporated.
3. In another bowl, thoroughly combine the almond flour, coconut flour, sea salt, lemon pepper, and chili powder.
4. Dredge the fillets in the egg mixture, shaking off any excess, then roll in the flour mixture to coat well.

5. Place the fillets in the air fryer basket and bake at 390ºF (199ºC) for 7 minutes. Flip the fillets and spray with cooking spray. Continue cooking for 5 minutes, or until the fish is flaky.
6. Serve warm.

Golden Crab and Fish Patties

Prep time: 20 minutes | Cook time: 10 to 12 minutes | Serves 4

8 ounces (227 g) imitation crab meat
4 ounces (113 g) leftover cooked fish (such as cod, pollock, or haddock)
2 tablespoons minced celery
2 tablespoons minced green onion
2 tablespoons light mayonnaise
1 tablespoon plus 2 teaspoons Worcestershire sauce
¾ cup crushed saltine cracker crumbs
2 teaspoons dried parsley flakes
1 teaspoon prepared yellow mustard
½ teaspoon garlic powder
½ teaspoon dried dill weed, crushed
½ teaspoon Old Bay seasoning
½ cup panko bread crumbs
Cooking spray

1. Pulse the crab meat and fish in a food processor until finely chopped.
2. Transfer the meat mixture to a large bowl, along with the celery, green onion, mayo, Worcestershire sauce, cracker crumbs, parsley flakes, mustard, garlic powder, dill weed, and Old Bay seasoning. Stir to mix well.
3. Scoop out the meat mixture and form into 8 equal-sized patties with your hands.
4. Place the panko bread crumbs on a plate. Roll the patties in the bread crumbs until they are evenly coated on both sides. Spritz the patties with cooking spray.
5. Put the patties in the air fryer basket and bake at 390ºF (199ºC) for 10 to 12 minutes, flipping them halfway through, or until they are golden brown and cooked through.
6. Divide the patties among four plates and serve.

Simple Blackened Shrimp Tacos

Prep time: 10 minutes | Cook time: 10 to 15 minutes | Serves 4

12 ounces (340 g) medium shrimp, deveined, with tails off	8 corn tortillas, warmed
1 teaspoon olive oil	1 (14-ounce / 397-g) bag coleslaw mix
1 to 2 teaspoons Blackened seasoning	2 limes, cut in half
	Cooking spray

1. Spray the air fryer basket lightly with cooking spray.
2. Dry the shrimp with a paper towel to remove excess water.
3. In a medium bowl, toss the shrimp with olive oil and Blackened seasoning.
4. Place the shrimp in the air fryer basket and air fry at 400°F (204°C) for 5 minutes. Shake the basket, lightly spray with cooking spray, and cook until the shrimp are cooked through and starting to brown, 5 to 10 more minutes.
5. Fill each tortilla with the coleslaw mix and top with the blackened shrimp. Squeeze fresh lime juice over top and serve.

Air-Fried Chili Prawns

Prep time: 10 minutes | Cook time: 8 minutes | Serves 2

8 prawns, cleaned	powder
Salt and black pepper, to taste	½ teaspoon ground cumin
½ teaspoon ground cayenne pepper	½ teaspoon red chili flakes
½ teaspoon garlic	Cooking spray

1. Spritz the air fryer basket with cooking spray.
2. Toss the remaining ingredients in a large bowl until the prawns are well coated.
3. Spread the coated prawns evenly in the basket and spray them with cooking spray.
4. Air fry at 340°F (171°C) for 8 minutes, flipping the prawns halfway through, or until the prawns are pink.
5. Remove the prawns from the basket to a plate.

Lemony Tilapia Fillet

Prep time: 5 minutes | Cook time: 10 to 15 minutes | Serves 4

1 tablespoon lemon juice	½ teaspoon chili powder
1 tablespoon olive oil	4 (6-ounce / 170-g) tilapia fillets
1 teaspoon minced garlic	

1. Line the air fryer basket with parchment paper.
2. In a large, shallow bowl, mix together the lemon juice, olive oil, garlic, and chili powder to make a marinade. Place the tilapia fillets in the bowl and coat evenly.
3. Place the fillets in the basket in a single layer, leaving space between each fillet. You may need to cook in more than one batch.
4. Air fry at 380°F (193°C) until the fish is cooked and flakes easily with a fork, 10 to 15 minutes.
5. Serve hot.

Cheesy Balsamic Shrimp

Prep time: 15 minutes | Cook time: 7 to 8 minutes | Serves 2

1 pound (454 g) shrimp, deveined	taste
1½ tablespoons olive oil	1 teaspoon Dijon mustard
1½ tablespoons balsamic vinegar	½ teaspoon smoked cayenne pepper
1 tablespoon coconut aminos	½ teaspoon garlic powder
½ tablespoon fresh parsley, roughly chopped	Salt and ground black peppercorns, to taste
Sea salt flakes, to	1 cup shredded goat cheese

1. Except for the cheese, stir together all the ingredients in a large bowl until the shrimp are evenly coated.
2. Arrange the shrimp in the air fryer basket and air fry at 385°F (196°C) for 7 to 8 minutes, shaking the basket halfway through, or until the shrimp are pink and cooked through.
3. Serve the shrimp with the shredded goat cheese sprinkled on top.

Air-Fried Breaded Scallops

Prep time: 5 minutes | Cook time: 6 to 8 minutes | Serves 4

1 egg
3 tablespoons flour
1 cup bread crumbs
1 pound (454 g) fresh scallops
2 tablespoons olive oil
Salt and black pepper, to taste

1. In a bowl, lightly beat the egg. Place the flour and bread crumbs into separate shallow dishes.
2. Dredge the scallops in the flour and shake off any excess. Dip the flour-coated scallops in the beaten egg and roll in the bread crumbs.
3. Brush the scallops generously with olive oil and season with salt and pepper, to taste.
4. Arrange the scallops in the air fryer basket and air fry at 360ºF (182ºC) for 6 to 8 minutes, or until the scallops are firm and reach an internal temperature of just 145ºF (63ºC) on a meat thermometer. Shake the basket halfway through the cooking time.
5. Let the scallops cool for 5 minutes and serve.

Crab Cake Sandwich with Cajun Mayo

Prep time: 15 minutes | Cook time: 10 minutes | Serves 4

Crab Cakes:
½ cup panko bread crumbs
1 large egg, beaten
1 large egg white
1 tablespoon mayonnaise
1 teaspoon Dijon mustard
¼ cup minced fresh parsley
1 tablespoon fresh lemon juice
½ teaspoon Old Bay seasoning
⅛ teaspoon sweet paprika
⅛ teaspoon kosher salt
Freshly ground black pepper, to taste
10 ounces (283 g) lump crab meat
Cooking spray

Cajun Mayo:
¼ cup mayonnaise
1 tablespoon minced dill pickle
1 teaspoon fresh lemon juice
¾ teaspoon Cajun seasoning

For Serving:
4 Boston lettuce leaves
4 whole wheat potato buns or gluten-free buns

1. For the crab cakes: In a large bowl, combine the panko, whole egg, egg white, mayonnaise, mustard, parsley, lemon juice, Old Bay, paprika, salt, and pepper to taste and mix well. Fold in the crab meat, being careful not to over mix. Gently shape into 4 round patties, about ½ cup each, ¾ inch thick. Spray both sides with oil.
2. Working in batches, place the crab cakes in the air fryer basket. Air fry at 370ºF (188ºC) for about 10 minutes, flipping halfway, until the edges are golden.
3. Meanwhile, for the Cajun mayo: In a small bowl, combine the mayonnaise, pickle, lemon juice, and Cajun seasoning.
4. To serve: Place a lettuce leaf on each bun bottom and top with a crab cake and a generous tablespoon of Cajun mayonnaise. Add the bun top and serve.

Cajun Tilapia Fillets Tacos

Prep time: 5 minutes | Cook time: 10 to 15 minutes | Serves 6

2 teaspoons avocado oil
1 tablespoon Cajun seasoning
4 tilapia fillets
1 (14-ounce / 397-g) package coleslaw mix
12 corn tortillas
2 limes, cut into wedges

1. Line the air fryer basket with parchment paper.
2. In a medium, shallow bowl, mix the avocado oil and the Cajun seasoning to make a marinade. Add the tilapia fillets and coat evenly.
3. Place the fillets in the basket in a single layer, leaving room between each fillet. You may need to cook in batches.
4. Air fry at 380ºF (193ºC) until the fish is cooked and easily flakes with a fork, 10 to 15 minutes.
5. Assemble the tacos by placing some of the coleslaw mix in each tortilla. Add ⅓ of a tilapia fillet to each tortilla. Squeeze some lime juice over the top of each taco and serve.

Air-Fried Shrimp Patties

Prep time: 15 minutes | Cook time: 10 to 12 minutes | Serves 4

½ pound (227 g) raw shrimp, shelled, deveined, and chopped finely
2 cups cooked sushi rice
¼ cup chopped red bell pepper
¼ cup chopped celery
¼ cup chopped green onion
2 teaspoons Worcestershire sauce
½ teaspoon salt
½ teaspoon garlic powder
½ teaspoon Old Bay seasoning
½ cup plain bread crumbs
Cooking spray

1. Put all the ingredients except the bread crumbs and oil in a large bowl and stir to incorporate.
2. Scoop out the shrimp mixture and shape into 8 equal-sized patties with your hands, no more than ½-inch thick. Roll the patties in the bread crumbs on a plate and spray both sides with cooking spray.
3. Place the patties in the air fryer basket. You may need to work in batches to avoid overcrowding.
4. Air fry at 390ºF (199ºC) for 10 to 12 minutes, flipping the patties halfway through, or until the outside is crispy brown.
5. Divide the patties among four plates and serve warm.

Breaded Salmon Burgers

Prep time: 10 minutes | Cook time: 10 to 15 minutes | Serves 4

4 (5-ounce / 142-g) cans pink salmon in water, any skin and bones removed, drained
2 eggs, beaten
1 cup whole-wheat bread crumbs
4 tablespoons light mayonnaise
2 teaspoons Cajun seasoning
2 teaspoons dry mustard
4 whole-wheat buns
Cooking spray

1. In a medium bowl, mix the salmon, egg, bread crumbs, mayonnaise, Cajun seasoning, and dry mustard. Cover with plastic wrap and refrigerate for 30 minutes.
2. Spray the air fryer basket lightly with cooking spray.
3. Shape the mixture into four ½-inch-thick patties about the same size as the buns.
4. Place the salmon patties in the air fryer basket in a single layer and lightly spray the tops with cooking spray. You may need to cook them in batches.
5. Air fry at 360ºF (182ºC) for 6 to 8 minutes. Turn the patties over and lightly spray with cooking spray. Air fry until crispy on the outside, 4 to 7 more minutes.
6. Serve on whole-wheat buns.

Crispy Old Bay Shrimp

Prep time: 15 minutes | Cook time: 10 to 15 minutes | Serves 4

2 teaspoons Old Bay seasoning, divided
½ teaspoon garlic powder
½ teaspoon onion powder
1 pound (454 g) large shrimp, deveined, with tails on
2 large eggs
½ cup whole-wheat panko bread crumbs
Cooking spray

1. Spray the air fryer basket lightly with cooking spray.
2. In a medium bowl, mix together 1 teaspoon of Old Bay seasoning, garlic powder, and onion powder. Add the shrimp and toss with the seasoning mix to lightly coat.
3. In a separate small bowl, whisk the eggs with 1 teaspoon water.
4. In a shallow bowl, mix together the remaining 1 teaspoon Old Bay seasoning and the panko bread crumbs.
5. Dip each shrimp in the egg mixture and dredge in the bread crumb mixture to evenly coat.
6. Place the shrimp in the air fryer basket, in a single layer. Lightly spray the shrimp with cooking spray. You many need to cook the shrimp in batches.
7. Air fry at 380ºF (193ºC) for 10 to 15 minutes, or until the shrimp is cooked through and crispy, shaking the basket at 5-minute intervals to redistribute and evenly cook.
8. Serve immediately.

Crab Meat and Ratatouille

Prep time: 15 minutes | Cook time: 11 to 14 minutes | Serves 4

1½ cups peeled and cubed eggplant
2 large tomatoes, chopped
1 red bell pepper, chopped
1 onion, chopped
1 tablespoon olive oil
½ teaspoon dried
basil
½ teaspoon dried thyme
Pinch salt
Freshly ground black pepper, to taste
1½ cups cooked crab meat

1. In a metal bowl, stir together the eggplant, tomatoes, bell pepper, onion, olive oil, basil and thyme. Season with salt and pepper.
2. Place the bowl in the air fryer and roast at 400ºF (204ºC) for 9 minutes.
3. Remove the bowl from the air fryer. Add the crab meat and stir well and roast for another 2 to 5 minutes, or until the vegetables are softened and the ratatouille is bubbling.
4. Serve warm.

Air-Fried Scallops

Prep time: 5 minutes | Cook time: 4 minutes | Serves 2

12 medium sea scallops, rinsed and patted dry
1 teaspoon fine sea salt
¾ teaspoon ground
black pepper, plus more for garnish
Fresh thyme leaves, for garnish (optional)
Avocado oil spray

1. Coat the air fryer basket with avocado oil spray.
2. Place the scallops in a medium bowl and spritz with avocado oil spray. Sprinkle the salt and pepper to season.
3. Transfer the seasoned scallops to the air fryer basket, spacing them apart. You may need to work in batches to avoid overcrowding.
4. Air fry at 390ºF (199ºC) for 4 minutes, flipping the scallops halfway through, or until the scallops are firm and reach an internal temperature of just 145ºF (63ºC) on a meat thermometer.

5. Remove from the basket and repeat with the remaining scallops.
6. Sprinkle the pepper and thyme leaves on top for garnish, if desired. Serve immediately.

Shrimp Tacos with Spicy Mayo

Prep time: 10 minutes | Cook time: 6 minutes | Serves 4

Spicy Mayo:
3 tablespoons mayonnaise
1 tablespoon Louisiana-style hot pepper sauce
Cilantro-Lime Slaw:
2 cups shredded green cabbage
½ small red onion,
Shrimp:
1 large egg, beaten
1 cup crushed tortilla chips
24 jumbo shrimp (about 1 pound / 454 g), peeled and
thinly sliced
1 small jalapeño, thinly sliced
2 tablespoons chopped fresh cilantro
Juice of 1 lime
¼ teaspoon kosher salt

deveined
⅛ teaspoon kosher salt
Cooking spray
8 corn tortillas, for serving

1. For the spicy mayo: In a small bowl, mix the mayonnaise and hot pepper sauce.
2. For the cilantro-lime slaw: In a large bowl, toss together the cabbage, onion, jalapeño, cilantro, lime juice, and salt to combine. Cover and refrigerate to chill.
3. For the shrimp: Place the egg in a shallow bowl and the crushed tortilla chips in another. Season the shrimp with the salt. Dip the shrimp in the egg, then in the crumbs, pressing gently to adhere. Place on a work surface and spray both sides with oil.
4. Working in batches, arrange a single layer of the shrimp in the air fryer basket. Air fry at 360ºF (182ºC) for 6 minutes, flipping halfway, until golden and cooked through in the center.
5. To serve, place 2 tortillas on each plate and top each with 3 shrimp. Top each taco with ¼ cup slaw, then drizzle with spicy mayo.

Breaded Cod Cakes with Salad Greens

Prep time: 15 minutes | Cook time: 12 minutes | Serves 4

1 pound (454 g) cod fillets, cut into chunks
⅓ cup packed fresh basil leaves
3 cloves garlic, crushed
½ teaspoon smoked paprika
¼ teaspoon salt
¼ teaspoon pepper
1 large egg, beaten
1 cup panko bread crumbs
Cooking spray
Salad greens, for serving

1. In a food processor, pulse cod, basil, garlic, smoked paprika, salt, and pepper until cod is finely chopped, stirring occasionally. Form into 8 patties, about 2 inches in diameter. Dip each first into the egg, then into the panko, patting to adhere. Spray with oil on one side.
2. Working in batches, place half the cakes in the basket, oil-side down; spray with oil. Air fry at 400ºF (204ºC) for 12 minutes, until golden brown and cooked through.
3. Serve cod cakes with salad greens.

Golden Shrimp Empanadas

Prep time: 10 minutes | Cook time: 8 minutes | Serves 5

½ pound (227g) raw shrimp, peeled, deveined and chopped
¼ cup chopped red onion
1 scallion, chopped
2 garlic cloves, minced
2 tablespoons minced red bell pepper
2 tablespoons chopped fresh cilantro
½ tablespoon fresh lime juice
¼ teaspoon sweet paprika
⅛ teaspoon kosher salt
⅛ teaspoon crushed red pepper flakes (optional)
1 large egg, beaten
10 frozen Goya Empanada Discos, thawed
Cooking spray

1. In a medium bowl, combine the shrimp, red onion, scallion, garlic, bell pepper, cilantro, lime juice, paprika, salt, and pepper flakes (if using).
2. In a small bowl, beat the egg with 1 teaspoon water until smooth.

3. Place an empanada disc on a work surface and put 2 tablespoons of the shrimp mixture in the center. Brush the outer edges of the disc with the egg wash. Fold the disc over and gently press the edges to seal. Use a fork and press around the edges to crimp and seal completely. Brush the tops of the empanadas with the egg wash.
4. Spray the bottom of the air fryer basket with cooking spray to prevent sticking. Working in batches, arrange a single layer of the empanadas in the air fryer basket and air fry at 380ºF (193ºC) for about 8 minutes, flipping halfway, until golden brown and crispy.
5. Serve hot.

Crispy Cajun Catfish Fillet

Prep time: 5 minutes | Cook time: 16 to 18 minutes | Serves 4

1 cup buttermilk
5 catfish fillets, cut into 1½-inch strips
Cooking spray
1 cup cornmeal
1 tablespoon Creole, Cajun, or Old Bay seasoning

1. Pour the buttermilk into a shallow baking dish. Place the catfish in the dish and refrigerate for at least 1 hour to help remove any fishy taste.
2. Spray the air fryer basket lightly with cooking spray.
3. In a shallow bowl, combine cornmeal and Creole seasoning.
4. Shake any excess buttermilk off the catfish. Place each strip in the cornmeal mixture and coat completely. Press the cornmeal into the catfish gently to help it stick.
5. Place the strips in the air fryer basket in a single layer. Lightly spray the catfish with cooking spray. You may need to cook the catfish in more than one batch.
6. Air fry at 400ºF (204ºC) for 8 minutes. Turn the catfish strips over and lightly spray with cooking spray. Air fry until golden brown and crispy, 8 to 10 more minutes.
7. Serve warm.

Air-Fried Coconut Chili Fish

Prep time: 10 minutes | Cook time: 20 to 22 minutes | Serves 4

2 tablespoons sunflower oil, divided
1 pound (454 g) fish, chopped
1 ripe tomato, pureéd
2 red chilies, chopped
1 shallot, minced
1 garlic clove, minced
1 cup coconut milk
1 tablespoon coriander powder
1 teaspoon red curry paste
½ teaspoon fenugreek seeds
Salt and white pepper, to taste

1. Coat the air fryer basket with 1 tablespoon of sunflower oil.
2. Place the fish in the basket and air fry at 380ºF (193ºC) for 10 minutes. Flip the fish halfway through the cooking time.
3. When done, transfer the cooked fish to a baking pan greased with the remaining 1 tablespoon of sunflower oil. Stir in the remaining ingredients and return to the air fryer.
4. Reduce the temperature to 350ºF (177ºC) and air fry for another 10 to 12 minutes until heated through.
5. Cool for 5 to 8 minutes before serving.

Old Bay Crab Cakes

Prep time: 5 minutes | Cook time: 10 minutes | Serves 4

8 ounces (227 g) jumbo lump crab meat
1 egg, beaten
Juice of ½ lemon
1/3 cup bread crumbs
¼ cup diced green bell pepper
¼ cup diced red bell pepper
¼ cup mayonnaise
1 tablespoon Old Bay seasoning
1 teaspoon flour
Cooking spray

1. Make the crab cakes: Place all the ingredients except the flour and oil in a large bowl and stir until well incorporated.
2. Divide the crab mixture into four equal portions and shape each portion into a patty with your hands. Top each patty with a sprinkle of ¼ teaspoon of flour.
3. Arrange the crab cakes in the air fryer basket and spritz them with cooking spray.
4. Air fry at 375ºF (190ºC) for 10 minutes, flipping the crab cakes halfway through, or until they are cooked through.
5. Divide the crab cakes among four plates and serve.

Cheesy Hake Fillet with Garlic Sauce

Prep time: 5 minutes | Cook time: 10 minutes | Serves 3

Fish:
6 tablespoons mayonnaise
1 tablespoon fresh lime juice
1 teaspoon Dijon mustard
1 cup grated Parmesan cheese
Salt, to taste
¼ teaspoon ground black pepper, or more to taste
3 hake fillets, patted dry
Nonstick cooking spray
Garlic Sauce:
¼ cup plain Greek yogurt
2 tablespoons olive oil
2 cloves garlic, minced
½ teaspoon minced tarragon leaves

1. Mix the mayo, lime juice, and mustard in a shallow bowl and whisk to combine. In another shallow bowl, stir together the grated Parmesan cheese, salt, and pepper.
2. Dredge each fillet in the mayo mixture, then roll them in the cheese mixture until they are evenly coated on both sides.
3. Spray the air fryer basket with nonstick cooking spray. Arrange the fillets in the basket and air fry at 395ºF (202ºC) for 10 minutes, or until the fish flakes easily with a fork. Flip the fillets halfway through the cooking time.
4. Meanwhile, in a small bowl, whisk all the ingredients for the sauce until well incorporated.
5. Serve the fish warm alongside the sauce.

Fast Marinated Salmon Fillets

Prep time: 10 minutes | Cook time: 15 to 20 minutes | Serves 4

¼ cup soy sauce
¼ cup rice wine vinegar
1 tablespoon brown sugar
1 tablespoon olive oil
1 teaspoon mustard powder
1 teaspoon ground

ginger
½ teaspoon freshly ground black pepper
½ teaspoon minced garlic
4 (6-ounce / 170-g) salmon fillets, skin-on
Cooking spray

1. In a small bowl, combine the soy sauce, rice wine vinegar, brown sugar, olive oil, mustard powder, ginger, black pepper, and garlic to make a marinade.
2. Place the fillets in a shallow baking dish and pour the marinade over them. Cover the baking dish and marinate for at least 1 hour in the refrigerator, turning the fillets occasionally to keep them coated in the marinade.
3. Spray the air fryer basket lightly with cooking spray.
4. Shake off as much marinade as possible from the fillets and place them, skin-side down, in the air fryer basket in a single layer. You may need to cook the fillets in batches.
5. Air fry at 370°F (188°C) for 15 to 20 minutes for well done. The minimum internal temperature should be 145°F (63°C) at the thickest part of the fillets.
6. Serve hot.

Air-Fried Garlicky Scallops

Prep time: 10 minutes | Cook time: 10 to 15 minutes | Serves 4

2 teaspoons olive oil
1 packet dry zesty Italian dressing mix
1 teaspoon minced garlic

16 ounces (454 g) small scallops, patted dry
Cooking spray

1. Spray the air fryer basket lightly with cooking spray.
2. In a large zip-top plastic bag, combine the olive oil, Italian dressing mix, and garlic.

3. Add the scallops, seal the zip-top bag, and coat the scallops in the seasoning mixture.
4. Place the scallops in the air fryer basket and lightly spray with cooking spray.
5. Air fry at 400°F (204°C) for 5 minutes, shake the basket, and air fry for 5 to 10 more minutes, or until the scallops reach an internal temperature of 120°F (49°C).
6. Serve immediately.

Air-Fried Shrimp and Tomato Kebabs

Prep time: 15 minutes | Cook time: 5 minutes | Serves 4

1½ pounds (680 g) jumbo shrimp, cleaned, shelled and deveined
1 pound (454 g) cherry tomatoes
2 tablespoons butter, melted
1 tablespoons Sriracha sauce
Sea salt and ground

black pepper, to taste
1 teaspoon dried parsley flakes
½ teaspoon dried basil
½ teaspoon dried oregano
½ teaspoon mustard seeds
½ teaspoon marjoram

Special Equipment:
4 to 6 wooden skewers, soaked in water for 30 minutes

1. Put all the ingredients in a large bowl and toss to coat well.
2. Make the kebabs: Thread, alternating jumbo shrimp and cherry tomatoes, onto the wooden skewers that fit into the air fryer.
3. Arrange the kebabs in the air fryer basket. You may need to cook in batches depending on the size of your air fryer basket.
4. Air fry at 400°F (204°C) for 5 minutes, or until the shrimp are pink and the cherry tomatoes are softened. Repeat with the remaining kebabs.
5. Let the shrimp and cherry tomato kebabs cool for 5 minutes and serve hot.

Lemony Shrimp

Prep time: 5 minutes | Cook time: 8 minutes | Serves 4

Sauce:

¼ cup unsalted butter
2 tablespoons fish stock or chicken broth
2 cloves garlic, minced
2 tablespoons chopped fresh basil

leaves
1 tablespoon lemon juice
1 tablespoon chopped fresh parsley, plus more for garnish
1 teaspoon red pepper flakes

Shrimp:

1 pound (454 g) large shrimp, peeled and deveined, tails

removed
Fresh basil sprigs, for garnish

1. Put all the ingredients for the sauce in a baking pan and stir to incorporate.
2. Transfer the baking pan to the air fryer and air fry at 350ºF (177ºC) for 3 minutes, or until the sauce is heated through.
3. Once done, add the shrimp to the baking pan, flipping to coat in the sauce.
4. Return to the air fryer and cook for another 5 minutes, or until the shrimp are pink and opaque. Stir the shrimp twice during cooking.
5. Serve garnished with the parsley and basil sprigs.

Panko-Crusted Fish Sticks

Prep time: 15 minutes | Cook time: 10 to 15 minutes | Serves 4

4 fish fillets
½ cup whole-wheat flour
1 teaspoon seasoned salt
2 eggs

1½ cups whole-wheat panko bread crumbs
½ tablespoon dried parsley flakes
Cooking spray

1. Spray the air fryer basket lightly with cooking spray.
2. Cut the fish fillets lengthwise into "sticks."
3. In a shallow bowl, mix the whole-wheat flour and seasoned salt.
4. In a small bowl, whisk the eggs with 1 teaspoon of water.

5. In another shallow bowl, mix the panko bread crumbs and parsley flakes.
6. Coat each fish stick in the seasoned flour, then in the egg mixture, and dredge them in the panko bread crumbs.
7. Place the fish sticks in the air fryer basket in a single layer and lightly spray the fish sticks with cooking spray. You may need to cook them in batches.
8. Air fry at 400ºF (204ºC) for 5 to 8 minutes. Flip the fish sticks over and lightly spray with the cooking spray. Air fry until golden brown and crispy, 5 to 7 more minutes.
9. Serve warm.

Baked Shrimp and Veggies Paella

Prep time: 5 minutes | Cook time: 14 to 17 minutes | Serves 4

1 (10-ounce / 284-g) package frozen cooked rice, thawed
1 (6-ounce / 170-g) jar artichoke hearts, drained and chopped
¼ cup vegetable broth

½ teaspoon dried thyme
½ teaspoon turmeric
1 cup frozen cooked small shrimp
½ cup frozen baby peas
1 tomato, diced

1. Mix together the cooked rice, chopped artichoke hearts, vegetable broth, thyme, and turmeric in a baking pan and stir to combine.
2. Put the baking pan in the air fryer and bake at 340ºF (171ºC) for about 9 minutes, or until the rice is heated through.
3. Remove the pan from the air fryer and fold in the shrimp, baby peas, and diced tomato and mix well.
4. Return to the air fryer and continue cooking for 5 to 8 minutes, or until the shrimp are done and the paella is bubbling.
5. Cool for 5 minutes before serving.

Old Bay Shrimp and Sausage

Prep time: 10 minutes | Cook time: 15 to 20 minutes | Serves 4

1 pound (454 g) large shrimp, deveined, with tails on
1 pound (454 g) smoked turkey sausage, cut into thick slices
2 corn cobs, quartered
1 zucchini, cut into bite-sized pieces
1 red bell pepper, cut into chunks
1 tablespoon Old Bay seasoning
2 tablespoons olive oil
Cooking spray

1. Spray the air fryer basket lightly with cooking spray.
2. In a large bowl, mix the shrimp, turkey sausage, corn, zucchini, bell pepper, and Old Bay seasoning, and toss to coat with the spices. Add the olive oil and toss again until evenly coated.
3. Spread the mixture in the air fryer basket in a single layer. You will need to cook in batches.
4. Air fry at 400°F (204°C) for 15 to 20 minutes, or until cooked through, shaking the basket every 5 minutes for even cooking.
5. Serve immediately.

Golden Crab Sticks with Mayonnaise

Prep time: 5 minutes | Cook time: 12 minutes | Serves 4

Crab Sticks:
2 eggs
1 cup flour
⅓ cup panko bread crumbs
1 tablespoon old bay
seasoning
1 pound (454 g) crab sticks
Cooking spray
Mayo Sauce:
½ cup mayonnaise
1 lime, juiced
2 garlic cloves, minced

1. In a bowl, beat the eggs. In a shallow bowl, place the flour. In another shallow bowl, thoroughly combine the panko bread crumbs and old bay seasoning.
2. Dredge the crab sticks in the flour, shaking off any excess, then in the beaten eggs, finally press them in the bread crumb mixture to coat well.

3. Arrange the crab sticks in the air fryer basket and spray with cooking spray.
4. Air fry at 390°F (199°C) for 12 minutes until golden brown. Flip the crab sticks halfway through the cooking time.
5. Meanwhile, make the sauce by whisking together the mayo, lime juice, and garlic in a small bowl.
6. Serve the crab sticks with the mayo sauce on the side.

Sesame Glazed Salmon Fillet

Prep time: 5 minutes | Cook time: 12 to 16 minutes | Serves 4

3 tablespoons soy sauce
1 tablespoon rice wine or dry sherry
1 tablespoon brown sugar
1 tablespoon toasted sesame oil
1 teaspoon minced garlic
¼ teaspoon minced ginger
4 (6-ounce / 170-g) salmon fillets, skin-on
½ tablespoon sesame seeds
Cooking spray

1. In a small bowl, mix the soy sauce, rice wine, brown sugar, toasted sesame oil, garlic, and ginger.
2. Place the salmon in a shallow baking dish and pour the marinade over the fillets. Cover and refrigerate for at least 1 hour, turning the fillets occasionally to coat in the marinade.
3. Spray the air fryer basket lightly with cooking spray.
4. Shake off as much marinade as possible and place the fillets, skin-side down, in the air fryer basket in a single layer. Reserve the marinade. You may need to cook them in batches.
5. Air fry at 370°F (188°C) for 8 to 10 minutes. Brush the tops of the salmon fillets with the reserved marinade and sprinkle with sesame seeds.
6. Increase the temperature to 400°F (204°C) and air fry for 2 to 5 more minutes for medium, 1 to 3 minutes for medium rare, or 4 to 6 minutes for well done.
7. Serve warm.

Roasted Lemony Fish Fillet

Prep time: 10 minutes | Cook time: 7 to 8 minutes | Serves 4

½ cup raw whole almonds
1 scallion, finely chopped
Grated zest and juice of 1 lemon
½ tablespoon extra-virgin olive oil
¾ teaspoon kosher salt, divided
Freshly ground black pepper, to taste
4 (6 ounces / 170 g each) skinless fish fillets
Cooking spray
1 teaspoon Dijon mustard

1. In a food processor, pulse the almonds to coarsely chop. Transfer to a small bowl and add the scallion, lemon zest, and olive oil. Season with ¼ teaspoon of the salt and pepper to taste and mix to combine.
2. Spray the top of the fish with oil and squeeze the lemon juice over the fish. Season with the remaining ½ teaspoon salt and pepper to taste. Spread the mustard on top of the fish. Dividing evenly, press the almond mixture onto the top of the fillets to adhere.
3. Working in batches, place the fillets in the air fryer basket in a single layer. Air fry at 375ºF (191ºC) for 7 to 8 minutes, until the crumbs start to brown and the fish is cooked through.
4. Serve immediately.

Tangy Chili Shrimp Bowl

Prep time: 10 minutes | Cook time: 10 to 15 minutes | Serves 4

2 teaspoons lime juice
1 teaspoon olive oil
1 teaspoon honey
1 teaspoon minced garlic
1 teaspoon chili powder
Salt, to taste
12 ounces (340 g) medium shrimp,
peeled and deveined
2 cups cooked brown rice
1 (15-ounce / 425-g) can seasoned black beans, warmed
1 large avocado, chopped
1 cup sliced cherry tomatoes
Cooking spray

1. Spray the air fryer basket lightly with cooking spray.

2. In a medium bowl, mix together the lime juice, olive oil, honey, garlic, chili powder, and salt to make a marinade.
3. Add the shrimp and toss to coat evenly in the marinade.
4. Place the shrimp in the air fryer basket. Air fry at 400ºF (204ºC) for 5 minutes. Shake the basket and air fry until the shrimp are cooked through and starting to brown, an additional 5 to 10 minutes.
5. To assemble the bowls, spoon ¼ of the rice, black beans, avocado, and cherry tomatoes into each of four bowls. Top with the shrimp and serve.

Thai Green Curry Shrimp

Prep time: 15 minutes | Cook time: 5 minutes | Serves 4

1 to 2 tablespoons Thai green curry paste
2 tablespoons coconut oil, melted
1 tablespoon half-and-half or coconut milk
1 teaspoon fish sauce
1 teaspoon soy sauce
1 teaspoon minced
fresh ginger
1 clove garlic, minced
1 pound (454 g) jumbo raw shrimp, peeled and deveined
¼ cup chopped fresh Thai basil or sweet basil
¼ cup chopped fresh cilantro

1. In a baking pan, combine the curry paste, coconut oil, half-and-half, fish sauce, soy sauce, ginger, and garlic. Whisk until well combined.
2. Add the shrimp and toss until well coated. Marinate at room temperature for 15 to 30 minutes.
3. Place the pan in the air fryer basket. Air fry at 400ºF (204ºC) for 5 minutes, stirring halfway through the cooking time.
4. Transfer the shrimp to a serving bowl or platter. Garnish with the basil and cilantro. Serve immediately.

Herbed Scallops with Veggies

Prep time: 15 minutes | Cook time: 8 to 11 minutes | Serves 4

1 cup frozen peas
1 cup green beans
1 cup frozen chopped broccoli
2 teaspoons olive oil
½ teaspoon dried oregano
½ teaspoon dried basil
12 ounces (340 g) sea scallops, rinsed and patted dry

1. Put the peas, green beans, and broccoli in a large bowl. Drizzle with the olive oil and toss to coat well. Transfer the vegetables to the air fryer basket and air fry for 4 to 6 minutes, or until they are fork-tender.
2. Remove the vegetables from the basket to a serving bowl. Scatter with the oregano and basil and set aside.
3. Place the scallops in the air fryer basket and air fry at 400ºF (204ºC) for 4 to 5 minutes, or until the scallops are firm and just opaque in the center.
4. Transfer the cooked scallops to the bowl of vegetables and toss well. Serve warm.

Air-Fired Shrimp with Mayo Sauce

Prep time: 5 minutes | Cook time: 7 minutes | Serves 4

Shrimp
12 jumbo shrimp
½ teaspoon garlic salt
Sauce:
4 tablespoons mayonnaise
1 teaspoon grated lemon rind
1 teaspoon Dijon
¼ teaspoon freshly cracked mixed peppercorns
mustard
1 teaspoon chipotle powder
½ teaspoon cumin powder

1. In a medium bowl, season the shrimp with garlic salt and cracked mixed peppercorns.
2. Place the shrimp in the air fryer basket and air fry at 395ºF (202ºC) for 5 minutes. Flip the shrimp and cook for another 2 minutes until they are pink and no longer opaque.
3. Meanwhile, stir together all the ingredients for the sauce in a small bowl until well mixed.

4. Remove the shrimp from the basket and serve alongside the sauce.

Air-Fried Lemony Shrimp

Prep time: 10 minutes | Cook time: 5 minutes | Serves 4

18 shrimp, shelled and deveined
2 garlic cloves, peeled and minced
2 tablespoons extra-virgin olive oil
2 tablespoons freshly squeezed lemon juice
½ cup fresh parsley, coarsely chopped
1 teaspoon onion powder
1 teaspoon lemon-pepper seasoning
½ teaspoon hot paprika
½ teaspoon salt
¼ teaspoon cumin powder

1. Toss all the ingredients in a mixing bowl until the shrimp are well coated.
2. Cover and allow to marinate in the refrigerator for 30 minutes.
3. Arrange the shrimp in the air fryer basket and air fry at 400ºF (204ºC) for 5 minutes, or until the shrimp are pink on the outside and opaque in the center.
4. Remove from the basket and serve warm.

Air-Fried Lemony Shrimp

Prep time: 10 minutes | Cook time: 7 to 8 minutes | Serves 4

1 pound (454 g) shrimp, deveined
4 tablespoons olive oil
1½ tablespoons lemon juice
1½ tablespoons fresh parsley, roughly chopped
2 cloves garlic, finely minced
1 teaspoon crushed red pepper flakes, or more to taste
Garlic pepper, to taste
Sea salt flakes, to taste

1. Toss all the ingredients in a large bowl until the shrimp are coated on all sides.
2. Arrange the shrimp in the air fryer basket and air fry at 385ºF (196ºC) for 7 to 8 minutes, or until the shrimp are pink and cooked through.
3. Serve warm.

Air-Fried Lemony Shrimp and Zucchini

Prep time: 15 minutes | Cook time: 7 to 8 minutes | Serves 4

1¼ pounds (567 g) extra-large raw shrimp, peeled and deveined
2 medium zucchinis (about 8 ounces / 227 g each), halved lengthwise and cut into ½-inch-thick slices
1½ tablespoons olive oil
½ teaspoon garlic salt
1½ teaspoons dried oregano
⅛ teaspoon crushed red pepper flakes (optional)
Juice of ½ lemon
1 tablespoon chopped fresh mint
1 tablespoon chopped fresh dill

1. In a large bowl, combine the shrimp, zucchini, oil, garlic salt, oregano, and pepper flakes (if using) and toss to coat.
2. Working in batches, arrange a single layer of the shrimp and zucchini in the air fryer basket. Air fry at 350°F (177°C) for 7 to 8 minutes, shaking the basket halfway, until the zucchini is golden and the shrimp are cooked through.
3. Transfer to a serving dish and tent with foil while you air fry the remaining shrimp and zucchini.
4. Top with the lemon juice, mint, and dill and serve.

Paprika Tiger Shrimp

Prep time: 5 minutes | Cook time: 10 minutes | Serves 4

1 pound (454 g) tiger shrimp
2 tablespoons olive oil
½ tablespoon old bay seasoning
¼ tablespoon smoked paprika
¼ teaspoon cayenne pepper
A pinch of sea salt

1. Toss all the ingredients in a large bowl until the shrimp are evenly coated.
2. Arrange the shrimp in the air fryer basket and air fry at 380°F (193°C) for 10 minutes, shaking the basket halfway through, or until the shrimp are pink and cooked through.
3. Serve hot.

Cheesy Fish Fillets

Prep time: 8 minutes | Cook time: 17 minutes | Serves 4

⅓ cup grated Parmesan cheese
½ teaspoon fennel seed
½ teaspoon tarragon
⅓ teaspoon mixed peppercorns
2 eggs, beaten
4 (4-ounce / 113-g) fish fillets, halved
2 tablespoons dry white wine
1 teaspoon seasoned salt

1. Place the grated Parmesan cheese, fennel seed, tarragon, and mixed peppercorns in a food processor and pulse for about 20 seconds until well combined. Transfer the cheese mixture to a shallow dish.
2. Place the beaten eggs in another shallow dish.
3. Drizzle the dry white wine over the top of fish fillets. Dredge each fillet in the beaten eggs on both sides, shaking off any excess, then roll them in the cheese mixture until fully coated. Season with the salt.
4. Arrange the fillets in the air fryer basket and air fry at 345°F (174°C) for about 17 minutes, or until the fish is cooked through and no longer translucent. Flip the fillets once halfway through the cooking time.
5. Cool for 5 minutes before serving.

Roasted Honey Cod Fillet

Prep time: 5 minutes | Cook time: 7 to 9 minutes | Makes 1 fillet

1 tablespoon reduced-sodium soy sauce
2 teaspoons honey
Cooking spray
6 ounces (170 g) fresh cod fillet
1 teaspoon sesame seeds

1. In a small bowl, combine the soy sauce and honey.
2. Spray the air fryer basket with cooking spray, then place the cod in the basket, brush with the soy mixture, and sprinkle sesame seeds on top. Roast at 360°F (182°C) for 7 to 9 minutes or until opaque.
3. Remove the fish and allow to cool on a wire rack for 5 minutes before serving.

Cod Croquettes with Aioli

Prep time: 15 minutes | Cook time: 10 minutes | Serves 4

Croquettes:

3 large eggs, divided
12 ounces (340 g) raw cod fillet, flaked apart with two forks
¼ cup 1% milk
½ cup boxed instant mashed potatoes
2 teaspoons olive oil
⅓ cup chopped fresh dill
1 shallot, minced
1 large garlic clove, minced

¾ cup plus 2 tablespoons bread crumbs, divided
1 teaspoon fresh lemon juice
1 teaspoon kosher salt
½ teaspoon dried thyme
¼ teaspoon freshly ground black pepper
Cooking spray

Lemon-Dill Aioli:

5 tablespoons mayonnaise
Juice of ½ lemon

1 tablespoon chopped fresh dill

1. For the croquettes: In a medium bowl, lightly beat 2 of the eggs. Add the fish, milk, instant mashed potatoes, olive oil, dill, shallot, garlic, 2 tablespoons of the bread crumbs, lemon juice, salt, thyme, and pepper. Mix to thoroughly combine. Place in the refrigerator for 30 minutes.
2. For the lemon-dill aioli: In a small bowl, combine the mayonnaise, lemon juice, and dill. Set aside.
3. Measure out about 3½ tablespoons of the fish mixture and gently roll in your hands to form a log about 3 inches long. Repeat to make a total of 12 logs.
4. Beat the remaining egg in a small bowl. Place the remaining ¾ cup bread crumbs in a separate bowl. Dip the croquettes in the egg, then coat in the bread crumbs, gently pressing to adhere. Place on a work surface and spray both sides with cooking spray.
5. Working in batches, arrange a single layer of the croquettes in the air fryer basket. Air fry at 350ºF (177ºC) for about 10 minutes, flipping halfway, until golden.
6. Serve with the aioli for dipping.

Salmon Burgers with Rémoulade

Prep time: 15 minutes | Cook time: 12 minutes | Serves 5

Lemon-Caper Rémoulade:

½ cup mayonnaise
2 tablespoons minced drained capers
2 tablespoons

chopped fresh parsley
2 teaspoons fresh lemon juice

Salmon Patties:

1 pound (454 g) wild salmon fillet, skinned and pin bones removed
6 tablespoons panko bread crumbs
¼ cup minced red onion plus ¼ cup slivered for serving
1 garlic clove, minced

1 large egg, lightly beaten
1 tablespoon Dijon mustard
1 teaspoon fresh lemon juice
1 tablespoon chopped fresh parsley
½ teaspoon kosher salt

For Serving:

5 whole wheat potato buns or gluten-free buns

10 butter lettuce leaves

1. For the lemon-caper rémoulade: In a small bowl, combine the mayonnaise, capers, parsley, and lemon juice and mix well.
2. For the salmon patties: Cut off a 4-ounce / 113-g piece of the salmon and transfer to a food processor. Pulse until it becomes pasty. With a sharp knife, chop the remaining salmon into small cubes.
3. In a medium bowl, combine the chopped and processed salmon with the panko, minced red onion, garlic, egg, mustard, lemon juice, parsley, and salt. Toss gently to combine. Form the mixture into 5 patties about ¾ inch thick. Refrigerate for at least 30 minutes.
4. Working in batches, place the patties in the air fryer basket. Air fry at 400ºF (204ºC) for about 12 minutes, gently flipping halfway, until golden and cooked through.
5. To serve, transfer each patty to a bun. Top each with 2 lettuce leaves, 2 tablespoons of the rémoulade, and the slivered red onions.

Salmon and Bell Pepper Patty

Prep time: 15 minutes | Cook time: 10 to 15 minutes | Serves 4

4 (5-ounce / 142-g) cans pink salmon, skinless, boneless in water, drained
2 eggs, beaten
1 cup whole-wheat panko bread crumbs

4 tablespoons finely minced red bell pepper
2 tablespoons parsley flakes
2 teaspoons Old Bay seasoning
Cooking spray

1. Spray the air fryer basket lightly with cooking spray.
2. In a medium bowl, mix the salmon, eggs, panko bread crumbs, red bell pepper, parsley flakes, and Old Bay seasoning.
3. Using a small cookie scoop, form the mixture into 20 balls.
4. Place the salmon bites in the air fryer basket in a single layer and spray lightly with cooking spray. You may need to cook them in batches.
5. Air fry at 360ºF (182ºC) until crispy for 10 to 15 minutes, shaking the basket a couple of times for even cooking.
6. Serve immediately.

Spiced King Prawns

Prep time: 10 minutes | Cook time: 8 minutes | Serves 2

12 king prawns, rinsed
1 tablespoon coconut oil
Salt and ground black pepper, to taste
1 teaspoon onion powder

1 teaspoon garlic paste
1 teaspoon curry powder
½ teaspoon piri piri powder
½ teaspoon cumin powder

1. Combine all the ingredients in a large bowl and toss until the prawns are completely coated.
2. Place the prawns in the air fryer basket and air fry at 360ºF (182ºC) for 8 minutes, shaking the basket halfway through, or until the prawns turn pink.
3. Serve hot.

Spanish Garlicky Shrimp

Prep time: 10 minutes | Cook time: 10 to 15 minutes | Serves 4

2 teaspoons minced garlic
2 teaspoons lemon juice
2 teaspoons olive oil
½ to 1 teaspoon crushed red pepper

12 ounces (340 g) medium shrimp, deveined, with tails on
Cooking spray

1. In a medium bowl, mix together the garlic, lemon juice, olive oil, and crushed red pepper to make a marinade.
2. Add the shrimp and toss to coat in the marinade. Cover with plastic wrap and place the bowl in the refrigerator for 30 minutes.
3. Spray the air fryer basket lightly with cooking spray.
4. Place the shrimp in the air fryer basket. Air fry at 400ºF (204ºC) for 5 minutes. Shake the basket and air fry until the shrimp are cooked through and nicely browned, an additional 5 to 10 minutes. Cool for 5 minutes before serving.

Lemony Fish and Veggies Tacos

Prep time: 10 minutes | Cook time: 9 to 12 minutes | Serves 4

1 pound (454 g) white fish fillets
2 teaspoons olive oil
3 tablespoons freshly squeezed lemon juice, divided
1½ cups chopped red cabbage

1 large carrot, grated
½ cup low-sodium salsa
⅓ cup low-fat Greek yogurt
4 soft low-sodium whole-wheat tortillas

1. Brush the fish with the olive oil and sprinkle with 1 tablespoon of lemon juice. Air fry in the air fryer basket at 400ºF (204ºC) for 9 to 12 minutes, or until the fish just flakes when tested with a fork.
2. Meanwhile, in a medium bowl, stir together the remaining 2 tablespoons of lemon juice, the red cabbage, carrot, salsa, and yogurt.
3. When the fish is cooked, remove it from the air fryer basket and break it up into large pieces.
4. Offer the fish, tortillas, and the cabbage mixture, and let each person assemble a taco.
5. Serve immediately.

Panko-Crusted Coconut Shrimp

Prep time: 15 minutes | Cook time: 8 minutes | Serves 4

Sweet Chili Mayo:
3 tablespoons mayonnaise
3 tablespoons Thai sweet chili sauce
Shrimp:
⅔ cup sweetened shredded coconut
⅔ cup panko bread crumbs
Kosher salt, to taste
2 tablespoons all-purpose or gluten-free flour

1 tablespoon Sriracha sauce

2 large eggs
24 extra-jumbo shrimp (about 1 pound / 454 g), peeled and deveined
Cooking spray

1. In a medium bowl, combine the mayonnaise, Thai sweet chili sauce, and Sriracha and mix well.
2. In a medium bowl, combine the coconut, panko, and ¼ teaspoon salt. Place the flour in a shallow bowl. Whisk the eggs in another shallow bowl.
3. Season the shrimp with ⅛ teaspoon salt. Dip the shrimp in the flour, shaking off any excess, then into the egg. Coat in the coconut-panko mixture, gently pressing to adhere, then transfer to a large plate. Spray both sides of the shrimp with oil.
4. Working in batches, arrange a single layer of the shrimp in the air fryer basket. Air fry at 360ºF (182ºC) for about 8 minutes, flipping halfway, until the crust is golden brown and the shrimp are cooked through.
5. Serve with the sweet chili mayo for dipping.

Air-Fried Orange Shrimp

Prep time: 20 minutes | Cook time: 10 to 15 minutes | Serves 4

⅓ cup orange juice
3 teaspoons minced garlic
1 teaspoon Old Bay seasoning
¼ to ½ teaspoon cayenne pepper

1 pound (454 g) medium shrimp, peeled and deveined, with tails off
Cooking spray

1. In a medium bowl, combine the orange juice, garlic, Old Bay seasoning, and cayenne pepper.
2. Dry the shrimp with paper towels to remove excess water.
3. Add the shrimp to the marinade and stir to evenly coat. Cover with plastic wrap and place in the refrigerator for 30 minutes so the shrimp can soak up the marinade.
4. Spray the air fryer basket lightly with cooking spray.
5. Place the shrimp into the air fryer basket. Air fry at 400ºF (204ºC) for 5 minutes. Shake the basket and lightly spray with olive oil. Air fry until the shrimp are opaque and crisp, 5 to 10 more minutes.
6. Serve immediately.

Panko-Crusted Tuna Patty

Prep time: 15 minutes | Cook time: 10 to 15 minutes | Serves 4

3 (5-ounce / 142-g) cans tuna, packed in water
⅔ cup whole-wheat panko bread crumbs
⅓ cup shredded Parmesan cheese

1 tablespoon sriracha
¾ teaspoon black pepper
10 whole-wheat slider buns
Cooking spray

1. Spray the air fryer basket lightly with cooking spray.
2. In a medium bowl combine the tuna, bread crumbs, Parmesan cheese, sriracha, and black pepper and stir to combine.
3. Form the mixture into 10 patties.
4. Place the patties in the air fryer basket in a single layer. Spray the patties lightly with cooking spray. You may need to cook them in batches.
5. Air fry at 350ºF (177ºC) for 6 to 8 minutes. Turn the patties over and lightly spray with cooking spray. Air fry until golden brown and crisp, another 4 to 7 more minutes. Serve warm.

Chapter 12 Desserts

Air-Fried Sweet Apple Fritters

Prep time: 30 minutes | Cook time: 7 to 8 minutes | Serves 6

1 cup chopped, peeled Granny Smith apple
½ cup granulated sugar
1 teaspoon ground cinnamon
1 cup all-purpose flour
1 teaspoon baking powder
1 teaspoon salt
2 tablespoons milk
2 tablespoons butter, melted
1 large egg, beaten
Cooking spray
¼ cup confectioners' sugar (optional)

1. Mix together the apple, granulated sugar, and cinnamon in a small bowl. Allow to sit for 30 minutes.
2. Combine the flour, baking powder, and salt in a medium bowl. Add the milk, butter, and egg and stir to incorporate.
3. Pour the apple mixture into the bowl of flour mixture and stir with a spatula until a dough forms.
4. Make the fritters: On a clean work surface, divide the dough into 12 equal portions and shape into 1-inch balls. Flatten them into patties with your hands.
5. Line the air fryer basket with parchment paper and spray it with cooking spray.
6. Transfer the apple fritters onto the parchment paper, evenly spaced but not too close together. Spray the fritters with cooking spray.
7. Bake at 350ºF (177ºC) for 7 to 8 minutes until lightly browned. Flip the fritters halfway through the cooking time.
8. Remove from the basket to a plate and serve with the confectioners' sugar sprinkled on top, if desired.

Maple Buttered Pecan Pie

Prep time: 10 minutes | Cook time: 25 minutes | Serves 4

1 pie dough
½ teaspoons cinnamon
¾ teaspoon vanilla extract
2 eggs
¾ cup maple syrup
⅛ teaspoon nutmeg
3 tablespoons melted butter, divided
2 tablespoons sugar
½ cup chopped pecans

1. In a small bowl, coat the pecans in 1 tablespoon of melted butter.
2. Transfer the pecans to the air fryer and air fry at 370ºF (188ºC) for about 10 minutes.
3. Put the pie dough in a greased pie pan and add the pecans on top.
4. In a bowl, mix the rest of the ingredients. Pour this over the pecans.
5. Put the pan in the air fryer and bake for 25 minutes.
6. Serve immediately.

Baked Cinnamon Candied Apples

Prep time: 15 minutes | Cook time: 12 minutes | Serves 4

1 cup packed light brown sugar
2 teaspoons ground cinnamon
2 medium Granny Smith apples, peeled and diced

1. Thoroughly combine the brown sugar and cinnamon in a medium bowl.
2. Add the apples to the bowl and stir until well coated. Transfer the apples to a baking pan.
3. Bake in the air fryer at 350ºF (177ºC) for 9 minutes. Stir the apples once and bake for an additional 3 minutes until softened.
4. Serve warm.

Apricot and Apple Wedges

Prep time: 5 minutes | Cook time: 15 to 18 minutes | Serves 4

4 large apples, peeled and sliced into 8 wedges
2 tablespoons olive oil
½ cup dried apricots, chopped
1 to 2 tablespoons sugar
½ teaspoon ground cinnamon

1. Toss the apple wedges with the olive oil in a mixing bowl until well coated.
2. Place the apple wedges in the air fryer basket and air fry at 350ºF (180ºC) for 12 to 15 minutes.
3. Sprinkle with the dried apricots and air fry for another 3 minutes.
4. Meanwhile, thoroughly combine the sugar and cinnamon in a small bowl.
5. Remove the apple wedges from the basket to a plate. Serve sprinkled with the sugar mixture.

Simple Black and White Brownies

Prep time: 10 minutes | Cook time: 20 minutes | Makes 1 dozen brownies

1 egg
¼ cup brown sugar
2 tablespoons white sugar
2 tablespoons safflower oil
1 teaspoon vanilla
⅓ cup all-purpose flour
¼ cup cocoa powder
¼ cup white chocolate chips
Nonstick cooking spray

1. Spritz a baking pan with nonstick cooking spray.
2. Whisk together the egg, brown sugar, and white sugar in a medium bowl. Mix in the safflower oil and vanilla and stir to combine.
3. Add the flour and cocoa powder and stir just until incorporated. Fold in the white chocolate chips.
4. Scrape the batter into the prepared baking pan.
5. Bake in the air fryer at 340ºF (171ºC) for 20 minutes, or until the brownie springs back when touched lightly with your fingers.
6. Transfer to a wire rack and let cool for 30 minutes before slicing to serve.

Classic Black Forest Pies

Prep time: 10 minutes | Cook time: 15 minutes | Serves 6

3 tablespoons milk or dark chocolate chips
2 tablespoons thick, hot fudge sauce
2 tablespoons chopped dried cherries
1 (10-by-15-inch) sheet frozen puff pastry, thawed
1 egg white, beaten
2 tablespoons sugar
½ teaspoon cinnamon

1. In a small bowl, combine the chocolate chips, fudge sauce, and dried cherries.
2. Roll out the puff pastry on a floured surface. Cut into 6 squares with a sharp knife.
3. Divide the chocolate chip mixture into the center of each puff pastry square. Fold the squares in half to make triangles. Firmly press the edges with the tines of a fork to seal.
4. Brush the triangles on all sides sparingly with the beaten egg white. Sprinkle the tops with sugar and cinnamon.
5. Put in the air fryer basket and bake at 350ºF (177ºC) for 15 minutes or until the triangles are golden brown. The filling will be hot, so cool for at least 20 minutes before serving.

Baked Fruits Crisp

Prep time: 10 minutes | Cook time: 12 minutes | Serves 8

1 apple, peeled and chopped
2 peaches, peeled and chopped
⅓ cup dried cranberries
2 tablespoons honey
⅓ cup brown sugar
¼ cup flour
½ cup oatmeal
3 tablespoons softened butter

1. In a baking pan, combine the apple, peaches, cranberries, and honey, and mix well.
2. In a medium bowl, combine the brown sugar, flour, oatmeal, and butter, and mix until crumbly. Sprinkle this mixture over the fruit in the pan.
3. Bake at 370ºF (188ºC) for 10 to 12 minutes or until the fruit is bubbly and the topping is golden brown. Serve warm.

Baked Banana and Walnut Cake

Prep time: 10 minutes | Cook time: 25 minutes | Serves 6

1 pound (454 g) bananas, mashed
8 ounces (227 g) flour
6 ounces (170 g) sugar
3.5 ounces (99 g)

walnuts, chopped
2.5 ounces (71 g) butter, melted
2 eggs, lightly beaten
¼ teaspoon baking soda

1. In a bowl, combine the sugar, butter, egg, flour, and baking soda with a whisk. Stir in the bananas and walnuts.
2. Transfer the mixture to a greased baking dish. Put the dish in the air fryer and bake at 355ºF (179ºC) for 10 minutes.
3. Reduce the temperature to 330ºF (166ºC) and bake for another 15 minutes. Serve hot.

Baked Blackberry-Chocolate Cake

Prep time: 10 minutes | Cook time: 22 minutes | Serves 8

½ cup butter, at room temperature
2 ounces (57 g) Swerve
4 eggs
1 cup almond flour
1 teaspoon baking soda

⅓ teaspoon baking powder
½ cup cocoa powder
1 teaspoon orange zest
⅓ cup fresh blackberries

1. With an electric mixer or hand mixer, beat the butter and Swerve until creamy.
2. One at a time, mix in the eggs and beat again until fluffy.
3. Add the almond flour, baking soda, baking powder, cocoa powder, orange zest and mix well. Add the butter mixture to the almond flour mixture and stir until well blended. Fold in the blackberries.
4. Scrape the batter to a baking pan and bake in the air fryer at 335ºF (168ºC) for 22 minutes. Check the cake for doneness: If a toothpick inserted into the center of the cake comes out clean, it's done.
5. Allow the cake cool on a wire rack to room temperature. Serve immediately.

Chia Seed Pudding

Prep time: 5 minutes | Cook time: 4 minutes | Serves 2

1 cup chia seeds
1 cup unsweetened coconut milk
1 teaspoon liquid stevia

1 tablespoon coconut oil
1 teaspoon butter, melted

1. Mix together the chia seeds, coconut milk, and stevia in a large bowl. Add the coconut oil and melted butter and stir until well blended.
2. Divide the mixture evenly between the ramekins, filling only about ⅔ of the way.
3. Bake in the air fryer at 360ºF (182ºC) for 4 minutes.
4. Allow to cool for 5 minutes and serve warm.

Baked Coconut-Chocolate Cake

Prep time: 5 minutes | Cook time: 15 minutes | Serves 6

½ cup unsweetened chocolate, chopped
½ stick butter, at room temperature
1 tablespoon liquid stevia
1½ cups coconut

flour
2 eggs, whisked
½ teaspoon vanilla extract
A pinch of fine sea salt
Cooking spray

1. Place the chocolate, butter, and stevia in a microwave-safe bowl. Microwave for about 30 seconds until melted.
2. Let the chocolate mixture cool for 5 to 10 minutes.
3. Add the remaining ingredients to the bowl of chocolate mixture and whisk to incorporate.
4. Lightly spray a baking pan with cooking spray.
5. Scrape the chocolate mixture into the prepared baking pan.
6. Place the baking pan in the air fryer basket and bake at 330ºF (166ºC) for 15 minutes, or until the top springs back lightly when gently pressed with your fingers.
7. Let the cake cool for 5 minutes and serve.

Homemade Chocolate Coconut Brownies

Prep time: 15 minutes | Cook time: 15 minutes | Serves 8

½ cup coconut oil
2 ounces (57 g) dark chocolate
1 cup sugar
2½ tablespoons water
4 whisked eggs
¼ teaspoon ground cinnamon
½ teaspoons ground

anise star
¼ teaspoon coconut extract
½ teaspoons vanilla extract
1 tablespoon honey
½ cup flour
½ cup desiccated coconut
Sugar, for dusting

1. Melt the coconut oil and dark chocolate in the microwave.
2. Combine with the sugar, water, eggs, cinnamon, anise, coconut extract, vanilla, and honey in a large bowl.
3. Stir in the flour and desiccated coconut. Incorporate everything well.
4. Lightly grease a baking dish with butter. Transfer the mixture to the dish.
5. Put the dish in the air fryer and bake at 355ºF (179ºC) for 15 minutes.
6. Remove from the air fryer and allow to cool slightly.
7. Take care when taking it out of the baking dish. Slice it into squares.
8. Dust with sugar before serving.

Chocolate Lava Cake

Prep time: 5 minutes | Cook time: 10 minutes | Serves 4

3.5 ounces (99 g) butter, melted
3½ tablespoons sugar

3.5 ounces (99 g) chocolate, melted
1½ tablespoons flour
2 eggs

1. Grease four ramekins with a little butter.
2. Rigorously combine the eggs, butter, and sugar before stirring in the melted chocolate.
3. Slowly fold in the flour.
4. Spoon an equal amount of the mixture into each ramekin.
5. Put them in the air fryer and bake at 375ºF (191ºC) for 10 minutes
6. Put the ramekins upside-down on plates and let the cakes fall out. Serve hot.

Milk Chocolate-Pecan Pie

Prep time: 20 minutes | Cook time: 25 minutes | Serves 8

1 (9-inch) unbaked pie crust
Filling:
2 large eggs
⅓ cup butter, melted
1 cup sugar
½ cup all-purpose

flour
1 cup milk chocolate chips
1½ cups coarsely chopped pecans
2 tablespoons bourbon

1. Whisk the eggs and melted butter in a large bowl until creamy.
2. Add the sugar and flour and stir to incorporate. Mix in the milk chocolate chips, pecans, and bourbon and stir until well combined.
3. Use a fork to prick holes in the bottom and sides of the pie crust. Pour the prepared filling into the pie crust. Place the pie crust in the air fryer basket.
4. Bake at 350ºF (177ºC) for 25 minutes until a toothpick inserted in the center comes out clean.
5. Allow the pie cool for 10 minutes in the basket before serving.

Fast Chocolate S'mores

Prep time: 5 minutes | Cook time: 3 minutes | Serves 12

12 whole cinnamon graham crackers
2 (1.55-ounce / 44-

g) chocolate bars, broken into 12 pieces
12 marshmallows

1. Halve each graham cracker into 2 squares.
2. Put 6 graham cracker squares in the air fryer. Do not stack. Put a piece of chocolate into each. Bake at 350ºF (177ºC) for 2 minutes.
3. Open the air fryer and add a marshmallow onto each piece of melted chocolate. Bake for 1 additional minute.
4. Remove the cooked s'mores from the air fryer, then repeat steps 2 and 3 for the remaining 6 s'mores.
5. Top with the remaining graham cracker squares and serve.

Classic Vanilla Pound Cake

Prep time: 5 minutes | Cook time: 30 minutes | Serves 8

1 stick butter, at room temperature
1 cup Swerve
4 eggs
1½ cups coconut flour
½ cup buttermilk
½ teaspoon baking soda
½ teaspoon baking powder
¼ teaspoon salt
1 teaspoon vanilla essence
A pinch of ground star anise
A pinch of freshly grated nutmeg
Cooking spray

1. Spray a baking pan with cooking spray.
2. With an electric mixer or hand mixer, beat the butter and Swerve until creamy. One at a time, mix in the eggs and whisk until fluffy. Add the remaining ingredients and stir to combine.
3. Transfer the batter to the prepared baking pan. Bake in the air fryer at 320ºF (160ºC) for 30 minutes until the center of the cake is springy. Rotate the pan halfway through the cooking time.
4. Allow the cake to cool in the pan for 10 minutes before removing and serving.

Southern Fudge Pie

Prep time: 15 minutes | Cook time: 25 to 30 minutes | Serves 8

1½ cups sugar
½ cup self-rising flour
1/3 cup unsweetened cocoa powder
3 large eggs, beaten
12 tablespoons (1½ sticks) butter, melted
1½ teaspoons vanilla extract
1 (9-inch) unbaked pie crust
¼ cup confectioners' sugar (optional)

1. Thoroughly combine the sugar, flour, and cocoa powder in a medium bowl. Add the beaten eggs and butter and whisk to combine. Stir in the vanilla.
2. Pour the prepared filling into the pie crust and transfer to the air fryer basket.
3. Bake at 350ºF (177ºC) for 25 to 30 minutes until just set.
4. Allow the pie to cool for 5 minutes. Sprinkle with the confectioners' sugar, if desired. Serve warm.

Air-Fried Coconut Pineapple Sticks

Prep time: 10 minutes | Cook time: 10 minutes | Serves 4

½ fresh pineapple, cut into sticks
¼ cup desiccated coconut

1. Place the desiccated coconut on a plate and roll the pineapple sticks in the coconut until well coated.
2. Lay the pineapple sticks in the air fryer basket and air fry at 400ºF (204ºC) for 10 minutes until crisp-tender.
3. Serve warm.

Baked Coffee-Chocolate Cake

Prep time: 5 minutes | Cook time: 30 minutes | Serves 8

Dry Ingredients:
1½ cups almond flour
½ cup coconut meal
2/3 cup Swerve
1 teaspoon baking powder
¼ teaspoon salt
Wet Ingredients:
1 egg
1 stick butter, melted
½ cup hot strongly brewed coffee
Topping:
½ cup confectioner's Swerve
¼ cup coconut flour
3 tablespoons coconut oil
1 teaspoon ground cinnamon
½ teaspoon ground cardamom

1. In a medium bowl, combine the almond flour, coconut meal, Swerve, baking powder, and salt.
2. In a large bowl, whisk the egg, melted butter, and coffee until smooth.
3. Add the dry mixture to the wet and stir until well incorporated. Transfer the batter to a greased baking pan.
4. Stir together all the ingredients for the topping in a small bowl. Spread the topping over the batter and smooth the top with a spatula.
5. Bake in the air fryer at 330ºF (166ºC) for 30 minutes, or until the cake springs back when gently pressed with your fingers.
6. Rest for 10 minutes before serving.

Golden Pineapple Rings

Prep time: 5 minutes | Cook time: 6 to 8 minutes | Serves 6

1 cup rice milk
2/3 cup flour
1/2 cup water
1/4 cup unsweetened flaked coconut
4 tablespoons sugar
1/2 teaspoon baking soda
1/2 teaspoon baking powder

1/2 teaspoon vanilla essence
1/2 teaspoon ground cinnamon
1/4 teaspoon ground anise star
Pinch of kosher salt
1 medium pineapple, peeled and sliced

1. In a large bowl, stir together all the ingredients except the pineapple.
2. Dip each pineapple slice into the batter until evenly coated.
3. Arrange the pineapple slices in the basket and air fry at 380°F (193°C) for 6 to 8 minutes until golden brown.
4. Remove from the basket to a plate and cool for 5 minutes before serving.

Baked Curry Peach, Pear, and Plum

Prep time: 5 minutes | Cook time: 5 minutes | Serves 6 to 8

2 peaches
2 firm pears
2 plums
2 tablespoons melted

butter
1 tablespoon honey
2 to 3 teaspoons curry powder

1. Cut the peaches in half, remove the pits, and cut each half in half again. Cut the pears in half, core them, and remove the stem. Cut each half in half again. Do the same with the plums.
2. Spread a large sheet of heavy-duty foil on the work surface. Arrange the fruit on the foil and drizzle with the butter and honey. Sprinkle with the curry powder.
3. Wrap the fruit in the foil, making sure to leave some air space in the packet.
4. Put the foil package in the basket and bake at 325°F (163°C) for 5 to 8 minutes, shaking the basket once during the cooking time, until the fruit is soft.
5. Serve immediately.

Baked Blackberry Cobbler

Prep time: 15 minutes | Cook time: 25 to 30 minutes | Serves 6

3 cups fresh or frozen blackberries
1¾ cups sugar, divided
1 teaspoon vanilla

extract
8 tablespoons (1 stick) butter, melted
1 cup self-rising flour
Cooking spray

1. Spritz a baking pan with cooking spray.
2. Mix the blackberries, 1 cup of sugar, and vanilla in a medium bowl and stir to combine.
3. Stir together the melted butter, remaining sugar, and flour in a separate medium bowl.
4. Spread the blackberry mixture evenly in the prepared pan and top with the butter mixture.
5. Bake in the air fryer at 350°F (177°C) for 20 to 25 minutes. Check for doneness and bake for another 5 minutes, if needed.
6. Remove from the air fryer and place on a wire rack to cool to room temperature. Serve immediately.

Lemony Blackberry Granola Crumble

Prep time: 5 minutes | Cook time: 20 minutes | Serves 1

2 tablespoons lemon juice
1/3 cup powdered erythritol
1/4 teaspoon xantham

gum
2 cup blackberries
1 cup crunchy granola

1. In a bowl, combine the lemon juice, erythritol, xantham gum, and blackberries. Transfer to a round baking dish and cover with aluminum foil.
2. Put the dish in the air fryer and bake at 350°F (177°C) for 12 minutes.
3. Take care when removing the dish from the air fryer. Give the blackberries a stir and top with the granola.
4. Return the dish to the air fryer and bake for an additional 3 minutes, this time at 320°F (160°C). Serve once the granola has turned brown and enjoy.

Orange-Anise Bundt Cake

Prep time: 5 minutes | Cook time: 20 minutes | Serves 6

1 stick butter, at room temperature
5 tablespoons liquid monk fruit
2 eggs plus 1 egg yolk, beaten
1/3 cup hazelnuts, roughly chopped
3 tablespoons sugar-free orange marmalade
6 ounces (170 g)

unbleached almond flour
1 teaspoon baking soda
½ teaspoon baking powder
½ teaspoon ground cinnamon
½ teaspoon ground allspice
½ ground anise seed
Cooking spray

1. Lightly spritz a baking pan with cooking spray.
2. In a mixing bowl, whisk the butter and liquid monk fruit until the mixture is pale and smooth. Mix in the beaten eggs, hazelnuts, and marmalade and whisk again until well incorporated.
3. Add the almond flour, baking soda, baking powder, cinnamon, allspice, anise seed and stir to mix well.
4. Scrape the batter into the prepared baking pan. Bake in the air fryer at 310ºF (154ºC) for about 20 minutes, or until the top of the cake springs back when gently pressed with your fingers.
5. Transfer to a wire rack and let the cake cool to room temperature. Serve immediately.

Baked Orange Cake

Prep time: 10 minutes | Cook time: 23 minutes | Serves 8

Nonstick baking spray with flour
1¼ cups all-purpose flour
1/3 cup yellow cornmeal
¾ cup white sugar
1 teaspoon baking

soda
¼ cup safflower oil
1¼ cups orange juice, divided
1 teaspoon vanilla
¼ cup powdered sugar

1. Spray a baking pan with nonstick spray and set aside.

2. In a medium bowl, combine the flour, cornmeal, sugar, baking soda, safflower oil, 1 cup of the orange juice, and vanilla, and mix well.
3. Pour the batter into the baking pan and place in the air fryer. Bake at 350ºF (177ºC) for 23 minutes or until a toothpick inserted in the center of the cake comes out clean.
4. Remove the cake from the basket and place on a cooling rack. Using a toothpick, make about 20 holes in the cake.
5. In a small bowl, combine remaining ¼ cup of orange juice and the powdered sugar and stir well. Drizzle this mixture over the hot cake slowly so the cake absorbs it.
6. Cool completely, then cut into wedges to serve.

Tangy Coconut Cake

Prep time: 5 minutes | Cook time: 17 minutes | Serves 6

1 stick butter, melted
¾ cup granulated Swerve
2 eggs, beaten
¾ cup coconut flour
¼ teaspoon salt
1/3 teaspoon grated nutmeg

1/3 cup coconut milk
1¼ cups almond flour
½ teaspoon baking powder
2 tablespoons unsweetened orange jam
Cooking spray

1. Coat a baking pan with cooking spray. Set aside.
2. In a large mixing bowl, whisk together the melted butter and granulated Swerve until fluffy.
3. Mix in the beaten eggs and whisk again until smooth. Stir in the coconut flour, salt, and nutmeg and gradually pour in the coconut milk. Add the remaining ingredients and stir until well incorporated.
4. Scrape the batter into the baking pan.
5. Bake in the air fryer at 355ºF (179ºC) for 17 minutes until the top of the cake springs back when gently pressed with your fingers.
6. Remove from the air fryer to a wire rack to cool. Serve chilled.

Air-Fried Chocolate Donuts

Prep time: 5 minutes | Cook time: 8 minutes | Serves 8

1 (8-ounce / 227-g) can jumbo biscuits
Cooking oil

Chocolate sauce, for drizzling

1. Separate the biscuit dough into 8 biscuits and place them on a flat work surface. Use a small circle cookie cutter or a biscuit cutter to cut a hole in the center of each biscuit. You can also cut the holes using a knife.
2. Spray the air fryer basket with cooking oil.
3. Put 4 donuts in the air fryer. Do not stack. Spray with cooking oil. Air fry at 375ºF (191ºC) for 4 minutes.
4. Open the air fryer and flip the donuts. Air fry for an additional 4 minutes.
5. Remove the cooked donuts from the air fryer, then repeat steps 3 and 4 for the remaining 4 donuts.
6. Drizzle chocolate sauce over the donuts and enjoy while warm.

Golden Bananas with Chocolate Sauce

Prep time: 5 minutes | Cook time: 7 minutes | Serves 6

1 large egg
¼ cup cornstarch
¼ cup plain bread crumbs
3 bananas, halved

crosswise
Cooking oil
Chocolate sauce, for drizzling

1. In a small bowl, beat the egg. In another bowl, place the cornstarch. Put the bread crumbs in a third bowl.
2. Dip the bananas in the cornstarch, then the egg, and then the bread crumbs.
3. Spray the air fryer basket with cooking oil.
4. Put the bananas in the basket and spray them with cooking oil. Air fry at 350ºF (177ºC) for 5 minutes.
5. Open the air fryer and flip the bananas. Air fry for an additional 2 minutes.
6. Transfer the bananas to plates. Drizzle the chocolate sauce over the bananas, and serve.

Air-Fried Pineapple Sticks

Prep time: 5 minutes | Cook time: 10 minutes | Serves 4

½ fresh pineapple, cut into sticks
¼ cup desiccated coconut

1. Coat the pineapple sticks in the desiccated coconut and put each one in the air fryer basket.
2. Air fry at 400ºF (204ºC) for 10 minutes.
3. Serve immediately

Easy Graham Cracker Cheesecake

Prep time: 10 minutes | Cook time: 20 minutes | Serves 8

1 cup graham cracker crumbs
3 tablespoons softened butter
1½ (8-ounce / 227-g) packages cream cheese, softened

⅓ cup sugar
2 eggs
1 tablespoon flour
1 teaspoon vanilla
¼ cup chocolate syrup

1. For the crust, combine the graham cracker crumbs and butter in a small bowl and mix well. Press into the bottom of a baking pan and put in the freezer to set.
2. For the filling, combine the cream cheese and sugar in a medium bowl and mix well. Beat in the eggs, one at a time. Add the flour and vanilla.
3. Remove ⅔ cup of the filling to a small bowl and stir in the chocolate syrup until combined.
4. Pour the vanilla filling into the pan with the crust. Drop the chocolate filling over the vanilla filling by the spoonful. With a clean butter knife, stir the fillings in a zigzag pattern to marbleize them.
5. Bake at 450ºF (232ºC) for 20 minutes or until the cheesecake is just set.
6. Cool on a wire rack for 1 hour, then chill in the refrigerator until the cheesecake is firm.
7. Serve immediately.

Molten Chocolate Cupcakes

Prep time: 10 minutes | Cook time: 10 to 13 minutes | Serves 8

Nonstick baking spray with flour
1⅓ cups chocolate cake mix
1 egg
1 egg yolk
¼ cup safflower oil
¼ cup hot water
⅓ cup sour cream
3 tablespoons peanut butter
1 tablespoon powdered sugar

1. Double up 16 foil muffin cups to make 8 cups. Spray each lightly with nonstick spray; set aside.
2. In a medium bowl, combine the cake mix, egg, egg yolk, safflower oil, water, and sour cream, and beat until combined.
3. In a small bowl, combine the peanut butter and powdered sugar and mix well. Form this mixture into 8 balls.
4. Spoon about ¼ cup of the chocolate batter into each muffin cup and top with a peanut butter ball. Spoon remaining batter on top of the peanut butter balls to cover them.
5. Arrange the cups in the air fryer basket, leaving some space between each. Bake at 350ºF (177ºC) for 10 to 13 minutes or until the tops look dry and set.
6. Let the cupcakes cool for about 10 minutes, then serve warm.

Baked Honey Pumpkin Pudding

Prep time: 10 minutes | Cook time: 15 minutes | Serves 4

3 cups pumpkin purée
3 tablespoons honey
1 tablespoon ginger
1 tablespoon cinnamon
1 teaspoon clove
1 teaspoon nutmeg
1 cup full-fat cream
2 eggs
1 cup sugar

1. In a bowl, stir all the ingredients together to combine.
2. Scrape the mixture into the a greased dish and transfer to the air fryer. Bake at 390ºF (199ºC) for 15 minutes. Serve warm.

Lemony Ricotta Cheese Cake

Prep time: 5 minutes | Cook time: 25 minutes | Serves 6

17.5 ounces (496 g) ricotta cheese
5.4 ounces (153 g) sugar
3 eggs, beaten
3 tablespoons flour
1 lemon, juiced and zested
2 teaspoons vanilla extract

1. In a large mixing bowl, stir together all the ingredients until the mixture reaches a creamy consistency.
2. Pour the mixture into a baking pan and place in the air fryer.
3. Bake at 320ºF (160ºC) for 25 minutes until a toothpick inserted in the center comes out clean.
4. Allow to cool for 10 minutes on a wire rack before serving.

Pineapple and Dark Chocolate Cake

Prep time: 10 minutes | Cook time: 35 to 40 minutes | Serves 4

2 cups flour
4 ounces (113 g) butter, melted
¼ cup sugar
½ pound (227 g) pineapple, chopped
½ cup pineapple
juice
1 ounce (28 g) dark chocolate, grated
1 large egg
2 tablespoons skimmed milk

1. Grease a cake tin with a little oil or butter.
2. In a bowl, combine the butter and flour to create a crumbly consistency.
3. Add the sugar, chopped pineapple, juice, and grated dark chocolate and mix well.
4. In a separate bowl, combine the egg and milk. Add this mixture to the flour mixture and stir well until a soft dough forms.
5. Pour the mixture into the cake tin and transfer to the air fryer.
6. Bake at 370ºF (188ºC) for 35 to 40 minutes.
7. Serve immediately.

Pear-Apple Crisp with Whipped Cream

Prep time: 10 minutes | Cook time: 20 minutes | Serves 6

½ pound (227 g) apples, cored and chopped
½ pound (227 g) pears, cored and chopped
1 cup flour
1 cup sugar
1 tablespoon butter

1 teaspoon ground cinnamon
¼ teaspoon ground cloves
1 teaspoon vanilla extract
¼ cup chopped walnuts
Whipped cream, for serving

1. Lightly grease a baking dish and place the apples and pears inside.
2. Combine the rest of the ingredients, minus the walnuts and the whipped cream, until a coarse, crumbly texture is achieved.
3. Pour the mixture over the fruits and spread it evenly. Top with the chopped walnuts.
4. Bake at 340ºF (171ºC) for 20 minutes or until the top turns golden brown.
5. Serve at room temperature with whipped cream.

Best Coconut Chocolate Cake

Prep time: 5 minutes | Cook time: 15 minutes | Serves 10

1¼ cups unsweetened bakers' chocolate
1 stick butter
1 teaspoon liquid stevia
⅓ cup shredded coconut

2 tablespoons coconut milk
2 eggs, beaten
Cooking spray

1. Lightly spritz a baking pan with cooking spray.
2. Place the chocolate, butter, and stevia in a microwave-safe bowl. Microwave for about 30 seconds until melted. Let the chocolate mixture cool to room temperature.
3. Add the remaining ingredients to the chocolate mixture and stir until well incorporated. Pour the batter into the prepared baking pan.
4. Bake in the air fryer at 330ºF (166ºC) until a toothpick inserted in the center comes out clean, 15 minutes.
5. Remove from the pan and allow to cool for about 10 minutes before serving.

Peanut Buttered Chocolate Bread Pudding

Prep time: 10 minutes | Cook time: 10 to 12 minutes | Serves 8

1 egg
1 egg yolk
¾ cup chocolate milk
3 tablespoons brown sugar
3 tablespoons peanut butter

2 tablespoons cocoa powder
1 teaspoon vanilla
5 slices firm white bread, cubed
Nonstick cooking spray

1. Spritz a baking pan with nonstick cooking spray.
2. Whisk together the egg, egg yolk, chocolate milk, brown sugar, peanut butter, cocoa powder, and vanilla until well combined.
3. Fold in the bread cubes and stir to mix well. Allow the bread soak for 10 minutes.
4. When ready, transfer the egg mixture to the prepared baking pan.
5. Bake in the air fryer at 330ºF (166ºC) for 10 to 12 minutes, or until the pudding is just firm to the touch.
6. Serve at room temperature.

Baked Oatmeal-Carrot Cookies

Prep time: 10 minutes | Cook time: 8 minutes | Makes 16 cups

3 tablespoons unsalted butter, at room temperature
¼ cup packed brown sugar
1 tablespoon honey
1 egg white
½ teaspoon vanilla extract

⅓ cup finely grated carrot
½ cup quick-cooking oatmeal
⅓ cup whole-wheat pastry flour
½ teaspoon baking soda
¼ cup dried cherries

1. In a medium bowl, beat the butter, brown sugar, and honey until well combined.
2. Add the egg white, vanilla, and carrot. Beat to combine.
3. Stir in the oatmeal, pastry flour, and baking soda.
4. Stir in the dried cherries.
5. Double up 32 mini muffin foil cups to make 16 cups. Fill each with about 4 teaspoons of dough. Bake the cookie cups, 8 at a time, at 350ºF (177ºC) for 8 minutes, or until light golden brown and just set. Serve warm.

Fast Chocolate Cookie

Prep time: 10 minutes | Cook time: 9 minutes | Serves 4

Nonstick baking spray with flour
3 tablespoons softened butter
⅓ cup plus 1 tablespoon brown sugar
1 egg yolk
½ cup flour

2 tablespoons ground white chocolate
¼ teaspoon baking soda
½ teaspoon vanilla
¾ cup chocolate chips

1. In a medium bowl, beat the butter and brown sugar together until fluffy. Stir in the egg yolk.
2. Add the flour, white chocolate, baking soda, and vanilla, and mix well. Stir in the chocolate chips.
3. Line a baking pan with parchment paper. Spray the parchment paper with nonstick baking spray with flour.
4. Spread the batter into the prepared pan, leaving a ½-inch border on all sides.
5. Bake at 350ºF (177ºC) for about 9 minutes or until the cookie is light brown and just barely set.
6. Remove the pan from the air fryer and let cool for 10 minutes. Remove the cookie from the pan, remove the parchment paper, and let cool on a wire rack.
7. Serve immediately.

Chapter 13 Holiday Specials

Sugar and Bourbon-Glazed Monkey Bread

Prep time: 15 minutes | Cook time: 25 minutes | Serves 6 to 8

1 (16.3-ounce / 462-g) can store-bought refrigerated biscuit dough
¼ cup packed light brown sugar
1 teaspoon ground cinnamon
½ teaspoon freshly grated nutmeg
½ teaspoon ground ginger
½ teaspoon kosher salt
¼ teaspoon ground allspice
⅛ teaspoon ground cloves
4 tablespoons (½ stick) unsalted butter, melted
½ cup powdered sugar
2 teaspoons bourbon
2 tablespoons chopped candied cherries
2 tablespoons chopped pecans

1. Open the can and separate the biscuits, then cut each into quarters. Toss the biscuit quarters in a large bowl with the brown sugar, cinnamon, nutmeg, ginger, salt, allspice, and cloves until evenly coated. Transfer the dough pieces and any sugar left in the bowl to a round cake pan, metal cake pan, or foil pan and drizzle evenly with the melted butter. Put the pan in the air fryer and bake until the monkey bread is golden brown and cooked through in the middle, at 310ºF (154ºC) about 25 minutes. Transfer the pan to a wire rack and let cool completely. Unmold from the pan.
2. In a small bowl, whisk the powdered sugar and the bourbon into a smooth glaze. Drizzle the glaze over the cooled monkey bread and, while the glaze is still wet, sprinkle with the cherries and pecans to serve.

Golden Stromboli with Olive

Prep time: 25 minutes | Cook time: 25 minutes | Serves 8

4 large cloves garlic, unpeeled
3 tablespoons grated Parmesan cheese
½ cup packed fresh basil leaves
½ cup marinated, pitted green and black olives
¼ teaspoon crushed red pepper
½ pound (227 g) pizza dough, at room temperature
4 ounces (113 g) sliced provolone cheese (about 8 slices)
Cooking spray

1. Spritz the air fryer basket with cooking spray.
2. Put the unpeeled garlic in the air fryer basket.
3. Air fry for 10 minutes or until the garlic is softened completely. Remove them from the air fryer and allow to cool until you can handle.
4. Peel the garlic and place into a food processor with 2 tablespoons of Parmesan, basil, olives, and crushed red pepper. Pulse to mix well. Set aside.
5. Arrange the pizza dough on a clean work surface, then roll it out with a rolling pin into a rectangle. Cut the rectangle in half.
6. Sprinkle half of the garlic mixture over each rectangle half, and leave ½-inch edges uncover. Top them with the provolone cheese.
7. Brush one long side of each rectangle half with water, then roll them up. Spritz the air fryer basket with cooking spray. Transfer the rolls in the air fryer. Spritz with cooking spray and scatter with remaining Parmesan.
8. Air fry the rolls at 370ºF (188ºC) for 15 minutes or until golden brown. Flip the rolls halfway through.
9. Remove the rolls from the air fryer and allow to cool for a few minutes before serving.

Panko-Crusted Spicy Olives

Prep time: 10 minutes | Cook time: 5 minutes | Serves 4

12 ounces (340 g) pitted black extra-large olives
¼ cup all-purpose flour
1 cup panko bread crumbs
2 teaspoons dried thyme
1 teaspoon red pepper flakes
1 teaspoon smoked paprika
1 egg beaten with 1 tablespoon water
Vegetable oil for spraying

1. Drain the olives and place them on a paper towel–lined plate to dry.
2. Put the flour on a plate. Combine the panko, thyme, red pepper flakes, and paprika on a separate plate. Dip an olive in the flour, shaking off any excess, then coat with egg mixture. Dredge the olive in the panko mixture, pressing to make the crumbs adhere, and place the breaded olive on a platter. Repeat with the remaining olives.
3. Spray the olives with oil and place them in a single layer in the air fryer basket. Work in batches if necessary so as not to overcrowd the basket. Air fry at 400°F (204°C) for 5 minutes until the breading is browned and crispy. Serve warm

Air-Fried Golden Nuggets

Prep time: 15 minutes | Cook time: 4 minutes per batch | Makes 20 nuggets

1 cup all-purpose flour, plus more for dusting
1 teaspoon baking powder
½ teaspoon butter, at room temperature, plus more for brushing
¼ teaspoon salt
¼ cup water
⅛ teaspoon onion powder
¼ teaspoon garlic powder
⅛ teaspoon seasoning salt
Cooking spray

1. Line the air fryer basket with parchment paper.
2. Mix the flour, baking powder, butter, and salt in a large bowl. Stir to mix well. Gradually whisk in the water until a sanity dough forms.
3. Put the dough on a lightly floured work surface, then roll it out into a ½-inch thick rectangle with a rolling pin.
4. Cut the dough into about twenty 1- or 2-inch squares, then arrange the squares in a single layer in the air fryer. Spritz with cooking spray. You need to work in batches to avoid overcrowding.
5. Combine onion powder, garlic powder, and seasoning salt in a small bowl. Stir to mix well, then sprinkle the squares with the powder mixture.
6. Air fry the dough squares at 370°F (188°C) for 4 minutes or until golden brown. Flip the squares halfway through the cooking time.
7. Remove the golden nuggets from the air fryer and brush with more butter immediately. Serve warm.

Crispy Hasselback Potatoes

Prep time: 5 minutes | Cook time: 50 minutes | Serves 4

4 russet potatoes, peeled
Salt and freshly ground black pepper,
to taste
¼ cup grated Parmesan cheese
Cooking spray

1. Spray the air fryer basket lightly with cooking spray.
2. Make thin parallel cuts into each potato, ⅛-inch to ¼-inch apart, stopping at about ½ of the way through. The potato needs to stay intact along the bottom.
3. Spray the potatoes with cooking spray and use the hands or a silicone brush to completely coat the potatoes lightly in oil.
4. Put the potatoes, sliced side up, in the air fryer basket in a single layer. Leave a little room between each potato. Sprinkle the potatoes lightly with salt and black pepper.
5. Air fry at 400°F (204°C) for 20 minutes. Reposition the potatoes and spritz lightly with cooking spray again. Air fry until the potatoes are fork-tender and crispy and browned, another 20 to 30 minutes.
6. Sprinkle the potatoes with Parmesan cheese and serve.

Sweet Jewish Blintzes

Prep time: 5 minutes | Cook time: 10 minutes | Makes 8 blintzes

2 (7½-ounce / 213-g) packages farmer cheese, mashed
¼ cup cream cheese
¼ teaspoon vanilla extract
¼ cup granulated white sugar
8 egg roll wrappers
4 tablespoons butter, melted

1. Combine the farmer cheese, cream cheese, vanilla extract, and sugar in a bowl. Stir to mix well.
2. Unfold the egg roll wrappers on a clean work surface, spread ¼ cup of the filling at the edge of each wrapper and leave a ½-inch edge uncovering.
3. Wet the edges of the wrappers with water and fold the uncovered edge over the filling. Fold the left and right sides in the center, then tuck the edge under the filling and fold to wrap the filling.
4. Brush the wrappers with melted butter, then arrange the wrappers in a single layer in the air fryer, seam side down. Leave a little space between each two wrappers. Work in batches to avoid overcrowding.
5. Air fry at 375°F (191°C) for 10 minutes or until golden brown.
6. Serve immediately.

Panko-Crusted Sushi Rolls with Kale Salad

Prep time: 10 minutes | Cook time: 10 minutes | Serves 12

Kale Salad:

1½ cups chopped kale
1 tablespoon sesame seeds
¾ teaspoon soy sauce
¾ teaspoon toasted
sesame oil
½ teaspoon rice vinegar
¼ teaspoon ginger
⅛ teaspoon garlic powder

Sushi Rolls:

3 sheets sushi nori
1 batch cauliflower rice
½ avocado, sliced
Sriracha Mayonnaise:
¼ cup Sriracha sauce
¼ cup vegan mayonnaise

Coating:

½ cup panko breadcrumbs

1. In a medium bowl, toss all the ingredients for the salad together until well coated and set aside.
2. Place a sheet of nori on a clean work surface and spread the cauliflower rice in an even layer on the nori. Scoop 2 to 3 tablespoon of kale salad on the rice and spread over. Place 1 or 2 avocado slices on top. Roll up the sushi, pressing gently to get a nice, tight roll. Repeat to make the remaining 2 rolls.
3. In a bowl, stir together the Sriracha sauce and mayonnaise until smooth. Add breadcrumbs to a separate bowl.
4. Dredge the sushi rolls in Sriracha Mayonnaise, then roll in breadcrumbs till well coated.
5. Place the coated sushi rolls in the air fryer basket and air fry at 390°F (199°C) for 10 minutes, or until golden brown and crispy. Flip the sushi rolls gently halfway through to ensure even cooking..
6. Transfer to a platter and rest for 5 minutes before slicing each roll into 8 pieces. Serve warm.

Crescent Dogs

Prep time: 10 minutes | Cook time: 8 minutes per batch | Makes 16 rolls

1 can refrigerated crescent roll dough
1 small package mini smoked sausages, patted dry
2 tablespoons melted
butter
2 teaspoons sesame seeds
1 teaspoon onion powder

1. Place the crescent roll dough on a clean work surface and separate into 8 pieces. Cut each piece in half and you will have 16 triangles.
2. Make the pigs in the blanket: Arrange each sausage on each dough triangle, then roll the sausages up.
3. Brush the pigs with melted butter and place half of the pigs in the blanket in the air fryer. Sprinkle with sesame seeds and onion powder.
4. Bake at 330°F (166°C) for 8 minutes or until the pigs are fluffy and golden brown. Flip the pigs halfway through.
5. Serve immediately.

Caramel Pecan Tart

Prep time: 2hours 25 minutes | Cook time: 30 minutes | Serves 8

Tart Crust:

¼ cup firmly packed brown sugar

⅓ cup butter, softened

Filling:

¼ cup whole milk

4 tablespoons butter, diced

½ cup packed brown sugar

¼ cup pure maple syrup

1 cup all-purpose flour

¼ teaspoon kosher salt

1½ cups finely chopped pecans

¼ teaspoon pure vanilla extract

¼ teaspoon sea salt

1. Line a baking pan with aluminum foil, then spritz the pan with cooking spray.
2. Stir the brown sugar and butter in a bowl with a hand mixer until puffed, then add the flour and salt and stir until crumbled.
3. Pour the mixture in the prepared baking pan and tilt the pan to coat the bottom evenly.
4. Arrange the pan in the air fryer. Bake at 350°F (177°C) for 13 minutes or until the crust is golden brown.
5. Meanwhile, pour the milk, butter, sugar, and maple syrup in a saucepan. Stir to mix well. Bring to a simmer, then cook for 1 more minute. Stir constantly.
6. Turn off the heat and mix the pecans and vanilla into the filling mixture.
7. Pour the filling mixture over the golden crust and spread with a spatula to coat the crust evenly.
8. Bake in the air fryer for an additional 12 minutes or until the filling mixture is set and frothy.
9. Remove the baking pan from the air fryer and sprinkle with salt. Allow to sit for 10 minutes or until cooled.
10. Transfer the pan to the refrigerator to chill for at least 2 hours, then remove the aluminum foil and slice to serve.

Air- Fried Teriyaki Shrimp Skewers

Prep time: 10 minutes | Cook time: 6 minutes | Makes 12 skewered shrimp

1½ tablespoons mirin

1½ teaspoons ginger juice

1½ tablespoons soy sauce

12 large shrimp (about 20 shrimps per

pound), peeled and deveined

1 large egg

¾ cup panko breadcrumbs

Cooking spray

1. Combine the mirin, ginger juice, and soy sauce in a large bowl. Stir to mix well.
2. Dunk the shrimp in the bowl of mirin mixture, then wrap the bowl in plastic and refrigerate for 1 hour to marinate.
3. Spritz the air fryer basket with cooking spray.
4. Run twelve 4-inch skewers through each shrimp.
5. Whisk the egg in the bowl of marinade to combine well. Pour the breadcrumbs on a plate.
6. Dredge the shrimp skewers in the egg mixture, then shake the excess off and roll over the breadcrumbs to coat well.
7. Arrange the shrimp skewers in the air fryer and spritz with cooking spray. You need to work in batches to avoid overcrowding.
8. Air fry at 400°F (204°C) for 6 minutes or until the shrimp are opaque and firm. Flip the shrimp skewers halfway through.
9. Serve immediately.

Small Brazilian Cheese Bread

Prep time: 37 minutes | Cook time: 24 minutes | Makes 12 balls

2 tablespoons butter, plus more for greasing
½ cup milk
1½ cups tapioca flour

½ teaspoon salt
1 large egg
⅔ cup finely grated aged Asiago cheese

1. Put the butter in a saucepan and pour in the milk, heat over medium heat until the liquid boils. Keep stirring.
2. Turn off the heat and mix in the tapioca flour and salt to form a soft dough. Transfer the dough in a large bowl, then wrap the bowl in plastic and let sit for 15 minutes.
3. Break the egg in the bowl of dough and whisk with a hand mixer for 2 minutes or until a sanity dough forms. Fold the cheese in the dough. Cover the bowl in plastic again and let sit for 10 more minutes.
4. Grease a cake pan with butter.
5. Scoop 2 tablespoons of the dough into the cake pan. Repeat with the remaining dough to make dough 12 balls. Keep a little distance between each two balls. You may need to work in batches to avoid overcrowding.
6. Place the cake pan in the air fryer.
7. Bake at 375°F (191°C) for 12 minutes or until the balls are golden brown and fluffy. Flip the balls halfway through the cooking time.
8. Remove the balls from the air fryer and allow to cool for 5 minutes before serving.

Classic Butter Cake

Prep time: 25 minutes | Cook time: 20 minutes | Serves 8

1 cup all-purpose flour
1¼ teaspoons baking powder
¼ teaspoon salt
½ cup plus 1½ tablespoons granulated white sugar
9½ tablespoons butter, at room temperature

2 large eggs
1 large egg yolk
2½ tablespoons milk
1 teaspoon vanilla extract
Cooking spray

1. Spritz a cake pan with cooking spray.
2. Combine the flour, baking powder, and salt in a large bowl. Stir to mix well.
3. Whip the sugar and butter in a separate bowl with a hand mixer on medium speed for 3 minutes.
4. Whip the eggs, egg yolk, milk, and vanilla extract into the sugar and butter mix with a hand mixer.
5. Pour in the flour mixture and whip with hand mixer until sanity and smooth.
6. Scrape the batter into the cake pan and level the batter with a spatula.
7. Place the cake pan in the air fryer.
8. Bake at 325°F (163°C) for 20 minutes or until a toothpick inserted in the center comes out clean. Check the doneness during the last 5 minutes of the baking.
9. Invert the cake on a cooling rack and allow to cool for 15 minutes before slicing to serve.

Golden Honey Yeast Rolls

Prep time: 10 minutes | Cook time: 20 minutes | Makes 8 rolls

¼ cup whole milk, heated to 115ºF (46ºC) in the microwave
½ teaspoon active dry yeast
1 tablespoon honey
⅔ cup all-purpose flour, plus more for dusting
½ teaspoon kosher salt
2 tablespoons unsalted butter, at room temperature, plus more for greasing
Flaky sea salt, to taste

1. In a large bowl, whisk together the milk, yeast, and honey and let stand until foamy, about 10 minutes.
2. Stir in the flour and salt until just combined. Stir in the butter until absorbed. Scrape the dough onto a lightly floured work surface and knead until smooth, about 6 minutes. Transfer the dough to a lightly greased bowl, cover loosely with a sheet of plastic wrap or a kitchen towel, and let sit until nearly doubled in size, about 1 hour.
3. Uncover the dough, lightly press it down to expel the bubbles, then portion it into 8 equal pieces. Prep the work surface by wiping it clean with a damp paper towel (if there is flour on the work surface, it will prevent the dough from sticking lightly to the surface, which helps it form a ball). Roll each piece into a ball by cupping the palm of the hand around the dough against the work surface and moving the heel of the hand in a circular motion while using the thumb to contain the dough and tighten it into a perfectly round ball. Once all the balls are formed, nestle them side by side in the air fryer basket.
4. Cover the rolls loosely with a kitchen towel or a sheet of plastic wrap and let sit until lightly risen and puffed, 20 to 30 minutes.
5. Uncover the rolls and gently brush with more butter, being careful not to press the rolls too hard. Air fry at 270ºF (132ºC) until the rolls are light golden brown and fluffy, about 12 minutes.
6. Remove the rolls from the air fryer and brush liberally with more butter, if you like, and sprinkle each roll with a pinch of sea salt. Serve warm.

Spicy Shrimp and Worcestershire Sauce

Prep time: 15 minutes | Cook time: 10 minutes per batch | Serves 4

1 tablespoon Sriracha sauce
1 teaspoon Worcestershire sauce
2 tablespoons sweet chili sauce
¾ cup mayonnaise
1 egg, beaten
1 cup panko breadcrumbs
1 pound (454 g) raw shrimp, shelled and deveined, rinsed and drained
Lime wedges, for serving
Cooking spray

1. Spritz the air fryer basket with cooking spray.
2. Combine the Sriracha sauce, Worcestershire sauce, chili sauce, and mayo in a bowl. Stir to mix well. Reserve ⅓ cup of the mixture as the dipping sauce.
3. Combine the remaining sauce mixture with the beaten egg. Stir to mix well. Put the panko in a separate bowl.
4. Dredge the shrimp in the sauce mixture first, then into the panko. Roll the shrimp to coat well. Shake the excess off.
5. Place the shrimp in the air fryer, then spritz with cooking spray. You may need to work in batches to avoid overcrowding.
6. Air fry the shrimp at 360ºF (182ºC) for 10 minutes or until opaque. Flip the shrimp halfway through the cooking time.
7. Remove the shrimp from the air fryer and serve with reserve sauce mixture and squeeze the lime wedges over.

Cheesy Risotto Croquettes with Tomato Sauce

Prep time: 1 hour 40 minutes | Cook time: 1 hour | Serves 6

Risotto Croquettes:
4 tablespoons unsalted butter
1 small yellow onion, minced
1 cup Arborio rice
3½ cups chicken stock
½ cup dry white wine
3 eggs
Zest of 1 lemon
½ cup grated Parmesan cheese

2 ounces (57 g) fresh Mozzarella cheese
¼ cup peas
2 tablespoons water
½ cup all-purpose flour
1½ cups panko breadcrumbs
Kosher salt and ground black pepper, to taste
Cooking spray

Tomato Sauce:
2 tablespoons extra-virgin olive oil
4 cloves garlic, minced
¼ teaspoon red pepper flakes

1 (28-ounce / 794-g) can crushed tomatoes
2 teaspoons granulated sugar
Kosher salt and ground black pepper, to taste

1. Melt the butter in a pot over medium heat, then add the onion and salt to taste. Sauté for 5 minutes or until the onion in translucent.
2. Add the rice and stir to coat well. Cook for 3 minutes or until the rice is lightly browned. Pour in the chicken stock and wine.
3. Bring to a boil. Then cook for 20 minutes or until the rice is tender and liquid is almost absorbed.
4. Make the risotto: When the rice is cooked, break the egg into the pot. Add the lemon zest and Parmesan cheese. Sprinkle with salt and ground black pepper. Stir to mix well.
5. Pour the risotto in a baking sheet, then level with a spatula to spread the risotto evenly. Wrap the baking sheet in plastic and refrigerate for1 hour.
6. Meanwhile, heat the olive oil in a saucepan over medium heat until shimmering.
7. Add the garlic and sprinkle with red pepper flakes. Sauté for a minute or until fragrant.
8. Add the crushed tomatoes and sprinkle with sugar. Stir to mix well. Bring to a boil. Reduce the heat to low and simmer for 15 minutes or until lightly thickened. Sprinkle with salt and pepper to taste. Set aside until ready to serve.
9. Remove the risotto from the refrigerator. Scoop the risotto into twelve 2-inch balls, then flatten the balls with your hands.
10. Arrange a about ½-inch piece of Mozzarella and 5 peas in the center of each flattened ball, then wrap them back into balls.
11. Transfer the balls in a baking sheet lined with parchment paper, then refrigerate for 15 minutes or until firm.
12. Whisk the remaining 2 eggs with 2 tablespoons of water in a bowl. Pour the flour in a second bowl and pour the panko in a third bowl.
13. Dredge the risotto balls in the bowl of flour first, then into the eggs, and then into the panko. Shake the excess off.
14. Transfer the balls in the air fryer and spritz with cooking spray. You may need to work in batches to avoid overcrowding.
15. Bake at 400ºF (204ºC) for 10 minutes or until golden brown. Flip the balls halfway through.
16. Serve the risotto balls with the tomato sauce.

Chapter 14 Fast and Easy Everyday Favorites

Homemade Air-Fried Chicken Wings

Prep time: 5 minutes | Cook time: 19 minutes | Serves 6

2 pounds (907 g) chicken wings, tips removed
⅛ teaspoon salt

1. Season the wings with salt.
2. Working in 2 batches, place half the chicken wings in the basket and air fry for 15 minutes, or until the skin is browned and cooked through, turning the wings with tongs halfway through cooking.
3. Combine both batches in the air fryer and air fry at 400ºF (204ºC) for 4 minutes more. Transfer to a large bowl and serve immediately.

Cheesy Bacon-Wrapped Jalapeño

Prep time: 5 minutes | Cook time: 12 minutes | Serves 6

6 large jalapeños
4 ounces (113 g) ⅓-less-fat cream cheese
¼ cup shredded reduced-fat sharp Cheddar cheese
2 scallions, green tops only, sliced
6 slices center-cut bacon, halved

1. Wearing rubber gloves, halve the jalapeños lengthwise to make 12 pieces. Scoop out the seeds and membranes and discard.
2. In a medium bowl, combine the cream cheese, Cheddar, and scallions. Using a small spoon or spatula, fill the jalapeños with the cream cheese filling. Wrap a bacon strip around each pepper and secure with a toothpick.
3. Working in batches, place the stuffed peppers in a single layer in the air fryer basket. Bake at 325ºF (163ºC) for about 12 minutes, until the peppers are tender, the bacon is browned and crisp, and the cheese is melted.
4. Serve warm.

Cheesy Capicola Sandwich

Prep time: 5 minutes | Cook time: 8 minutes | Serves 2

2 tablespoons mayonnaise
4 thick slices sourdough bread
4 thick slices Brie cheese
8 slices hot capicola

1. Spread the mayonnaise on one side of each slice of bread. Place 2 slices of bread in the air fryer basket, mayonnaise-side down.
2. Place the slices of Brie and capicola on the bread and cover with the remaining two slices of bread, mayonnaise-side up.
3. Bake at 350ºF (177ºC) for 8 minutes, or until the cheese has melted.
4. Serve immediately.

Golden Knots with Parsley

Prep time: 10 minutes | Cook time: 10 minutes | Makes 8 knots

1 teaspoon dried parsley
¼ cup melted butter
2 teaspoons garlic powder
1 (11-ounce / 312-g) tube refrigerated French bread dough, cut into 8 slices

1. Combine the parsley, butter, and garlic powder in a bowl. Stir to mix well.
2. Place the French bread dough slices on a clean work surface, then roll each slice into a 6-inch long rope. Tie the ropes into knots and arrange them on a plate. Brush the knots with butter mixture.
3. Transfer the knots into the air fryer. You need to work in batches to avoid overcrowding.
4. Air fry at 350ºF (177ºC) for 5 minutes or until the knots are golden brown. Flip the knots halfway through the cooking time.
5. Serve immediately.

Greek Salsa with Halloumi Cheese

Prep time: 15 minutes | Cook time: 6 minutes | Serves 4

Salsa:

1 small shallot, finely diced
3 garlic cloves, minced
2 tablespoons fresh lemon juice
2 tablespoons extra-virgin olive oil
1 teaspoon freshly cracked black pepper
Pinch of kosher salt

½ cup finely diced English cucumber
1 plum tomato, deseeded and finely diced
2 teaspoons chopped fresh parsley
1 teaspoon snipped fresh dill
1 teaspoon snipped fresh oregano

Cheese:

8 ounces (227 g) Halloumi cheese, sliced into ½-inch-

thick pieces
1 tablespoon extra-virgin olive oil

1. For the salsa: Combine the shallot, garlic, lemon juice, olive oil, pepper, and salt in a medium bowl. Add the cucumber, tomato, parsley, dill, and oregano. Toss gently to combine; set aside.
2. For the cheese: Place the cheese slices in a medium bowl. Drizzle with the olive oil. Toss gently to coat. Arrange the cheese in a single layer in the air fryer basket. Bake at 375ºF (191ºC) for 6 minutes.
3. Divide the cheese among four serving plates. Top with the salsa and serve immediately.

Zucchini Noodles

Prep time: 10 minutes | Cook time: 10 minutes | Serves 4

2 large zucchinis, peeled and spiralized
2 large yellow summer squash, peeled and spiralized
1 tablespoon olive oil, divided

½ teaspoon kosher salt
1 garlic clove, whole
2 tablespoons fresh basil, chopped
Cooking spray

1. Spritz the air fryer basket with cooking spray.
2. Combine the zucchini and summer squash with 1 teaspoon olive oil and salt in a large bowl. Toss to coat well.
3. Transfer the zucchini and summer squash in the air fryer and add the garlic.
4. Air fry at 360ºF (182ºC) for 10 minutes or until tender and fragrant. Toss the spiralized zucchini and summer squash halfway through the cooking time.
5. Transfer the cooked zucchini and summer squash onto a plate and set aside.
6. Remove the garlic from the air fryer and allow to cool for a few minutes. Mince the garlic and combine with remaining olive oil in a small bowl. Stir to mix well.
7. Drizzle the spiralized zucchini and summer squash with garlic oil and sprinkle with basil. Toss to serve.

Crispy Green Tomato

Prep time: 5 minutes | Cook time: 6 to 8 minutes | Serves 4

4 medium green tomatoes
⅓ cup all-purpose flour
2 egg whites
¼ cup almond milk
1 cup ground

almonds
½ cup panko bread crumbs
2 teaspoons olive oil
1 teaspoon paprika
1 clove garlic, minced

1. Rinse the tomatoes and pat dry. Cut the tomatoes into ½-inch slices, discarding the thinner ends.
2. Put the flour on a plate. In a shallow bowl, beat the egg whites with the almond milk until frothy. And on another plate, combine the almonds, bread crumbs, olive oil, paprika, and garlic and mix well.
3. Dip the tomato slices into the flour, then into the egg white mixture, then into the almond mixture to coat.
4. Place four of the coated tomato slices in the air fryer basket. Air fry at 400ºF (204ºC) for 6 to 8 minutes, or until the tomato coating is crisp and golden brown. Repeat with remaining tomato slices and serve immediately.

Fast Cheesy Grits

Prep time: 10 minutes | Cook time: 12 minutes | Serves 6

¾ cup hot water
2 (1-ounce / 28-g) packages instant grits
1 large egg, beaten
1 tablespoon butter, melted

2 cloves garlic, minced
½ to 1 teaspoon red pepper flakes
1 cup shredded Cheddar cheese or jalapeño Jack cheese

1. In a baking pan, combine the water, grits, egg, butter, garlic, and red pepper flakes. Stir until well combined. Stir in the shredded cheese.
2. Place the pan in the air fryer basket and air fry at 400ºF (204ºC) for 12 minutes, or until the grits have cooked through and a knife inserted near the center comes out clean.
3. Let stand for 5 minutes before serving.

Lemony Beet Salad with Mixed Greens

Prep time: 10 minutes | Cook time: 12 to 15 minutes | Serves 4

6 medium red and golden beets, peeled and sliced
1 teaspoon olive oil
¼ teaspoon kosher salt
Vinaigrette:
2 teaspoons olive oil
2 tablespoons

salt
½ cup crumbled feta cheese
8 cups mixed greens
Cooking spray

chopped fresh chives
Juice of 1 lemon

1. In a large bowl, toss the beets, olive oil, and kosher salt.
2. Spray the air fryer basket with cooking spray, then place the beets in the basket and air fry at 360ºF (182ºC) for 12 to 15 minutes or until tender.
3. While the beets cook, make the vinaigrette in a large bowl by whisking together the olive oil, lemon juice, and chives.
4. Remove the beets from the air fryer, toss in the vinaigrette, and allow to cool for 5 minutes. Add the feta and serve on top of the mixed greens.

Spicy Cheese Toast

Prep time: 5 minutes | Cook time: 5 minutes | Serves 1

2 tablespoons grated Parmesan cheese
2 tablespoons grated Mozzarella cheese
2 teaspoons salted butter, at room temperature

10 to 15 thin slices serrano chile or jalapeño
2 slices sourdough bread
½ teaspoon black pepper

1. In a small bowl, stir together the Parmesan, Mozzarella, butter, and chiles.
2. Spread half the mixture onto one side of each slice of bread. Sprinkle with the pepper. Place the slices, cheese-side up, in the air fryer basket. Bake at 325ºF (163ºC) for 5 minutes, or until the cheese has melted and started to brown slightly.
3. Serve immediately.

Cheesy Jalapeño with Potato Chips

Prep time: 5 minutes | Cook time: 25 minutes | Serves 6

2 slices bacon, halved
¾ cup whole milk ricotta cheese
½ cup shredded sharp Cheddar cheese
1 green onion, finely

chopped
¼ teaspoon salt
6 large jalapeños, halved lengthwise and deseeded
½ cup finely crushed potato chips

1. Lay bacon in single layer in basket. Air fry at 400ºF (204ºC) for 5 minutes, or until crisp. Remove bacon and place on paper towels to drain. When cool, finely chop.
2. Stir together ricotta, Cheddar, green onion, bacon, and salt. Spoon into jalapeños; top with potato chips.
3. Place half the jalapeños in the basket and air fry for 8 minutes, or until tender. Repeat with the remaining jalapeños.
4. Serve immediately.

Classic Mexican Street Corn Casserole

Prep time: 5 minutes | Cook time: 7 minutes | Serves 4

4 medium ears corn, husked
Cooking spray
2 tablespoons mayonnaise
1 tablespoon fresh lime juice
½ teaspoon ancho chile powder
¼ teaspoon kosher salt
2 ounces (57 g) crumbled Cotija or feta cheese
2 tablespoons chopped fresh cilantro

1. Spritz the corn with cooking spray. Working in batches, arrange the ears of corn in the air fryer basket in a single layer. Air fry at 375ºF (191ºC) for about 7 minutes, flipping halfway, until the kernels are tender when pierced with a paring knife. When cool enough to handle, cut the corn kernels off the cob.
2. In a large bowl, mix together mayonnaise, lime juice, ancho powder, and salt. Add the corn kernels and mix to combine. Transfer to a serving dish and top with the Cotija and cilantro. Serve immediately.

Fast Devils on Horseback

Prep time: 5 minutes | Cook time: 7 minutes | Serves 12

24 petite pitted prunes (4½ ounces / 128 g)
¼ cup crumbled blue cheese, divided
8 slices center-cut bacon, cut crosswise into thirds

1. Halve the prunes lengthwise, but don't cut them all the way through. Place ½ teaspoon of cheese in the center of each prune. Wrap a piece of bacon around each prune and secure the bacon with a toothpick.
2. Working in batches, arrange a single layer of the prunes in the air fryer basket. Air fry at 400ºF (204ºC) for about 7 minutes, flipping halfway, until the bacon is cooked through and crisp.
3. Let cool slightly and serve warm.

Frothy Frico

Prep time: 5 minutes | Cook time: 5 minutes | Serves 2

1 cup shredded aged Manchego cheese
1 teaspoon all-purpose flour
½ teaspoon cumin seeds
¼ teaspoon cracked black pepper

1. Line the air fryer basket with parchment paper.
2. Combine the cheese and flour in a bowl. Stir to mix well. Spread the mixture in the basket into a 4-inch round.
3. Combine the cumin and black pepper in a small bowl. Stir to mix well. Sprinkle the cumin mixture over the cheese round.
4. Air fry at 375ºF (191ºC) for 5 minutes or until the cheese is lightly browned and frothy.
5. Use tongs to transfer the cheese wafer onto a plate and slice to serve.

Baked Cherry Tomato with Basil

Prep time: 5 minutes | Cook time: 4 to 6 minutes | Serves 2

2 cups cherry tomatoes
1 clove garlic, thinly sliced
1 teaspoon olive oil
⅛ teaspoon kosher
salt
1 tablespoon freshly chopped basil, for topping
Cooking spray

1. Spritz the air fryer baking pan with cooking spray and set aside.
2. In a large bowl, toss together the cherry tomatoes, sliced garlic, olive oil, and kosher salt. Spread the mixture in an even layer in the prepared pan.
3. Bake in the air fryer at 360ºF (182ºC) for 4 to 6 minutes, or until the tomatoes become soft and wilted.
4. Transfer to a bowl and rest for 5 minutes. Top with the chopped basil and serve warm.

Panko Salmon and Carrot Croquettes

Prep time: 15 minutes | Cook time: 10 minutes | Serves 6

2 egg whites
1 cup almond flour
1 cup panko breadcrumbs
1 pound (454 g) chopped salmon fillet
⅔ cup grated carrots
2 tablespoons minced garlic cloves
½ cup chopped onion
2 tablespoons chopped chives
Cooking spray

1. Spritz the air fryer basket with cooking spray.
2. Whisk the egg whites in a bowl. Put the flour in a second bowl. Pour the breadcrumbs in a third bowl. Set aside.
3. Combine the salmon, carrots, garlic, onion, and chives in a large bowl. Stir to mix well.
4. Form the mixture into balls with your hands. Dredge the balls into the flour, then egg, and then breadcrumbs to coat well.
5. Arrange the salmon balls in the air fryer and spritz with cooking spray.
6. Air fry at 350ºF (177ºC) for 10 minutes or until crispy and browned. Shake the basket halfway through.
7. Serve immediately.

Lush Sugar-Glazed Apple Fritters

Prep time: 5 minutes | Cook time: 25 minutes | Makes 15 fritters

Apple Fritters:
2 firm apples, peeled, cored, and diced
½ teaspoon cinnamon
Juice of 1 lemon
1 cup all-purpose flour
1½ teaspoons baking powder
½ teaspoon kosher
salt
2 eggs
¼ cup milk
2 tablespoons unsalted butter, melted
2 tablespoons granulated sugar
Cooking spray
Glaze:
½ teaspoon vanilla extract
1¼ cups powdered
sugar, sifted
¼ cup water

1. Line the air fryer basket with parchment paper.
2. Combine the apples with cinnamon and lemon juice in a small bowl. Toss to coat well.
3. Combine the flour, baking powder, and salt in a large bowl. Stir to mix well.
4. Whisk the egg, milk, butter, and sugar in a medium bowl. Stir to mix well.
5. Make a well in the center of the flour mixture, then pour the egg mixture into the well and stir to mix well. Mix in the apple until a dough forms.
6. Use an ice cream scoop to scoop 5 balls from the dough into the air fryer. Spritz with cooking spray.
7. Air fry at 360ºF (182ºC) for 8 minutes or until golden brown. Flip them halfway through. Remove the fritters from the air fryer and repeat with the remaining dough.
8. Meanwhile, combine the ingredients for the glaze in a separate small bowl. Stir to mix well.
9. Serve the fritters with the glaze on top or use the glaze for dipping.

Herbed Roasted Veggies

Prep time: 10 minutes | Cook time: 14 to 18 minutes | Serves 4

1 red bell pepper, sliced
1 (8-ounce / 227-g) package sliced mushrooms
1 cup green beans, cut into 2-inch pieces
⅓ cup diced red
onion
3 garlic cloves, sliced
1 teaspoon olive oil
½ teaspoon dried basil
½ teaspoon dried tarragon

1. In a medium bowl, mix the red bell pepper, mushrooms, green beans, red onion, and garlic. Drizzle with the olive oil. Toss to coat.
2. Add the herbs and toss again.
3. Place the vegetables in the air fryer basket. Roast at 350ºF (177ºC) for 14 to 18 minutes, or until tender. Serve immediately.

Brown Sugar Bartlett Pear

Prep time: 10 minutes | Cook time: 8 minutes | Serves 4

2 large Bartlett pears, peeled, cut in half, cored
3 tablespoons melted butter
½ teaspoon ground ginger
¼ teaspoon ground cardamom
3 tablespoons brown sugar
½ cup whole-milk ricotta cheese
1 teaspoon pure lemon extract
1 teaspoon pure almond extract
1 tablespoon honey, plus additional for drizzling

1. Toss the pears with butter, ginger, cardamom, and sugar in a large bowl. Toss to coat well.
2. Arrange the pears in the air fryer, cut side down. Air fry at 375ºF (191ºC) for 5 minutes, then flip the pears and air fry for 3 more minutes or until the pears are soft and browned.
3. In the meantime, combine the remaining ingredients in a separate bowl. Whip for 1 minute with a hand mixer until the mixture is puffed.
4. Divide the mixture into four bowls, then put the pears over the mixture and drizzle with more honey to serve.

Homemade Spciy Old Bay Shrimp

Prep time: 7 minutes | Cook time: 10 minutes | Makes 2 cups

½ teaspoon Old Bay Seasoning
1 teaspoon ground cayenne pepper
½ teaspoon paprika
1 tablespoon olive oil
⅛ teaspoon salt
½ pound (227 g) shrimps, peeled and deveined
Juice of half a lemon

1. Combine the Old Bay Seasoning, cayenne pepper, paprika, olive oil, and salt in a large bowl, then add the shrimps and toss to coat well.
2. Put the shrimps in the air fryer. Air fry at 390ºF (199ºC) for 10 minutes or until opaque. Flip the shrimps halfway through.
3. Serve the shrimps with lemon juice on top.

Classic Indian Masala Omelet

Prep time: 10 minutes | Cook time: 12 minutes | Serves 2

4 large eggs
½ cup diced onion
½ cup diced tomato
¼ cup chopped fresh cilantro
1 jalapeño, deseeded and finely chopped
½ teaspoon ground
turmeric
½ teaspoon kosher salt
½ teaspoon cayenne pepper
Olive oil, for greasing the pan

1. Generously grease a 3-cup Bundt pan.
2. In a large bowl, beat the eggs. Stir in the onion, tomato, cilantro, jalapeño, turmeric, salt, and cayenne.
3. Pour the egg mixture into the prepared pan. Place the pan in the air fryer basket. Bake at 250ºF (121ºC) for 12 minutes, or until the eggs are cooked through. Carefully unmold and cut the omelet into four pieces.
4. Serve immediately.

Crispy Indian Masala Sweet Potato Fries

Prep time: 5 minutes | Cook time: 8 minutes | Make 20 fries

Seasoning Mixture:
¾ teaspoon ground coriander
½ teaspoon garam masala
½ teaspoon garlic
powder
½ teaspoon ground cumin
¼ teaspoon ground cayenne pepper
Fries:
2 large sweet potatoes, peeled
2 teaspoons olive oil

1. In a small bowl, combine the coriander, garam masala, garlic powder, cumin, and cayenne pepper.
2. Slice the sweet potatoes into ¼-inch-thick fries.
3. In a large bowl, toss the sliced sweet potatoes with the olive oil and the seasoning mixture.
4. Transfer the seasoned sweet potatoes to the air fryer basket and fry at 400ºF (204ºC) for 8 minutes, until crispy.
5. Serve warm.

Cheesy Brown Rice and Pepper Fritters

Prep time: 10 minutes | Cook time: 8 to 10 minutes | Serves 4

1 (10-ounce / 284-g) bag frozen cooked brown rice, thawed
1 egg
3 tablespoons brown rice flour
1/3 cup finely grated carrots
1/3 cup minced red bell pepper
2 tablespoons minced fresh basil
3 tablespoons grated Parmesan cheese
2 teaspoons olive oil

1. In a small bowl, combine the thawed rice, egg, and flour and mix to blend.
2. Stir in the carrots, bell pepper, basil, and Parmesan cheese.
3. Form the mixture into 8 fritters and drizzle with the olive oil.
4. Put the fritters carefully into the air fryer basket. Air fry at 380°F (193°C) for 8 to 10 minutes, or until the fritters are golden brown and cooked through.
5. Serve immediately.

Simple Lemony Asparagus

Prep time: 5 minutes | Cook time: 10 minutes | Makes 10 spears

10 spears asparagus (about ½ pound / 227 g in total), snap the ends off
1 tablespoon lemon juice
2 teaspoons minced garlic
½ teaspoon salt
¼ teaspoon ground black pepper
Cooking spray

1. Line a parchment paper in the air fryer basket.
2. Put the asparagus spears in a large bowl. Drizzle with lemon juice and sprinkle with minced garlic, salt, and ground black pepper. Toss to coat well.
3. Transfer the asparagus in the air fryer and spritz with cooking spray. Air fryer at 400°F (204°C) for 10 minutes or until wilted and soft. Flip the asparagus halfway through.
4. Serve immediately.

Crispy Parsnip with Creamy Yogurt Dip

Prep time: 10 minutes | Cook time: 10 minutes | Serves 4

3 medium parsnips, peeled, cut into sticks
¼ teaspoon kosher salt
Dip:
¼ cup plain Greek yogurt
⅛ teaspoon garlic powder
1 tablespoon sour
1 teaspoon olive oil
1 garlic clove, unpeeled
Cooking spray

cream
¼ teaspoon kosher salt
Freshly ground black pepper, to taste

1. Spritz the air fryer basket with cooking spray.
2. Put the parsnip sticks in a large bowl, then sprinkle with salt and drizzle with olive oil.
3. Transfer the parsnip into the air fryer and add the garlic.
4. Air fry for 5 minutes, then remove the garlic from the air fryer and shake the basket. Air fry at 360°F (182°C) for 5 more minutes or until the parsnip sticks are crisp.
5. Meanwhile, peel the garlic and crush it. Combine the crushed garlic with the ingredients for the dip. Stir to mix well.
6. When the frying is complete, remove the parsnip fries from the air fryer and serve with the dipping sauce.

Spicy Chicken Wing

Prep time: 5 minutes | Cook time: 30 minutes | Makes 16 wings

16 chicken wings
3 tablespoons hot
sauce
Cooking spray

1. Spritz the air fryer basket with cooking spray.
2. Arrange the chicken wings in the air fryer. You need to work in batches to avoid overcrowding.
3. Cook at 360°F (182°C) for 15 minutes or until well browned. Shake the basket at lease three times during the cooking.
4. Transfer the air fried wings on a plate and serve with hot sauce.

Purple Potato Chips with Chipotle Sauce

Prep time: 10 minutes | Cook time: 9 to 14 minutes | Serves 6

1 cup Greek yogurt
2 chipotle chiles, minced
2 tablespoons adobo sauce
1 teaspoon paprika
1 tablespoon lemon juice
10 purple fingerling potatoes
1 teaspoon olive oil
2 teaspoons minced fresh rosemary leaves
⅛ teaspoon cayenne pepper
¼ teaspoon coarse sea salt

1. In a medium bowl, combine the yogurt, minced chiles, adobo sauce, paprika, and lemon juice. Mix well and refrigerate.
2. Wash the potatoes and dry them with paper towels. Slice the potatoes lengthwise, as thinly as possible. You can use a mandoline, a vegetable peeler, or a very sharp knife.
3. Combine the potato slices in a medium bowl and drizzle with the olive oil; toss to coat.
4. Air fry the chips in batches at 400°F (204°C) for 9 to 14 minutes. Use tongs to gently rearrange the chips halfway during cooking time.
5. Sprinkle the chips with the rosemary, cayenne pepper, and sea salt. Serve with the chipotle sauce for dipping.

Fast Air-Fried Okra Chips

Prep time: 5 minutes | Cook time: 16 minutes | Serves 6

2 pounds (907 g) fresh okra pods, cut into 1-inch pieces
2 tablespoons canola
oil
1 teaspoon coarse sea salt

1. Stir the oil and salt in a bowl to mix well. Add the okra and toss to coat well.
2. Place the okra in the air fryer. Air fry at 400°F (204°C) for 16 minutes or until lightly browned. Shake the basket at least three times during the cooking time.
3. Serve immediately.

Garlicky Roasted Carrot Chips

Prep time: 5 minutes | Cook time: 15 minutes | Makes 3 cups

3 large carrots, peeled and sliced into long and thick chips diagonally
1 tablespoon granulated garlic
1 teaspoon salt
¼ teaspoon ground black pepper
1 tablespoon olive oil
1 tablespoon finely chopped fresh parsley

1. Toss the carrots with garlic, salt, ground black pepper, and olive oil in a large bowl to coat well.
2. Place the carrots in the air fryer. Roast at 360°F (182°C) for 15 minutes or until the carrot chips are soft. Shake the basket halfway through.
3. Serve the carrot chips with parsley on top.

Baked Sweet Potato Soufflé

Prep time: 10 minutes | Cook time: 30 minutes | Serves 4

1 sweet potato, baked and mashed
2 tablespoons unsalted butter, divided
1 large egg, separated
¼ cup whole milk
½ teaspoon kosher salt

1. In a medium bowl, combine the sweet potato, 1 tablespoon of melted butter, egg yolk, milk, and salt. Set aside.
2. In a separate medium bowl, whisk the egg white until stiff peaks form.
3. Using a spatula, gently fold the egg white into the sweet potato mixture.
4. Coat the inside of four 3-inch ramekins with the remaining 1 tablespoon of butter, then fill each ramekin halfway full. Place 2 ramekins in the air fryer basket and bake at 330°F (166°C) for 15 minutes. Repeat this process with the remaining ramekins.
5. Remove the ramekins from the air fryer and allow to cool on a wire rack for 10 minutes before serving

Scalloped Vegetable Casserole

Prep time: 10 minutes | Cook time: 15 minutes | Serves 4

1 Yukon Gold potato, thinly sliced
1 small sweet potato, peeled and thinly sliced
1 medium carrot, thinly sliced
¼ cup minced onion
3 garlic cloves, minced
¾ cup 2 percent milk
2 tablespoons cornstarch
½ teaspoon dried thyme

1. In a baking pan, layer the potato, sweet potato, carrot, onion, and garlic.
2. In a small bowl, whisk the milk, cornstarch, and thyme until blended. Pour the milk mixture evenly over the vegetables in the pan.
3. Bake at 380ºF (193ºC) for 15 minutes. Check the casserole—it should be golden brown on top, and the vegetables should be tender.
4. Serve immediately.

Easy Air-Fried Brussels Sprouts

Prep time: 5 minutes | Cook time: 20 minutes | Serves 4

¼ teaspoon salt
⅛ teaspoon ground black pepper
1 tablespoon extra-virgin olive oil
1 pound (454 g) Brussels sprouts, trimmed and halved
Lemon wedges, for garnish

1. Combine the salt, black pepper, and olive oil in a large bowl. Stir to mix well.
2. Add the Brussels sprouts to the bowl of mixture and toss to coat well.
3. Arrange the Brussels sprouts in the air fryer. Air fry at 350ºF (177ºC) for 20 minutes or until lightly browned and wilted. Shake the basket two times during the air frying.
4. Transfer the cooked Brussels sprouts to a large plate and squeeze the lemon wedges on top to serve.

Crispy Green Beans

Prep time: 5 minutes | Cook time: 10 minutes | Makes 2 cups

½ teaspoon lemon pepper
2 teaspoons granulated garlic
½ teaspoon salt
1 tablespoon olive oil
2 cups fresh green beans, trimmed and snapped in half

1. Combine the lemon pepper, garlic, salt, and olive oil in a bowl. Stir to mix well.
2. Add the green beans to the bowl of mixture and toss to coat well.
3. Arrange the green beans in the air fryer. Bake at 370ºF (188ºC) for 10 minutes or until tender and crispy. Shake the basket halfway through to make sure the green beans are cooked evenly.
4. Serve immediately.

Garlicky Parmesan Shrimps

Prep time: 10 minutes | Cook time: 16 minutes | Serves 4 to 6

⅔ cup grated Parmesan cheese
4 minced garlic cloves
1 teaspoon onion powder
½ teaspoon oregano
1 teaspoon basil
1 teaspoon ground
black pepper
2 tablespoons olive oil
2 pounds (907 g) cooked large shrimps, peeled and deveined
Lemon wedges, for topping
Cooking spray

1. Spritz the air fryer basket with cooking spray.
2. Combine all the ingredients, except for the shrimps, in a large bowl. Stir to mix well.
3. Dunk the shrimps in the mixture and toss to coat well. Shake the excess off.
4. Arrange the shrimps in the air fryer. Air fry at 350ºF (177ºC) for 8 minutes or until opaque. Flip the shrimps halfway through. You may need to work in batches to avoid overcrowding.
5. Transfer the cooked shrimps on a large plate and squeeze the lemon wedges over before serving.

Southwest Roasted Corn Salad

Prep time: 10 minutes | Cook time: 10 minutes | Serves 4

For the Corn:
1½ cups thawed frozen corn kernels
1 cup mixed diced bell peppers
1 jalapeño, diced
1 cup diced yellow onion
½ teaspoon ancho chile powder

1 tablespoon fresh lemon juice
1 teaspoon ground cumin
½ teaspoon kosher salt
Cooking spray

For Serving:
¼ cup feta cheese
¼ cup chopped fresh cilantro

1 tablespoon fresh lemon juice

1. Spritz the air fryer with cooking spray.
2. Combine the ingredients for the corn in a large bowl. Stir to mix well.
3. Pout the mixture into the air fryer. Air fry at 375ºF (191ºC) for 10 minutes or until the corn and bell peppers are soft. Shake the basket halfway through the cooking time.
4. Transfer them onto a large plate, then spread with feta cheese and cilantro. Drizzle with lemon juice and serve.

Air-Fired Sweet-Spicy Peanuts

Prep time: 5 minutes | Cook time: 5 minutes | Serves 9

3 cups shelled raw peanuts
1 tablespoon hot red pepper sauce

3 tablespoons granulated white sugar

1. Put the peanuts in a large bowl, then drizzle with hot red pepper sauce and sprinkle with sugar. Toss to coat well.
2. Pour the peanuts in the air fryer. Air at 400ºF (204ºC) fry for 5 minutes or until the peanuts are crispy and browned. Shake the basket halfway through.
3. Serve immediately.

Queso Fundido with Chorizo

Prep time: 10 minutes | Cook time: 25 minutes | Serves 4

4 ounces (113 g) fresh Mexican chorizo, casings removed
1 medium onion, chopped
3 cloves garlic, minced
1 cup chopped tomato
2 jalapeños, deseeded and diced

2 teaspoons ground cumin
2 cups shredded Oaxaca or Mozzarella cheese
½ cup half-and-half
Celery sticks or tortilla chips, for serving

1. In a baking pan, combine the chorizo, onion, garlic, tomato, jalapeños, and cumin. Stir to combine.
2. Place the pan in the air fryer basket. Air fry for 15 minutes, or until the sausage is cooked, stirring halfway through the cooking time to break up the sausage.
3. Add the cheese and half-and-half; stir to combine. Air fry at 400ºF (204ºC) for 10 minutes, or until the cheese has melted.
4. Serve with celery sticks or tortilla chips.

Greek Spinach Pie

Prep time: 5 minutes | Cook time: 25 minutes | Serves 6

½ (10-ounce / 284-g) package frozen
spinach, thawed and squeezed dry
1 egg, lightly beaten
¼ cup pine nuts, toasted
¼ cup grated Parmesan cheese
¾ cup crumbled feta cheese

⅛ teaspoon ground nutmeg
½ teaspoon salt
Freshly ground black pepper, to taste
6 sheets phyllo dough
½ cup butter, melted

1. Combine all the ingredients, except for the phyllo dough and butter, in a large bowl. Whisk to combine well. Set aside.
2. Place a sheet of phyllo dough on a clean work surface. Brush with butter then top with another layer sheet of phyllo. Brush with butter, then cut the layered sheets into six 3-inch-wide strips.
3. Top each strip with 1 tablespoon of the spinach mixture, then fold the bottom left corner over the mixture towards the right strip edge to make a triangle. Keep folding triangles until each strip is folded over.
4. Brush the triangles with butter and repeat with remaining strips and phyllo dough.
5. Place six triangles in the air fryer. Air fry at 350ºF (177ºC) for 8 minutes or until golden brown. Flip the triangles halfway through. Repeat with the remaining triangles.
6. Serve immediately.

Low-Country Shrimp Boil

Prep time: 10 minutes | Cook time: 18 minutes | Serves 2

1 ear corn, husk and silk removed, cut into
2-inch rounds
8 ounces (227 g) red potatoes, unpeeled, cut
into 1-inch pieces
2 teaspoons Old Bay Seasoning, divided
2 teaspoons vegetable oil, divided
¼ teaspoon ground black pepper

8 ounces (227 g) large shrimps (about 12
shrimps), deveined
6 ounces (170 g) andouille or chorizo
sausage, cut into 1-inch pieces
2 garlic cloves, minced
1 tablespoon chopped fresh parsley

1. Put the corn rounds and potatoes in a large bowl. Sprinkle with 1 teaspoon of Old Bay seasoning and drizzle with vegetable oil. Toss to coat well.
2. Transfer the corn rounds and potatoes on a baking sheet, then put in the air fryer.
3. Bake at 400ºF (204ºC) for 12 minutes or until soft and browned. Shake the basket halfway through the cooking time.
4. Meanwhile, cut slits into the shrimps but be careful not to cut them through. Combine the shrimps, sausage, remaining Old Bay seasoning, and remaining vegetable oil in the large bowl. Toss to coat well.
5. When the baking of the potatoes and corn rounds is complete, add the shrimps and sausage and bake for 6 more minutes or until the shrimps are opaque. Shake the basket halfway through the cooking time.
6. When the baking is finished, serve them on a plate and spread with parsley before serving.

Appendix 1: Measurement Conversion Chart

VOLUME EQUIVALENTS(DRY)

US STANDARD	METRIC (APPROXIMATE)
1/8 teaspoon	0.5 mL
1/4 teaspoon	1 mL
1/2 teaspoon	2 mL
3/4 teaspoon	4 mL
1 teaspoon	5 mL
1 tablespoon	15 mL
1/4 cup	59 mL
1/2 cup	118 mL
3/4 cup	177 mL
1 cup	235 mL
2 cups	475 mL
3 cups	700 mL
4 cups	1 L

VOLUME EQUIVALENTS(LIQUID)

US STANDARD	US STANDARD (OUNCES)	METRIC (APPROXIMATE)
2 tablespoons	1 fl.oz.	30 mL
1/4 cup	2 fl.oz.	60 mL
1/2 cup	4 fl.oz.	120 mL
1 cup	8 fl.oz.	240 mL
1 1/2 cup	12 fl.oz.	355 mL
2 cups or 1 pint	16 fl.oz.	475 mL
4 cups or 1 quart	32 fl.oz.	1 L
1 gallon	128 fl.oz.	4 L

TEMPERATURES EQUIVALENTS

FAHRENHEIT(F)	CELSIUS(C) (APPROXIMATE)
225 °F	107 °C
250 °F	120 °C
275 °F	135 °C
300 °F	150 °C
325 °F	160 °C
350 °F	180 °C
375 °F	190 °C
400 °F	205 °C
425 °F	220 °C
450 °F	235 °C
475 °F	245 °C
500 °F	260 °C

WEIGHT EQUIVALENTS

US STANDARD	METRIC (APPROXIMATE)
1 ounce	28 g
2 ounces	57 g
5 ounces	142 g
10 ounces	284 g
15 ounces	425 g
16 ounces (1 pound)	455 g
1.5 pounds	680 g
2 pounds	907 g

Appendix 2: Air Fryer Cooking Chart

Beef

Item	Temp (°F)	Time (mins)	Item	Temp (°F)	Time (mins)
Beef Eye Round Roast (4 lbs.)	400 °F	45 to 55	Meatballs (1-inch)	370 °F	7
Burger Patty (4 oz.)	370 °F	16 to 20	Meatballs (3-inch)	380 °F	10
Filet Mignon (8 oz.)	400 °F	18	Ribeye, bone-in (1-inch, 8 oz)	400 °F	10 to 15
Flank Steak (1.5 lbs.)	400 °F	12	Sirloin steaks (1-inch, 12 oz)	400 °F	9 to 14
Flank Steak (2 lbs.)	400 °F	20 to 28			

Chicken

Item	Temp (°F)	Time (mins)	Item	Temp (°F)	Time (mins)
Breasts, bone in (1 ¼ lb.)	370 °F	25	Legs, bone-in (1 ¾ lb.)	380 °F	30
Breasts, boneless (4 oz)	380 °F	12	Thighs, boneless (1 ½ lb.)	380 °F	18 to 20
Drumsticks (2 ½ lb.)	370 °F	20	Wings (2 lb.)	400 °F	12
Game Hen (halved 2 lb.)	390 °F	20	Whole Chicken	360 °F	75
Thighs, bone-in (2 lb.)	380 °F	22	Tenders	360 °F	8 to 10

Pork & Lamb

Item	Temp (°F)	Time (mins)	Item	Temp (°F)	Time (mins)
Bacon (regular)	400 °F	5 to 7	Pork Tenderloin	370 °F	15
Bacon (thick cut)	400 °F	6 to 10	Sausages	380 °F	15
Pork Loin (2 lb.)	360 °F	55	Lamb Loin Chops (1-inch thick)	400 °F	8 to 12
Pork Chops, bone in (1-inch, 6.5 oz)	400 °F	12	Rack of Lamb (1.5 – 2 lb.)	380 °F	22

Fish & Seafood

Item	Temp (°F)	Time (mins)	Item	Temp (°F)	Time (mins)
Calamari (8 oz)	400 °F	4	Tuna Steak	400 °F	7 to 10
Fish Fillet (1-inch, 8 oz)	400 °F	10	Scallops	400 °F	5 to 7
Salmon, fillet (6 oz)	380 °F	12	Shrimp	400 °F	5
Swordfish steak	400 °F	10			

Vegetables

INGREDIENT	AMOUNT	PREPARATION	OIL	TEMP	COOK TIME
Asparagus	2 bunches	Cut in half, trim stems	2 Tbsp	420°F	12-15 mins
Beets	1½ lbs	Peel, cut in ½-inch cubes	1Tbsp	390°F	28-30 mins
Bell peppers (for roasting)	4 peppers	Cut in quarters, remove seeds	1Tbsp	400°F	15-20 mins
Broccoli	1 large head	Cut in 1-2-inch florets	1Tbsp	400°F	15-20 mins
Brussels sprouts	1lb	Cut in half, remove stems	1Tbsp	425°F	15-20 mins
Carrots	1lb	Peel, cut in ¼-inch rounds	1 Tbsp	425°F	10-15 mins
Cauliflower	1 head	Cut in 1-2-inch florets	2 Tbsp	400°F	20-22 mins
Corn on the cob	7 ears	Whole ears, remove husks	1 Tbps	400°F	14-17 mins
Green beans	1 bag (12 oz)	Trim	1 Tbps	420°F	18-20 mins
Kale (for chips)	4 oz	Tear into pieces,remove stems	None	325°F	5-8 mins
Mushrooms	16 oz	Rinse, slice thinly	1 Tbps	390°F	25-30 mins
Potatoes, russet	1½ lbs	Cut in 1-inch wedges	1 Tbps	390°F	25-30 mins
Potatoes, russet	1lb	Hand-cut fries, soak 30 mins in cold water, then pat dry	½ -3 Tbps	400°F	25-28 mins
Potatoes, sweet	1lb	Hand-cut fries, soak 30 mins in cold water, then pat dry	1 Tbps	400°F	25-28 mins
Zucchini	1lb	Cut in eighths lengthwise, then cut in half	1 Tbps	400°F	15-20 mins

Appendix 3: Recipe Index